D0164444

2e

Marketing
Yourself

Dorene Ciletti

SOUTH-WESTERN
CENGAGE Learning

Australia • Brazil • Japan • Korea • Mexico • Singapore • Spain • United Kingdom • United States

SOUTH-WESTERN
CENGAGE Learning™

Marketing Yourself, 2nd Edition
Dorene Ciletti

Vice President of Editorial, Business: Jack W. Calhoun

Vice President/Editor-in-Chief: Karen Schmohe

Vice President/Marketing: Bill Hendee

Executive Editor: Eve Lewis

Senior Developmental Editor: Dr. Inell Bolls

Marketing Specialist: Linda Kuper

Content Project Manager: D. Jean Buttrom

Senior Media Editor: Sally Nieman

Frontlist Buyer, Manufacturing: Kevin Kluck

Production Service: MPS Limited, A Macmillan Company

Compositor: MPS Limited, A Macmillan Company

Senior Art Director: Tippy McIntosh

Internal Designer: Lou Ann Thesing

Cover Designer: Lou Ann Thesing

Cover Image: ©iStock

Photography Manager: John Hill

Photo Researcher: Darren Wright

© 2011, 2004 South-Western, Cengage Learning

ALL RIGHTS RESERVED. No part of this work covered by the copyright herein may be reproduced, transmitted, stored or used in any form or by any means graphic, electronic, or mechanical, including but not limited to photocopying, recording, scanning, digitizing, taping, Web distribution, information networks, or information storage and retrieval systems, except as permitted under Section 107 or 108 of the 1976 United States Copyright Act, without the prior written permission of the publisher.

For product information and technology assistance, contact us at
Cengage Learning Customer & Sales Support, 1-800-354-9706

For permission to use material from this text or product, submit all requests online at **cengage.com/permissions**
Further permissions questions can be emailed to
permissionrequest@cengage.com

ExamView® is a registered trademark of eInstruction Corp. Windows is a registered trademark of the Microsoft Corporation used herein under license. Macintosh and Power Macintosh are registered trademarks of Apple Computer, Inc. used herein under license.

© 2008 Cengage Learning. All Rights Reserved.

Library of Congress Control Number: 2009943131

Student Edition ISBN 13: 978-0-538-45011-9

Student Edition ISBN 10: 0-538-45011-8

South-Western Cengage Learning
5191 Natorp Boulevard
Mason, OH 45040
USA

Cengage Learning products are represented in Canada by Nelson Education, Ltd.

For your course and learning solutions, visit **www.cengage.com/school**

Purchase any of our products at your local college store or at our preferred online store **www.CengageBrain.com**

Printed in the United States of America
1 2 3 4 5 6 7 13 12 11 10 09

CONTENTS

HOW TO USE THIS BOOK

CAREERS IN MARKETING

American Airlines Center

Opened in 2001, American Airlines Center in Dallas, Texas, is home to the Dallas Mavericks NBA team and Dallas Stars NHL team. The unique design of this facility allows for a smooth transition from basketball games to hockey games, and even for use as a concert hall.

The Premium Sales Associate is responsible for creating revenue for suite and club seats and related products for this entertainment venue. The Associate generates sales leads, sells accounts, and provides customer service and follow-up to build and maintain long-term relationships with clients.

The position requires a college degree, sales experience, strong communicati... skills, and excellent product knowled... Candidates should have proven busir... development experience, problem-so... standing of customer relationship ma...

Think *Critically*

1. For a position such as this, what
2. Why do you think it is important long-term client relationships?

Careers in Marketing highlights today's fascinating companies and the careers they offer.

PORTFOLIO BUILDER PROJECT
Involving Others in Your Portfolio

Project Objectives

The key to involving others in your portfolio is **networking**. Networking is actively making as many people as possible aware of your job search. In this project, you will:

- Create an extensive contact list of people you know.
- Compile a list of qualified references.
- Request letters of recommendation.

Getting Started

Read the Project Process below. Look at the resources on the Portfolio Builder CD.

- Study the sample contact list.
- Plan how to model your own list of references on the sample references list.
- Look over the sample letter of recommendation.

Project Process

Part 1   Lesson 5.1 Your network begins with personal contacts who link to others. List at least 25 people in your network and compare your list with your classmates' lists. Did their lists remind you of anyone you missed? Create a final list with contact information.

Part 2   Lesson 5.2 Identify three people, unrelated to you, who can vouch for the qualities that will make you a good employee. Contact these individuals and update them on your career plans. Ask for permission to use them as a

Part 3   Lesson 5.3 Ask those three references for a letter of recommendation. Be sure to tell these individuals about any new skills you have as well as your target job objective. Display the letters in your portfolio.

Project Wrap-Up

Think about what your references wrote about you. Did they point out any job skills or personal assets you had previously overlooked?

Portfolio Builder Project supplies activities for self-knowledge, self-marketing, and the job search, showcasing work readiness.

Goals
- Analyze your personality and interests
- Define a method for self-improvement

Key Terms
- accomplishment
- self-aware
- benefit selling
- benefits
- extravert
- features

Goals and Key Terms

Goals are clearly stated learning objectives to guide learning. **Terms** appear in bold and in color and are defined in the section.

Marketing Matters offers a thought-provoking introductory scenario that connects to chapter content and demonstrates relevance.

marketing matters

Luis Lopez, a high school senior, is unsure of his future. He has gone to the career center at school for an assessment. How can his interests, as well as his likes and dislikes, help him select a career path?

marketing math connection

The Americans with Disabilities Act of 1990 defines disability as a "substantial limitation in a major life activity." In 2005, the United States Census Bureau published a study about Americans with disabilities. This bar chart shows the percentage of the 2005 population in each age group that was disabled. The total population of the United States that year was 291.1 million people.

Disability Prevalence by Age: 2005

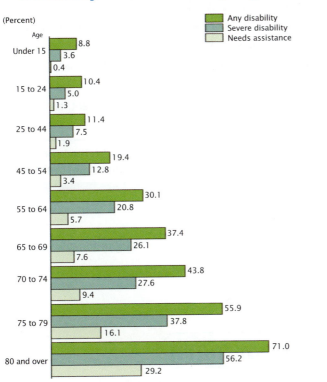

Source: U.S. Census Bureau, Survey of Income and Program Participation, June–September 2005.

1. In 2005, there were approximately 42,300,000 Americans between the ages of 15 and 24. How many Americans in that age group had a severe disability?

2. In 2005, 54.4 million people had some type of disability. What percentage of the total population had a disability?

SOLUTION

1. 42,300,000 × 0.053 = 2,241,900
2. 54,400,000 ÷ 291,100,000 = 0.187 = 18.7 percent

Did You Know?

"If you don't know what you want, you will probably never get it." Oliver Wendell Holmes had the right idea about setting goals!

Did You Know? presents an interesting fact connecting the section topic to the real world.

com·mu·ni·cate

Create a flyer that depicts and describes the four American values mentioned in this chapter: freedom, individualism, equality, education, and inclusion

Communicate provides activities to reinforce, review, and practice communication skills.

Marketing Math Connection teaches mathematical concepts important for success in the workplace.

Workshop

Go to **www.cengage.com/ school/marketing/yourself** and click on the link in Chapter 3 to the personality test. Complete the test and then click on the trait description link and read about the MBTI® traits.

Divide into small groups and discuss how you can identify the personality types of others at school and in the workplace.

Workshop activities promote class participation and teamwork.

diversity in the workplace

The Multicultural Economy

Buying power, or disposable income, refers to the income an individual or group has available to spend on goods and services after paying taxes. If you were a marketer, how would you use the following statistics about predicted changes in buying power in the years 2007–2012?

- The African-American, Asian-American, Native-American, and Hispanic markets will grow faster than the white market.

- The African-American population will grow by 6.7 percent, and its buying power will increase by 34.2 percent.

- Asian Americans' buying power will increase by 45.9 percent. By 2012, 16.2 million Americans will claim Asian ancestry.

- The Native-American population will grow by 8.2 percent, and its buying power will increase by 35.6 percent.

- The Hispanic population will grow by 15.3 percent, and its buying power will increase by 46.3 percent.

"The Multicultural Economy, 2002." Selig Center for Economic Growth, Terry College of Business, The University of Georgia. Reprinted by permission.

Diversity in the Workplace offers examples and tips for getting along in today's multi-cultural workplace.

Net Bookmark features online activities that encourage Internet research and supply the practice needed to improve online researching skills.

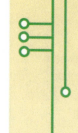

NETBookmark

Online self-assessments can be a helpful starting point for understanding how your skills and interests may point to career choices. To complete an online self-assessment, access **www.cengage.com/school/marketing/yourself** and click on the link for Chapter 3 to be directed to several self-assessment sites. After completing an assessment, provide a one-page review about it. State which assessment site you accessed, the information it provided about you, and how you can use this information to plan your job search.

Check ▶ Point

What are two important steps for individual self-awareness?

Check Point
questions are found throughout the text to help gauge comprehension of concepts.

3.1 Assessment

THINK CRITICALLY

1. What is self-awareness and why is it important?
2. Compare and contrast extraverts and introverts.
3. Why would it be helpful to have someone who knows you well describe your personality?

MAKE ACADEMIC CONNECTIONS

4. **PROBLEM SOLVING** Choose one personality trait that you would like to change. Use the process outlined in the text to develop a change strategy. For two weeks, keep a journal tracking your progress. In your first entry, name the personality trait you plan to change and explain the strategy you've developed. In each additional entry, discuss what, if any, progress you've made. In your fina[l]
results of your strategy: Were you able to chang[e]
trait? Which parts of the strategy were helpful?

End of Lesson Activities
Think Critically questions offer opportunities to apply concepts.

Make Academic Connections activities provide connections to other disciplines.

Internet Icon
indicates opportunities to research on the web.

Vocabulary Builder
matches terms with definitions to confirm understanding of key terms.

VOCABULARY BUILDER

Choose the term that best fits the definition. Write the letter of the answer in the space provided. Some terms may not be used.

_____ 1. Someone who likes to work alone

_____ 2. Things you want to accomplish

_____ 3. The advantages a customer gets from buying the product

_____ 4. When a marketer promotes products by considering the needs and wants of the customer

a. accomplishment
b. benefit selling
c. benefits
d. extravert
e. features
f. goals

Winning Edge
activities prepare students for BPA, DECA, and FBLA competitive events, increasing critical-thinking and presentation skills.

REVIEW CONCEPTS

www.cengage.com/school/marketing/yourself

12. List five career options that an extravert might consider and five that an introvert might consider.

_____

_____

_____

Planning a Career in Marketing Management

Economics may not seem like a career area, but economists can be found in all types of industries and businesses. The need for people with an understanding of the intri-cate workings of the national and world economies is vital to the suc-cess of companies and the eco-nomic health of our country. People with the capability to gather and analyze economic data, predict economic changes and the effects of those changes on busi-ness deci-sions, and communicate complex mathematical informa-tion to busi-ness and government leaders will be in high demand in the future.

Employment Outlook

Employment of economists is expected to grow more slowly than average for all occupations over the next 10 years. Demand is rising for economic analysis in virtually every industry. More than half of all economists are employed by the

entific, and technical consulting services.

Job Titles
- economist
- financial analyst
- market analyst

Ne
- sk
- m
- a

Wh
in

Planning a Career in ...
incorporates Career Clusters and presents the skills, education, work experience, and industry opportunities for a variety of business-related career paths.

SKILLS FOR OCCUPATIONAL SUCCESS

Using Communications Technology Professionally

Economics may not seem like a career area, but economists can be found in all types of industries and businesses. The need for people with an understanding of the intri-cate workings of the national and world economies is vital to the suc-cess of companies and the eco-nomic health of our coun-try. People with the capability to

be the fastest in private industry, espe-cially in management, sci-entific, and technical consulting services.
- economist
- financial analyst
- market analyst
- public policy consultant
- researcher or research assistant
- econometrician

Well-developed quantita-tive skills and preparation in mathematics, statistics, survey design, and computers.
Minimum of a bachelor's de-gree with increasing demand for an MBA. Top economists hold a PhD.
Excellent communication skills to present quantitative data and make understandable recom-mendations to decision-makers.

evelop Your Skill
The real estate market has

---

careerbuilder®

Are You Employable?

Excerpted from "Career Building: Your Total Handbook for Finding a Job and Making It Work" the Editors at CareerBuilder.com

Here's the bottom line: You have to get a job, you have to go to work and someday, you'll probably have to change jobs. "CAREER BUILDING: Your Total Handbook for Finding a Job and Making It Work" (Collins Business) is a one-stop guide for navigating all those times in your career.

For some people, "If it ain't broke, don't fix it" is a guiding principle. And if you've found one job, you can certainly find another. You know all you need to know about job hunting, right?

If you find your job hunt isn't giving you anything but a stress head-ache, maybe it's time for a refresher. Ask yourself these questions:

Is my résumé targeted?

Just because you're applying for multiple jobs, don't assume the same résumé works for every position. Each job posting will stress different qualities over others, so rework each résumé to highlight the experience and skills that correspond to that particular employer. Your résumé will prove not only that you're qualified for the job but that you also pay atten-tion to detail.

Am I networking?

We've said it once; we'll say it again -- networking is crucial. Think about this: There is only one of you and there are thousands of job openings. The

careerbuilder®
articles are included in every chapter and offer career tips and advice on searching for a job.

Skills for Occupational Success
introduces basic skills needed in everyday business and teaches students how to market themselves.

The Marketplace

1.1 The Marketing Connection

1.2 The Changing Marketplace

1.3 The Current Marketplace

CAREERS IN MARKETING

American Eagle Outfitters

American Eagle Outfitters (AEO), a well-known apparel company, opened its first store in 1977. Known for private-label clothing and accessories for men and women, AEO has expanded to include aerie by American Eagle, Martin & Osa, and 77kids. AEO operates more than 800 stores in the United States and Canada, as well as an online store.

AEO has a 10-week paid corporate summer internship program for college students at its Pittsburgh World Headquarters. The program focuses on achieving excellence in store operations, finance, merchandising, planning and allocation, marketing, information technology, and human resources. Interns work in various corporate departments, learning about trends, fashion, marketing, and business operations. They also work in retail stores, learning about store design, visual display, and inventory.

Think *Critically*

1. How do you think American Eagle Outfitters' internship program applies to marketing?

2. Marketing can be a highly interpersonal skill. How do you think this internship program would support an intern's development of the necessary interpersonal skills?

Brand X Pictures/Jupiter Images

PORTFOLIO BUILDER PROJECT
What Is a Portfolio?

Project Objectives

A **portfolio** is a collection of work samples that represent your abilities and accomplishments. It can be used to demonstrate your work readiness, show your eligibility for admission to a college or other organization, or showcase a special talent. In the Portfolio Projects in this text, you will have opportunities to assess your skills and develop different sections of your own portfolio. In this project you will:

- Learn the importance of a complete, attractive, and well-organized portfolio
- Identify appropriate content for a portfolio
- Understand that a variety of materials can be used to present a portfolio

Getting Started

- Discuss why developing a portfolio that demonstrates your work readiness is important even before you start a career.

- Brainstorm the types of materials you might use to display and organize the variety of information in your portfolio.
- List everything you can think of that would be an asset in your portfolio. What would a potential employer or admissions officer want to know about you? What examples of your work would he or she want to see?

Project Process

Part 1 Lesson 1.1 Look at your content list. How does each of these components help you market yourself? Now, look at the Portfolio Checklist on the Portfolio Builder CD. What other elements should you include? Write a short paragraph describing how the processes of marketing products/services and marketing yourself are similar.

Part 2 Lesson 1.2 In a market economy, competition can be stiff. The same is true when applying to a school or applying for a job. Other applicants are your competitors, and a great portfolio could be the thing that sets you apart. Why is it important for your portfolio to be complete, attractive, and well-organized?

Part 3 Lesson 1.3 Information, technology, and communication are important in today's global world. Identify several ways you could demonstrate your information management and communication skills in your portfolio.

Project Wrap-Up

Hold a class discussion about the best type of notebook to use to display and organize the contents of your portfolio. Make a list of things you did not know about portfolios before completing this project. Why is it important to review and evaluate your portfolio regularly to keep it up-to-date?

© iofoto, 2009/Used under license from Shutterstock.com

3

The Marketing Connection

Goals

- Understand key marketing concepts
- Learn the nine key marketing functions
- Explain how marketing relates to the job search and career development

Key Terms

- marketing
- satisfaction
- idea marketing
- social marketing

Marketing Is Everywhere

Ever since you were a small child, your purchasing decisions have been shaped by marketing. Do you remember passing a popular restaurant and asking to stop and eat there? You probably recognized the restaurant's logo. Perhaps you remembered watching a commercial on television or seeing a friend's toy from the kid's meal.

Marketing is a part of your daily life, although you usually do not notice it. Look around you. Do you have any classmates wearing T-shirts with logos? Do they have the same hairstyles as famous athletes or entertainers? Those brand names and celebrity "looks" are examples of marketing's influence.

Maybe you have already used marketing skills at work. Have you worked as a sales associate in a retail store? Have you answered phones for an organization? Have you posted flyers advertising your lawn-mowing service? These are just a few examples of marketing activities. You have experienced it regularly, but can you define "marketing"? This section looks at some basic marketing concepts.

The Meaning of Marketing

The American Marketing Association defines **marketing** as "the activity, set of institutions, and processes for creating, communicating, delivering, and exchanging offerings that have value for customers, clients, partners, and society at large."

marketing matters

Maria Ruiz is moving from her home in a small town in Texas to attend college in Maine. To prepare for the new climate, she decides to visit the mall to buy some "cold weather" clothes. Clothes, especially for harsh weather, were originally designed for protection against the elements. In addition to protection, what other qualities will shape Maria's wardrobe choices? How will the stores and brands try to make these qualities attractive?

© Monkey Business Images, 2009/Used under license from Shutterstock.com

You will read about the individual marketing functions, such as pricing and distribution, later in this chapter. For now, think of marketing as the process of making one product more attractive than the other products a person may choose. Marketing also involves making that product satisfactory to both the consumer who buys it and the producer who makes it.

Exchange and Satisfaction

All marketing involves some kind of *exchange* where two parties see *value* in what the other has to offer. Monetary transactions and barter transactions are two types of exchange.

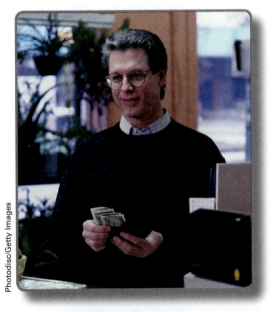

Photodisc/Getty Images

You make a monetary exchange when you go to the store and exchange a dollar for a chilled bottle of water. The water is valuable to you because you are hot and thirsty, and the dollar is valuable to the store because it makes money by selling the water. But the exchange must provide **satisfaction**: the performance of the product or service must meet expectations. If the "chilled" water turns out to be lukewarm, the exchange is not satisfactory. You may even return to the store to complain.

Money is the best-known currency, but it is not the only one. You have many other forms of currency available to you—including time, talent, and knowledge—which you can *barter*, or exchange for other goods or services. To barter, you exchange something of value, such as a DVD, for something else, perhaps a computer game. For this kind of exchange to occur, the person who owns the game must want to acquire your DVD, and you must want to acquire the computer game.

Money is a scarce resource, but it has no value until it is exchangeable for goods and services. Goods and services used in barter are still valuable and useful whether you exchange them or not.

Check ▶ Point

Have you had any recent experiences with bartering? What generalizations can you make about bartering?

Workshop

In small groups, make a list of all your marketing transactions in the last week. Compare your list to those of other groups.

Key Marketing Functions

If you think that marketing only involves selling physical products at a retail store, you are mistaken. Many other activities must take place before a consumer buys a product or service. All marketing activities fall into at least one of nine key functions:

- Market planning
- Product and service management
- Promotion
- Selling
- Pricing

- Distribution
- Marketing-information management
- Financing
- Risk management

- **Market planning** is understanding the market a company wants to serve, and identifying the problems or needs experienced by the customers in that market. For example, with increased awareness of global warming and concern for the environment, car companies have recognized that there is a need in the market for cars that are powered by alternatives to gasoline, such as electricity or biofuels.

- **Product/service management** is designing, creating, improving, and maintaining products and services that satisfy customers' needs. Twenty years ago museums and malls did not have diaper-changing tables in the men's restroom. But as family roles have changed, many

places now provides changing tables in both restrooms. Businesses adapt their goods and services to keep their customers coming back.

- **Promotion** refers to communications to inform, persuade, and remind consumers of a product's benefit and encourage them to buy it. When people think of marketing, they often think of advertising and selling. There are many other types of promotional activities, such as writing press releases for news organizations and sponsoring charitable events.

- **Selling** refers to direct contact with potential customers to determine their needs and satisfy these needs. A web site that sells income tax software might feature a service where you can talk directly to an accountant or tax lawyer while you are preparing your taxes electronically. By providing this direct contact, the company hopes that consumers are more likely to buy the product.

- **Pricing** is the process of deciding how much a product or service will cost the consumer. Price is the value placed on the product. Businesses have to think about many things when determining a price: Is the price low enough to attract a lot of buyers? Is it high enough that people won't assume the product is poorly made?

- **Distribution** involves getting products and services to the customers in the best way possible. Many electronics companies sell their products online and in large electronics stores. This way they get the business of those who like to shop online as well as the business of those who like to see a product before purchasing it.

- **Marketing-information management** is the process of gathering and using information about customers to improve business decisions. Have you ever answered a phone survey about a product? The company is gathering information from you so they can make product decisions based on what consumers really say.

    This step can also be applied to marketing yourself. In the future, you will probably select a job or higher education opportunity that is appropriate to what you have to offer. You wouldn't try to convince an organization or recruiter to place you in a role that isn't appropriate for its needs or your skills and experience. Just as a producer must present a beneficial product to consumers, you must shape yourself into an attractive product that is attractive to future schools and employers.

- **Financing** is the process of acquiring the financial resources to market the product/service. Financing also involves giving consumers payment options. Yvonne wants to buy a motor scooter, but she doesn't have the full amount. She may be able to get a low-interest loan from the seller so that she can purchase the scooter now.

- **Risk management** involves reducing the risks associated with marketing decisions and activities. Organizations should be aware of the potential risks involving products, personnel, or customers, and seek to reduce them.

Did You Know?

Nearly anything can be marketed. Post-it® Notes, for example, began as a mistake when a scientist was trying to create a strong adhesive. When the scientist later used the resulting weak adhesive to mark his place in a church hymnal, a star product was born. Sales of the product began in 1980. Today, Post-it® Notes can be found in every office in the United States.

com-mu-ni-cate

Imagine that you are a marketer conducting surveys about products. Develop a survey for a digital music player or cell phone. Then survey five of your friends to see which features they value most in the product.

Check Point

Can the nine marketing functions be ranked in order of importance? Why or why not?

Marketing, Society, and You

Marketing is everywhere. It impacts media, popular culture, and, of course, business. Every business is involved in marketing, either directly or indirectly. Every business produces a product or service, and that product or service must be made available and attractive to potential customers. Marketing efforts provide for an abundance of products, services, ideas, and even lifestyles. Marketing is a very visible business activity. We see examples of marketing communication, such as billboards, television commercials, and store displays, every day. We see products being transported by truck or train to locations where customers can buy them, we see the impact of pricing decisions at the checkout counter, and we feel a sense of need or want for particular goods or services.

When you think of marketing, do you think of physical products (such as soap, computers, and clothes) and services (such as day care, online banking, and dry cleaning)? Have you considered that ideas and individuals can also be marketed?

Marketing Ideas

Does your family recycle newspapers? Can you describe the ideas of a particular political party? If you answer yes, it's probably because of **idea marketing**. Recycling is an accepted social practice because the importance of preserving the environment has been marketed for the past 30 years. Political parties "sell" their plans and values to voters. The marketing of ideas—particularly ideas that can benefit individuals, groups, or society—is known as **social marketing.**

Marketing ideas is similar to marketing a product or a service. First, the need for the information is determined: "We should reuse many of our materials to save our natural resources." Second, the service of recycling is suggested to meet that need. Finally, a plan is put in place for promoting and distributing the idea of recycling through press releases, advertisements, community recycling programs, and so on.

Marketing Individuals

Individuals also use marketing. Star athletes market their athletic ability and success, college applicants market their potential as students, and job seekers market their potential as contributing members of an organization.

Doesn't everyone spend some time marketing themselves to the people around them? As a student you might market yourself to your math teacher by turning in all your homework and answering questions in class. You market yourself so that in exchange for being a disciplined and responsible student you will get a good grade in geometry. Does that sound strange? You may do this without realizing it, but you do it.

Marketing Yourself in the Workplace

You aren't a box of laundry detergent or the local cable service, but you will still need to market yourself as you move into the workplace and other opportunities. You will need to "sell" yourself to get into the college you want to attend, get a scholarship, get a job or promotion, keep a job, convince other people of your ideas, and more.

Earlier you read that marketing involves an exchange where two parties see value in what the other has to offer. Employment is one type of exchange. Once you are hired, your employer will expect you to provide value to the organization. You go to work and in exchange for your time and skills, an employer pays you and perhaps provides benefits such as health insurance and paid vacation days.

You will need to understand your employer's needs and wants so that your job performance meets, or even exceeds, your employer's expectations. To build a strong, mutually beneficial relationship, you should seek out organizations and positions that can meet *your* expectations. Through research, you can develop a target market of organizations that are most likely to desire your skills and abilities, as well as determine which companies can most likely satisfy your employment expectations.

As you progress through this text, you will learn more about marketing while you are preparing your portfolio and planning your self-marketing strategy. Each chapter covers key marketing concepts and activities and relates them to your future school and job roles. For example, you will evaluate what makes you attractive to employers and which types of job situations you might be happiest working in. You will learn how you can get an edge by targeting organizations that offer a good match between their needs and your skills. You also will learn how to present yourself in the best light and showcase your value in your resume, job correspondence, and interviews.

Most importantly, you'll learn that closing the sale is just the beginning: successful marketing *maintains* a strong product impression and customer relationship. After all your hard work, you want to make sure your customers always think of you as the *best* choice.

Check Point

How is a job an exchange?

careerbuilder®

Advice for Workers of Every Age, at Every Stage

By Anthony Balderrama, CareerBuilder.com writer

Copyright 2009 CareerBuilder, LLC.—Reprinted with permission.

"Where is this relationship going?" is a question that can mean several things for a romance. It can signal demise or it can reignite long-lost passion. Whatever the outcome, asking it means you're taking control of things. Your career isn't exactly like having a significant other, but some of the same rules apply. Coasting through your professional life without asking any questions of yourself or taking into account your ambitions can limit what you achieve. And it doesn't matter if you're at your first job or you're about to retire, you should always be thinking about where you are and what you want out of your job.

With that in mind, we put together some suggestions for workers at every stage of their careers. Many issues you face as a high school student aren't the same as what you'll face midcareer. But you'll also notice that some advice is relevant to you no matter what your age is. So here are some topics to think about as you navigate your career when...

... you're still in high school:

Pick a job that doesn't interfere with school. First jobs can teach you about the value of work and earning a paycheck, but the real benefit is learning how to balance personal and work lives. At this age, you should be more focused on getting your education and a diploma than on climbing the corporate ladder.

Take your job seriously. Don't become a teenage workaholic, but don't shirk your responsibilities, either. Show up on time, perform your tasks and treat your boss with respect. It never hurts to have a good reference and a boss willing to have you back, maybe during your summer breaks during college or full-time when starting your career.

... you're still in college:

Find a job that relates to your major or your interests. Working and going to school isn't easy, and you'll be even less inclined to enjoy your job if it bores you. While you may not find your dream job right now, any opportunity to see if you enjoy working in your ideal industry is a good learning experience.

Look for internships. Now is a prime opportunity to get experience that can build into a full-time job after graduation, and it's also the one time in your life when you can live very cheaply. Internships don't often pay well or anything at all, but they often count for course credit and always build your résumé, so take advantage of them while you can.

Start job hunting a semester (or more) before graduation. Every May, the job market is flooded with new graduates ready and eager to find work. If you start sending out résumés, going on interviews and networking ahead of your classmates, you can have a job lined up before you even get your diploma. You can really enjoy walking across that stage even more when you've already accepted an offer.

Remember that you're a working student. Although a lot changes from high school to college, some things stay the same, namely, the need to remain focused on school and taking the job

continued on page 11

seriously. Don't forget to study for an exam because of work. (And don't forget to show up for work because you were having too much fun.)

... you're at your first "grown-up" job:

Learn from others. You're a sophisticated, likable person with great ideas; you're also the newbie. Don't be afraid to speak up and contribute to the team, but remember that you have a lot to learn from colleagues and your boss. They can teach you what to do and what not to do at that particular company and in the professional world.

Look for a good foundation. For the average worker, an entry-level job does not mark the beginning of a lifelong relationship with that particular employer. You're likely to have several jobs throughout your career, so don't look at a first job as if you're going to be there forever. Look for a job that interests you, offers networking opportunities and, most importantly, lets you develop skills that will help you down the road.

Don't burn your bridges. When you move on to a new job, do not e-mail your boss with a diatribe about what an incompetent fool she is. Don't tell your colleague how sorry you feel for him because he's still stuck in that prison of a company. Peaceful partings can ensure you have good references and a good reputation. (This advice is good for everyone, regardless of age.)

... you're in the middle of your career:

Assess your life goals. For a second, forget about your career and think about what you want your life to be, both now and in the future. Are you on track to achieve what you want? This isn't just about a work/life balance, but also an opportunity to see if your job situation helps you achieve the personal goals and lifestyle you want.

Take stock of your professional worth. Midcareer is a vague period because it comes at different points for many people and not everyone's professional life progresses at the same pace. So, this period isn't about your specific age as it is about the status of your career.

At this stage, you've had at least one job, if not several, and are accruing experience and expertise in a field. Ask yourself what your résumé would look like if you were to job hunt right now. What are your strongest skills? Where do you need improvement? What career opportunities would be available to you? Now is the time for you to decide if you need to change directions or if you're happy with your situation.

... you can retire:

Decide what you want your golden years to look like. The template of what retirement should look like is long gone. Today, mature workers are taking different paths when it comes to their careers, and you can decide what works best for you.

Because people are living longer, many older workers have no desire to leave the work force and spend another 10 or 20 years at home. Instead, some are scaling back to part-time jobs with their current employers. They still get a paycheck and the company retains their expertise. Others are switching professions entirely and venturing into their dream jobs now that they have the time and money to do so.

Decide what you need to have the life you want: Some mature workers can't afford to leave their full-time jobs, even if they wanted to, due to financial needs. As you get older, you have to plan for the cost of health care, medicine and other living expenses, none of which is cheap. Deciding what your future looks like should account for your ideal situation and inevitable factors.

1.1 Assessment

THINK CRITICALLY

1. Why is satisfaction an important component of exchange in terms of marketing?

2. What are some of the pros and cons of marketing in society?

3. Match each marketing function with the activity in that function:

   1. Market Planning; 2. Product/Service Management;
   3. Promotion; 4. Selling; 5. Pricing; 6. Distribution; 7. Marketing-Information Management; 8. Financing; 9. Risk Management

   a. Calling prospective customers at dinnertime

   b. Manufacturing a machine that hangs up on telemarketers

   c. Giving patrons of your delicatessen a frequent buyer card

   d. Deciding how much to charge for donuts

   e. Setting up a Saturday car wash at the community center

   f. Writing the script that telemarketers read over the phone

   g. Offering "unbelievable savings" to people who buy vinyl siding from a telemarketer

   h. Recognizing a need in the market for a new product offering

   i. A store owner buying liability insurance to manage the risk of a customer falling and injuring him- or herself while shopping

MAKE ACADEMIC CONNECTIONS

4. **TIME TRAVEL** The year is 1903, and you and your brother Orville have just flown your 605-pound wooden airplane for 12 seconds! How will you apply the nine marketing functions to your new invention? Present your marketing plans in a PowerPoint presentation or a series of flip charts.

5. **BUSINESS PRACTICES** Companies in certain industries, such as clothing manufacturing and mining, have been criticized for *exploitation*. Exploitation can be defined in two ways: (1) the act of employing to the greatest possible advantage and (2) utilizing another person or group for selfish purposes. Which definition describes a situation you have seen in the news? Are these positive or negative business practices? Why? What are the short-term consequences and long-term consequences of these actions? Write a short report to explain your ideas and defend your point of view.

The Changing Marketplace

Goals
- Explain the development of markets
- Recognize four economic systems that have affected economic development
- Describe the U.S. market economy

Key Terms
- traditional economy
- command economy
- market economy
- mixed economy

Marketing and Society

As you embark upon your future, it is helpful to understand the past. As you begin your journey of self-marketing, understanding the story of the marketplace will make it easier for you to live and work in it.

Until fairly recent times, a "market" was a physical place where buyers and sellers gathered to conduct exchanges. Throughout history, people have used markets to acquire personal and national wealth. Along the way, humans have acquired communication skills and critical thinking skills to enhance these ventures.

The timeline on the next page shows the various stages in the history of the marketplace. Starting at the bottom of the timeline, read about the characteristics, technologies, and values of each era. Think about the qualities you would have needed to be an effective "employee" in each period.

Since its beginning, the United States has significantly influenced marketplace development. Early colonists wanted to manage trade and businesses without heavy taxation from the English government. After the Civil War, the financial center of the world shifted from London to New York City. Many of the technical innovations of the Industrial Revolution were developed or perfected in this country. For example, Eli Whitney was the first inventor to successfully mass produce an item using interchangeable parts—he manufactured 10,000 muskets for the American Army in 1798.

marketing matters

After moving to a new apartment in Connecticut, Asif Haq met his neighbor, Maryann Carson. Maryann explained that every Saturday she visits the Central District to buy fresh produce and other groceries. How does Maryann's shopping preference relate to the development of marketplaces?

© Brandon Seidel, 2009/ Used under license from Shutterstock.com

HISTORY OF THE MARKETPLACE

1950s to present ⬆	**The Evolving Marketplace**	**Information Age**	**Characteristics:** Shift from the manufacturing sector of the economy to the service sector; information management **Technology:** Computers, Internet, and digital technology **Values:** Global commerce, access to information, and communication skills
1700 A.D. ⬆		**Industrialization**	**Characteristics:** Technological advances, mass production, expanding commercial markets **Technology:** Steam engine, cotton gin, electricity **Values:** Self-interest placed ahead of the common good; labor organization
1400 A.D. ⬆		**Early Modern Period**	**Characteristics:** Closing of land routes between East and West; exploration by sea; colonization **Technology:** Telescope, printing press, gunpowder **Values:** Mobile labor
800 B.C. ⬆	**Early Trade**		**Characteristics:** Improved techniques of transportation and communication; marketplaces developed to provide central location for trade **Technology:** Caravans and, later, sea routes **Values:** Items that could be bartered and traded; coined money
7000 B.C. ⬆	**Development of Society**	**Agrarian Society**	**Characteristics:** Permanent settlements, work separate from family life, bartering between groups, agriculture/crops on a larger scale, and specialization of labor **Technology:** Plows and the wheel **Values:** Agriculture; variety in social structures and personality types
10,000 B.C. ⬆		**Horticultural Society**	**Characteristics:** Cultivated plants and domesticated animals, bartering and trading within tribal groups **Technology:** Hand tools needed to grow food **Values:** Strength, hard work, interference with natural selection
Before 10,000 B.C. ⬆		**Hunters and Gatherers**	**Characteristics:** Nomadic people followed herds and vegetation and lived in family groups **Technology:** Tools necessary for finding food—spears, bows and arrows **Values:** Family groups and survival skills

Check ▶ Point

List three types of societies and an important value for a worker from each.

Economic Systems

Economic systems, like the marketplace itself, have developed over time. Four economic systems that have affected the worldwide market include the traditional economy, command economy, market economy, and mixed economy. Economic systems answer three questions:

1. What goods and services will be produced?
2. How will they be produced?
3. For whom will they be produced?

Traditional Economy

In a **traditional economy**, the three economic questions are answered according to custom or tradition. This type of economy is found in less-developed countries that are not yet involved in the global economy. A traditional economy is based on meeting people's basic needs for food, clothing, and shelter.

Command Economy

In a **command economy** the government provides answers to the three economic questions. A centralized government controls all re-sources and determines what should be produced. Individuals do not directly benefit from their work. A command economy also is referred to as communism. Cuba and North Korea have communist economies. China and the former Soviet Union had communist economies until the 1990s.

Market Economy

In a **market economy** the three economic questions are answered by individuals through buying and selling goods and services in the marketplace. Market forces such as supply and demand move the economy. Individuals have the freedom to choose the products they want to buy, choose their schooling, and choose their careers. The potential for risk and reward is an outcome of the availability of these choices.

Digital Vision, Getty Images

Mixed Economy

Most countries in the world have mixed economies. **Mixed economies** have elements of both command and market economies. Worldwide there has been a shift away from command economies and toward market economies. The resulting economies have various degrees of government involvement in the marketplace. Also, as countries with traditional economies evolve, most develop mixed economies.

Ask students how learning about an agrarian society could be useful to a student in the 21st century? (Although it's not likely that students will be confronted with having to learn to become successful in an agrarian society, such skills would be necessary if they decide to pursue humanitarian work in less-developed countries.)

Check ▶ Point

What three questions do economic systems answer?

The U.S. Market Economy

The United States is a mixed economy. It is a market economy because markets play a large role. However, the government provides programs to help members of society, regulates businesses, and owns some businesses. Congress and state governments also regulate entire industries, such as the insurance industry.

The U.S. market economy also is referred to as *capitalism*. With capitalism, individuals are free to own property; individuals and companies are allowed to compete for their own economic gain; and free market forces determine the prices of goods and services. Supply and demand, discussed in more detail in Chapter 2, determine which products are produced and the prices at which they will be sold.

As an employee in the U.S. economy, you are free to work for the organization of your choice—provided, of course, that the organization will hire you. You also are free to change jobs or start your own business.

Each era of U.S. economic development has had particular characteristics that demonstrate the focus of the market at that time. These characteristics reflect the technology and values of the people during each era.

Production Era (Through 1925)

As the Industrial Revolution introduced economic changes to society, the Production Era emerged. During this era, companies believed that products would sell themselves. They focused on mass production and the affordability of products. When assembly lines made the manufacturing of cars more efficient, for example, the number of cars increased, and manufacturers assumed that people would buy more cars.

Hutton Archive/Getty Images

Sales Era (1925 to Early 1950s)

As the business environment became more competitive, companies realized that it takes more than an available product to stimulate sales. The philosophy of the Sales Era was to *find* customers for products. Instead of expecting products to sell themselves, companies developed advertising campaigns to boost sales and hired salespeople to convince customers to buy their products. Maybe your grandparents remember door-to-door salespeople coming to their homes to sell encyclopedias and household items.

NETBookmark

The Bureau of Consumer Protection, a branch of the Federal Trade Commission (FTC), works to protect consumers against "unfair, deceptive, or fraudulent practices" and to enforce truth-in-advertising standards. The huge growth of the Internet, along with its millions of advertisements, has given the Bureau the challenge of patrolling cyberspace. Learn how the Bureau has faced the challenge by reading its guidelines for advertising on the Internet. Access the Bureau's web site through **www.cengage.com/school/marketing/yourself**. Choose one of the Rules listed, and rewrite it in paragraph form in your own words.

Marketing Era (1950s to Early 1990s)

Businesses gradually realized that consumers would buy their products if they produced items and services that consumers wanted. This was the underlying philosophy of the Marketing Era. Products were increasingly visible in advertising campaigns, and consumers had more access to credit, making purchases seem more affordable.

Some organizations exploited consumers through the use of high-pressure sales tactics and misleading advertisements. Consumers became concerned that organizations could take advantage of them, and issues of trust and product benefits became more important.

Relationship Marketing Era (Early 1990s to Present)

The current era in the evolution of marketing is the Relationship Marketing Era. Building relationships that benefit buyers and sellers is increasingly important. Satisfaction—the feeling that the good or service has met expectations—influences these relationships. The goal of marketing is to attract new customers, keep current customers, and anticipate customers' needs.

Communication is more important than ever because identifying and then satisfying customers' needs and wants are crucial to a business's survival. Marketing is no longer confined to one department. Everyone in an organization becomes a marketer, creating and delivering satisfaction and value to customers.

Photodisc/Getty Images

Check Point

What are the four eras in the evolution of the U.S. market economy?

1.2 Assessment

THINK CRITICALLY

1. Using information from the History of the Marketplace chart on page 14, compare and contrast the characteristics, technology, and values of the early traders with those of the Information Age.

2. Some nations resent the power that the U.S. has over global economic development. Discuss why you think that is.

3. You are moving to a country with a command economic system. What practical assumptions might you make about government and economics in that country?

MAKE ACADEMIC CONNECTIONS

4. **MARKETING MATH** Brenna is looking for a part-time job while in high school. She wants to work at the mall to get retail marketing experience. Shop A offers her $5.50 per hour with a promise of 15 hours per week of scheduled work. Shop B offers her $6.25 per hour with a guarantee of 12 hours per week. Which position offers a higher weekly base salary?

5. **TECHNOLOGY** The U.S. market economy differs from a pure capitalist economy. Conduct research on the Internet to develop a list of some of the services the U.S. government provides to citizens and some of the services it provides to companies.

6. **COMMUNICATION** The first paper money produced in the colonies that later became the United States was issued by the Massachusetts Bay colony around 1690. Research the history of money in the United States and create a flip chart or PowerPoint presentation that illustrates the evolution of money in the U.S. marketplace.

The Current Marketplace

Goals
- Describe the importance of information and communication in the U.S. market economy and in global business
- State current employment workplace trends

Key Terms
- global village
- mass customization
- e-commerce
- individualism

Information and Communication

You live in the Information Age. You are witnessing the shift from a society focused on the production of goods and services to a post-industrial society in which access to information is vital and production of knowledge is a key economic factor.

In this new economic framework, information and communication skills continue to increase in importance. In the 19th and 20th centuries, mechanical and industrial skills helped workers get ahead. Today, your information and communication skills—including speaking, interpreting written information, writing, and computer skills—can help you move ahead in your career. Let's look at the ways information and knowledge are affecting service businesses and the global economy.

Service Sector Growth

Two-thirds of the total value of the goods and services produced in the United States—called the *gross domestic product (GDP)*—is produced by businesses that provide services (known as "the service sector"). Banks, insurance companies, childcare facilities, cleaning services, customer service centers, and information processing are all examples of businesses that provide services.

Information and knowledge drive the growth of services. Technology, including electronic communication and information technology, has

marketing matters

Eva Brukowski would like to move from Tennessee to Arizona to be closer to her daughter's family. She has worked as a legal assistant for 35 years. How can she use technology to continue working for her current employer after she moves?

© Elliot Westacott, 2009/Used under license from Shutterstock.com

changed the way services are provided. You can use an automated teller machine (ATM) to withdraw money from your bank account. If you want to find your account balance or billing date, you don't even need to visit the ATM. You can log onto the bank's web site, type your password, and review your account over the Internet.

According to the U.S. Department of Labor, the service sector will produce 15.7 million new jobs in the decade between 2006 and 2016. Training and continued skill development will be important values in workforce development.

Global Business

Was your stereo system manufactured in Japan? Can a French citizen eat at an American restaurant chain in Paris? Developed countries such as the United States have seen the rapid creation and adoption of new technologies open up new markets and create greater global competition. In the early years of the current century, nearly 60 percent of families in the United States have a home computer.

From a business perspective, this connectedness opens up new markets that may not have been accessible because of limits on time or distance. The phenomenon of drawing people and businesses together from across the planet has been termed the **global village**.

The lowering of these barriers has allowed businesses to expand their operations to meet market needs and also to make the best use of available resources around the globe. An example is a foreign automobile company that builds manufacturing sites in the United States. Manufacturing the

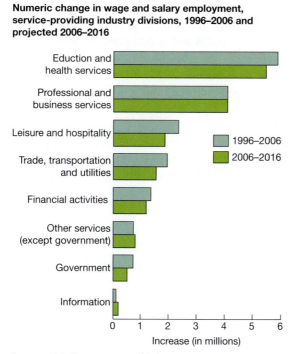

Numeric change in wage and salary employment, service-providing industry divisions, 1996–2006 and projected 2006–2016

Source: U.S. Department of Labor

cars closer to American consumers reduces the time and expense of shipping steel and other materials overseas. The foreign manufacturer also has access to American employees who have engineering, production, and managerial experience in the American automobile industry.

Mass customization, the process of providing products and services that more closely meet the needs and wants of individual customers, is becoming more commonplace. Technological advancements are improving production systems and customer research methods. Instead of mass producing the same products for everyone, businesses can use technology to learn more about customers and personalize products more affordably. It is easier to enter new markets and practice global business with products that are tailored to the needs of customers. Nike offers mass customization through NIKEiD. Customers choose a shoe style (the upper), and then make choices such as base shoe color, type of outsole, and laces—even the color of the swoosh!

Check▸Point

Does mass customization enable producers to bring highly individualized products to market faster or more slowly than previous processes?

marketing math connection

You are considering two different marketing occupations: One is as a marketing manager, and the other is as a marketing designer. According to a local job resource center, the number of jobs for marketing managers in your area was 5,000 in 2008 and is projected to be 6,200 by 2012. The number of marketing designer positions in your area was 8,100 in 2008 and is projected to be 9,500 by 2012. Which occupation has the greatest percentage increase projected for jobs?

SOLUTION

To calculate a percentage increase, subtract the number of jobs available in 2008 from the number projected for 2012. Next, divide the difference by the number of jobs in 2008. Express the answer in percentage form.

Percentage increase (manager) $= \dfrac{(6200 - 5000)}{5000} = 0.24 = 24\%$

Percentage increase (designer) $= \dfrac{(9500 - 8100)}{8100} = 0.173 = 17.3\%$

The marketing manager position has a greater percentage increase projected for jobs.

Employment Trends

As you prepare to enter the workforce, consider some important trends that affect the workforce of the 21st century, including diversity, education, e-commerce, ethics and social responsibility, and focus on the individual.

Diversity

The composition of the workforce is changing, and you are likely to work alongside people of different experiences, races, ages, and ethnicities. These differences can strengthen an organization by making a variety of skills and backgrounds available to support the organization's mission.

An example of workplace diversity can be found in the aging U.S. population, which is providing one element of growth in the service sector. Retirees are working at fast-food restaurants and serving as greeters and sales associates in retail stores.

Education

The concept of lifelong, or continuous, learning is becoming critically important in the service sector. Technology produces change, so employees should prepare themselves to adapt to changes in the ways their jobs are performed and the ways their employers conduct business.

Photodisc/Getty Images

Technology is changing the way education is delivered as well. Students can receive all or part of their advanced education over the Internet. Most colleges, universities, and trade schools offer "distance learning programs" with videotaped lectures, online exercises and exams, and virtual discussion groups between instructors and students.

E-Commerce

E-commerce is the process of conducting business transactions over the Internet. The Internet and e-commerce have rapidly changed the way consumers and businesses buy products and services. Customers have 24-hour access via the Internet to view product information and make purchases. A customer in India can buy products from a company in Nebraska without leaving home.

Did You Know?

Advanced technology allows Wal-Mart's "Alarm Central" emergency operations center to monitor fire and burglar alarms at the more than 3,000 Wal-Mart and Sam's Club stores. The "Alarm Central" employees also watch news stations for information about events such as bad weather that could affect store operations.

Ethics and Social Responsibility

In 1962, Milton Friedman argued that a business's only social responsibility was to make a profit. Many others, including marketing scholar Philip Kotler and management guru Peter Drucker, believed that businesses also had a responsibility to society. In today's business climate, high-profile incidents of unethical and even unlawful behavior have led to an emphasis on ethics and corporate social responsibility.

The influential role marketing plays makes the issue of ethics even more important to the discipline. Marketing influences many decisions within its organization as well as those made by consumers and other organizations. Marketing decisions, which ultimately affect the decisions of others, often involve ethical dilemmas, as morals and standards generally are not universal, and competing interests need to be balanced. For example, marketing may be involved in product labeling decisions, persuasive promotional media, and pricing decisions. These marketing decisions influence the decisions of others, and this interaction allows for ethical dilemmas. The American Marketing Association (AMA) has its own statement of ethics for marketers. This code covers ethical issues in promotions, distribution, pricing, and marketing research.

The World Business Council for Sustainable Development defines corporate social responsibility as "the continuing commitment by business to behave ethically and contribute to economic development while improving the quality of life of the workforce and their families as well as of the local community and society at large." As a student, for example, social responsibility might mean respecting the comments other students make in the classroom, avoiding cheating or plagiarizing in your class work, and joining a student organization that contributes in some way to the overall high school experience for all students.

Focus on the Individual

Because we are an information-driven economy and society, we tend to focus on the development of individuals' skills, knowledge, experience, and accomplishments rather than on the collective efforts of society. **Individualism** is defined by the 19th century German philosopher Max Stirner as "the free association of unique individuals who cooperate as equals in order to maximize their freedom and satisfy their desires."

You already participate in individualistic situations. For example, as a student you are responsible for your own grades. As part of a larger classroom community, such as a team project, your efforts affect the learning experience of the group. When you are in class, your participation (answering questions, working on group projects, giving presentations) helps other students learn. Their participation, in turn, helps you learn. Though as an individual you must take responsibility and be accountable for your personal efforts, the collective efforts of the group can serve to benefit everyone.

The U.S. market economy has freedom of choice at its core. But if individuals see this freedom as the ability to promote their own self-interests

diversity in the workplace

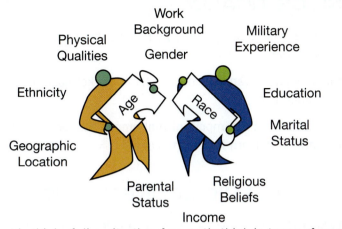

When people think of diversity, they frequently think in terms of race, age, or gender. But because people can have many qualities, diversity is a complex issue. The graphic above illustrates dimensions of humanity that can be found in the workplace.

List the similarities and differences among the people in each example:

1. Three female graduate students in mathematics in a class total of 200

2. A young white male Peace Corps officer working in Nairobi with medical professionals who are native black Africans

3. A Wall Street trader who studied the stock market growing up on a farm in Nebraska

without consideration of the consequences to society, they may make choices that have negative consequences. A business owner may choose to pay him- or herself a sizable salary with bonuses while the company is heading toward bankruptcy, for example.

As a 21st century employee or business owner, you may want to consider how you can be a productive member of the workforce *and* the community, satisfying your own needs while considering the needs of others. You have the opportunity to develop and direct yourself and create your own achievements, but only by recognizing the assets and contributions of others can you preserve your own uniqueness and liberty.

Check Point

Select one of the four workplace trends described in this section and explain its impact on your life or your parents' lives.

THINK CRITICALLY

1. List several ways that your lifestyle reflects the increased technology available today.

2. What are some advantages of the global marketplace to consumers and businesses?

3. Why do you think it's important that employees today be flexible and continue to learn new technology?

MAKE ACADEMIC CONNECTIONS

4. **COMMUNICATION** Locate an article about a company that has used technology to market its products. Prepare and present a five-minute oral report on your findings.

5. **SOCIAL STUDIES** Society has changed as a result of more women entering the workforce. Research the changing role of women and some of the ways society has changed as a result.

6. **INTERNATIONAL BUSINESS** Many goods and services we enjoy are the products of multiple countries. For example, the corporate headquarters may be in one country, a primary supply source may be in another country, and the final assembly may be in a third country. Think of some examples in which "one" is actually a product of "many," and how.

7. **COMMUNICATION** People from different groups may speak the same language differently. Role-play specific examples in which communication issues may surface between same-language speakers who are of different generations, geographic backgrounds, education levels, ethnicities, work backgrounds, o r physical abilities.

VOCABULARY BUILDER

Choose the term that best fits the definition. Some terms are not used.

_____ 1. Drawing people and businesses together from across the planet

_____ 2. Getting product and services to customers in the best possible way

_____ 3. Nine key activities that must occur in order to make a product or service available to consumers

_____ 4. Marketing communications that inform, persuade, and remind customers of a product's benefit and encourage them to buy it

_____ 5. The activity, set of institutions, and processes for creating, communicating, delivering, and exchanging offerings that have value for customers, clients, partners, and society at large

a. barter

b. distribution

c. global village

d. market economy

e. marketing

f. marketing functions

g. mass customization

h. pricing

i. promotion

j. relationship marketing

k. satisfaction

_____ 6. The process of providing products and services that more closely meet the needs and wants of individual customers

_____ 7. The process of exchanging products and services; does not involve a monetary exchange

_____ 8. Deciding how much a product or service will cost the consumer

_____ 9. Marketing approach that attracts new customers, keeps current customers, and anticipates customer needs

REVIEW CONCEPTS

www.cengage.com/school/ marketing/yourself

Read the terms and definitions for the four types of promotional activities, and then match the following groups of activities with the appropriate promotional activity.

a. **sales promotions** Communicating through a variety of non-personal, non-media vehicles, such as samples and coupons

b. **advertising** Communicating through non-personal, paid media

c. **publicity** Communicating through personal or non-personal media that is not explicitly paid for delivering the message

d. **personal selling** Communicating through paid sales personnel

10. _____
   - Print ads
   - Broadcast ads
   - Billboard ads
   - Direct mail ads
   - Packaging logos and information

11. _____
   - In-person sales presentations
   - Telemarketing

12. _____
   - Print media news stories
   - Broadcast media news stories
   - Annual reports
   - Speeches by employees

13. _____
   - Games, contests
   - Free samples
   - Trade shows
   - Coupons
   - Trading stamps
   - Reduced prices
   - Signs and displays

14. List four economic systems that operate in markets.

15. What are the three key factors that define capitalism?

16. How does promotion differ from selling?

17. What are the four eras in the marketing evolution of the United States?

18. Provide an example of the use of technology in global business.

19. List three major employment trends for the 21st century.

20. List three examples of advertising.

21. What is the service sector? List two service businesses that market to individual consumers, and two service businesses that market to other businesses. Use examples not mentioned in the text.

22. Why are posting flyers and having friends wear special T-shirts considered forms of advertising when the advertiser does not have to pay for the bulletin board space or for his or her friends to wear the T-shirts? Why aren't these activities considered to be other forms of promotion?

23. How does the Relationship Marketing Era differ from the Marketing Era?

24. Explain the concept of a global village.

25. How can diversity strengthen a workplace?

26. How can marketing information management be used as you market yourself?

27. Why is lifelong learning important in the service sector?

APPLY WHAT YOU LEARNED

28. How will you market yourself when you look for a job?

29. Can you think of something you purchased in the last month? Identify how the purchase involved the nine marketing functions.

30. Look at several TV commercials or magazine ads for a variety of vehicles. Describe specific features of each commercial or ad that indicate who the manufacturer is trying to appeal to.

31. Think of some values that are important in your society. Have any of them been "marketed"? Which ones? How have they been marketed?

32. How has the growth of the Internet increased global business opportunities?

33. How can technology impact retailers?

34. How might ethics impact your job search?

MAKE ACADEMIC CONNECTIONS

35. **COMMUNICATION** Predict the future of technological impact. Do you think on-ground businesses such as retail stores will eventually disappear? Explain your thoughts in a two-page persuasive paper that gives clear reasons for your predictions.

36. **ART/DESIGN** Create a poster to educate students and employees about workplace diversity. Provide at a glance an education in diversity.

37. **TECHNOLOGY** Search the Internet for information about e-commerce privacy and security (the ways in which organizations protect customer data). What are the main methods of ensuring secure transactions, and what are the advantages and issues surrounding secure transactions? Write a one-page summary of your findings.

38. **SOCIAL STUDIES** The growing availability of personal and financial information troubles many people. In groups, research privacy issues as they apply to businesses and the

Internet. Present a report on current problems in consumer privacy, possible solutions to these problems, and potential legislation to protect consumers' privacy.

39. **CREATIVE WRITING** Think of a problem that you have on a regular basis. Brainstorm the perfect product that would eliminate your problem. Use your imagination! Then, develop an advertisement for that product that would appeal to students your age.

40. **SOCIAL STUDIES** Research the various ethnic and cultural groups in your community, and create a map that shows the different parts of the world that these groups came from. In what ways have these groups contributed to the development and growth of your community?

41. **TECHNOLOGY** Search the Internet for two examples of mass customization. Write a short comparison paper explaining how these examples illustrate mass customization, comparing and contrasting them.

BUSINESS PRESENTATION

Multimedia presentations have become a common form of marketing for businesses and organizations. Each year FBLA will select a multimedia national topic for one, two, or three students to prepare. Multimedia presentations must be two to four minutes in length, and teams will be allowed nine minutes to describe the project. Judges have an additional three minutes to ask questions about the multimedia presentation.

TOPIC You have been asked to create a presentation on how individuals can stay safe on the Internet. An increasing number of individuals are paying bills and viewing financial information online. Online banking and shopping have allowed consumers to complete business transactions without leaving home. Many young people share personal information through web sites such as Facebook, Second Life, and YouTube. Your presentation must give individuals safety guidelines for conducting business and sharing personal information online.

Your presentation will be evaluated for implementing innovative technology into a convincing multimedia presentation that respects copyright issues.

Make a Persuasive Presentation

Effective persuasive presentations are designed to appeal to your audience. Using evidence, you explain to your audience the reasons for believing or acting the way you suggest. While you may think of persuasion as being negative or manipulative, persuasion is not in itself unethical. It is about changing a belief or encouraging action. This means that you must prepare for your presentation by conducting research, referring to credible sources, and planning to present your argument in a way that is believable and appealing to your audience. You can learn to be an effective speaker. Just remember the three P's—Prepare, Practice, and finally, Present!

Prepare

Before making a persuasive presentation, you need to prepare. Begin by writing a proposition, or persuasive speech goal, that you design either to impact a belief or to encourage action. As you write the proposition, consider your audience. For example, a presentation you give to a group of high school students will differ from a presentation you give on the same topic to school board members. Be specific—what do you want your audience to take away from your presentation? As you prepare, you should remember that an effective presentation includes an introduction, body, and conclusion. Using outline format is an effective way of organizing and preparing your presentation. You also will want to prepare visual aids, such as charts or graphs, to support your proposition.

The introduction sets the stage for your presentation. It should get attention, establish your credibility as a presenter, and build your relationship with your audience. The body includes your main points. Your persuasive presentation should not be based on opinion alone. You need to conduct research, using evidence and argument to support your proposition. Effective main points can be supported with facts. The conclusion gives you one more opportunity to make your point with your audience. Your conclusion should remind the audience of your key points. It

also should connect with your audience so they will remember your presentation and be impacted by your proposition.

Practice

You would not expect to swim like a pro the first time you jump in the water, and you cannot expect to give an effective persuasive presentation without practice. Good delivery, coupled with a believable and appealing argument based on credible sources, can help you to connect with and persuade your audience. You can improve delivery and become a more effective presenter through practice.

As you review your presentation outline, consider how you can use language, both verbal and nonverbal, to effectively present to your audience. Your voice will allow you to present your argument, and how you use it can impact your ability to persuade. You may want to record yourself so you become aware of your voice and speech patterns. Be aware of your facial expressions and gestures, as your body language acts as nonverbal communication. Practicing your presentation in front of a mirror can help you feel more comfortable with your delivery. You can even ask a friend or family member to watch your presentation and provide suggestions.

Present

On presentation day, bring your outline or notes as well as any visual aids. You have prepared and practiced, so you can shine during your presentation. Come to the presentation well-rested, and present with enthusiasm.

Develop Your Skill

Marketing, especially marketing communication, typically involves some element of persuasion. Social marketing, often done by not-for-profit or governmental organizations, is designed to influence the behavior of consumers to provide benefit to the target market and to society. Identify an issue that relates to social marketing and prepare a persuasive presentation with your classmates as your intended audience. Don't forget to follow the three P's model!

Chapter 2

The Character of the Market

2.1 The Economic Environment

2.2 Business Development

2.3 Management and Leadership

CAREERS IN MARKETING

The Green Building Alliance

Founded in 1993, the Green Building Alliance (GBA) is a regional organization driving innovation and awareness of environmentally sustainable building practices. The GBA seeks to advance economic prosperity and well-being through a focus on green building. GBA is affiliated with the U.S. Green Building Council.

© Anthony Harris, 2009/ Used under license from Shutterstock.com

The Executive Director oversees daily operations and implements programs and services consistent with GBA's mission. The Executive Director will serve as spokesperson for GBA, grow its membership, make educational and promotional presentations, and have a passion for sustainable building.

The position requires a college degree, knowledge of marketing, fundraising and strategic planning experience, and strong communication skills. The candidate should be a proven leader, proactive and responsive to the needs of the community, and passionate about the GBA's mission.

Think *Critically*

1. Why do you think knowledge of marketing is a requirement for the Executive Director position?

2. Why do you think the Executive Director needs to know management principles?

Project Objectives

How do you keep track of all the items that go into your portfolio? How do you document what you learn in class so you can put it into practice? Marketing yourself requires good organizational skills. As you do the assignments in this book, you will complete activities that help you market yourself. You will also produce items for your portfolio. In this project, you will:

- Assemble an organizational binder.
- Plan the completion of assignments and portfolio items.
- Incorporate daily to-do lists, job search information, and other essential career development items into an organizer.

Getting Started

Read the Project Process below. Make a list of any materials you will need. Decide how you will get the needed materials or information.

- From the Portfolio Builder CD, print the templates you will use to plan the completion of assignments and portfolio items.
- Use the Assignment Checklist from the Portfolio Builder CD to list each item you need to complete.
- Schedule the tasks and their due dates.

Project Process

Part 1   Lesson 2.1 Create your own organizer by reusing an empty three-ring binder or by buying a new binder. Look through the organizer templates on the Portfolio Builder CD, and decide which ones you want to use. Consider the different options for calendars, task lists, and so on and select a format that will be easy to use.

Part 2   Lesson 2.2 List the due dates for *Marketing Yourself* assignments and portfolio deadlines on your calendar. Create daily task lists based on upcoming assignments and deadlines. Do you have any job search contacts yet? If you do, record that information in your organizer's address section.

Part 3   Lesson 2.3 You can use your organizer to plan other areas of your life. Do you already have a job? If so, use a section of your organizer to list your work schedule.

Project Wrap-Up

Choose a partner and commit to keeping each other accountable for completing the *Marketing Yourself* assignments.

© mattomedia, 2009/Used under license from Shutterstock.com

The Economic Environment

Goals

- Understand several basic economic concepts
- Recognize the four types of economic utility

Key Terms

- economics
- need
- want
- scarcity
- consumers
- producers
- good
- service
- labor
- capital
- land
- entrepreneurship
- law of supply
- law of demand
- economic utility

Economics 101

Everyone has economic experience. Each household is its own *economic institution*, whether there is one member or twenty. Have you bought products such as a cell phone, a new notebook, an Internet service provider, or lunch at a deli? If so, you have made *economic choices* as a consumer. Do you have a job? Labor—your work—is a *resource* in the economy.

How is economics defined? **Economics** is the social science that deals with the production, distribution, and consumption of goods and services. Economics is very important to marketers because economic factors such as consumer spending, income, and purchasing power directly influence marketing. If you see a clever commercial for a new computer and you've just gotten a promotion and a raise, you may decide to buy the computer. If your neighbor who just lost her job sees the same clever commercial, she will probably resist the marketing efforts of the computer company and decide to keep using her current computer.

©Diego Cervo, 2009/Used under license from Shutterstock.com

marketing matters

On weekends, Bharat Patel works at a men's clothing store in the mall. In addition to his hourly pay and a commission for sales, Bharat receives a 20 percent discount on any purchase he makes at the store. He is not required to wear a uniform to work, but he does have to wear clothes that are currently for sale at the store, which he must buy with his own money. What are the economic implications of this policy for the store? What are the implications for Bharat?

Needs, Wants, and Scarcity

You probably never feel completely satisfied with your wardrobe or your music system or your book collection or even your dinner! You might like a few more shirts, CDs, books, or mashed potatoes. Most people have many *needs* and *wants*. In economic terms, a **need** is something that is required to live. A **want** is an unfulfilled desire. The resources for fulfilling everyone's needs and wants are limited. Unlimited needs and wants and limited resources make up the basic premise of economics: **scarcity**.

When resources are scarce, people have to make economic choices. Jonas may choose to go to the bookstore to buy a book he needs for a class project instead of buying a new video game. He has satisfied one need/want but has had to forego another. Businesses work to make *their* products and services the ones that people choose.

Consumers and Producers

Consumers are people who choose to spend resources on goods and services intended for personal use and not for manufacture or resale.

- Your family recently purchased a pick-up truck. Your parents are the consumers if they decided to spend their money on this particular truck. Although you and your siblings may benefit from using the truck, most marketing efforts focus on consumers.

©Brad Remy, 2009/ Used under license from Shutterstock.com

Producers are individuals or companies who create valued products and exchange these products with consumers for scarce resources (money). A product may be a **good** (a physical product) or a **service** (specific skills or knowledge).

- A car manufacturing company is the producer of your family's new truck, which is a good.

- Your driver education teacher is a producer who delivers a service: teaching students how to drive. The resulting benefit is a driver who has learned how to operate a car safely according to the rules of the road and who is ready to be officially licensed because of this knowledge.

Workshop

Think of a product that you would consume more of if the price were lower. Do you know of any products whose prices have been lowered to attract consumers?

Economic Resources

Economists refer to resources as *factors of production*. The resources of labor, capital, land, and entrepreneurship are used to produce goods and services that consumers want.

Labor refers to human effort, or work. The labor force includes full- and part-time workers, those who do physical work, and those who are knowledge workers. If you hold a job, you sell your labor in the marketplace.

Capital includes those items necessary to produce goods and services, including physical capital, such as buildings, machines, and tools. A dentist's drill would be physical capital. *Human capital* refers to an individual's knowledge and skills. The dentist's knowledge of teeth and gums and her dentistry skills are human capital.

Land includes the ground itself, as well as natural resources, such as water and minerals, used in production.

Entrepreneurship refers to the ability to envision new opportunities and undertake them. An *entrepreneur* is someone who organizes the start-up and takes the risks necessary to get a business started. If successful, an entrepreneur can increase the value of resources. Most businesses that you recognize began with entrepreneurship. Henry Ford recognized the opportunity for automotive transportation and acted on it by starting a business. Without entrepreneurship, new products and services are not developed.

Supply and Demand

Once a business has developed a product or service, how does it know how much of the product or service to produce? What keeps a business from producing too many notebook computers and not enough graphing calculators? Why does a computer programmer earn more than a data entry worker? Understanding supply and demand can help answer these questions.

Businesses tend to produce more of products that they can sell at higher prices. The **law of supply** says that the amount of a product supplied is directly related to price: the higher the price, the more supplied. If a product can be sold at a higher price, entrepreneurs might consider entering the market, and companies already producing the product may be able to expand production.

How much are consumers willing to pay for products? Consumers tend to buy more of a product when it is sold at a lower price. The **law of demand** says that the amount of a product demanded relates inversely to price: the lower the price, the more demanded. For instance, if Sunita enjoys baseball, she might attend one game during the season if the ticket price is $35. If the ticket price was only $15, she might be willing to attend three games.

Check Point

Define economics. Describe a recent situation in your life that had economic implications. What were those implications?

Economic Utility

When you watch a movie that has poor sound quality, you probably don't want to hurry back to that theater. On the other hand, when you order a cookbook on the Internet and it arrives in two days, you will be pleased. People choose products and services that give them the most *satisfaction*.

Economic utility is the amount of satisfaction a person gets from using a product or service. Because businesses know that satisfied customers lead to greater profitability, they want to provide high economic utility. Businesses, including marketing departments, work to provide utility in time, place, form, and possession.

©Stockbyte/Getty Images

- *Time utility* means making a product available at a time when consumers want it. Examples of time utility include a company making its products available "24/7" through an Internet site, a retail store remaining open until midnight on the days before the Christmas holiday for last-minute shoppers, and a doctor's office offering early morning and weekend appointments.

- *Place utility* involves making products available *where* consumers want them. A vending machine with fruit juices and bottled water near a practice field provides place utility, as do automated teller machines in grocery stores, movie theaters, and malls.

- *Form utility* occurs when the actual *form* of the product attracts consumers. A backpack with wide, sturdy straps, pockets for pencils, and a calculator made of water-resistant material provides form utility. You may not be interested in eating oats, raisins, and almonds separately, but in the form of a granola bar, you may find them a tasty snack.

- *Possession utility* means providing different ways for consumers to own a product. Possession utility may involve making products more affordable by offering credit, layaway, or debit cards. Some businesses rent or lease cars, furniture, electronics, camping supplies, tools, filled aquariums—you name it—to enable customers to consume products they would not otherwise find valuable.

Check Point

Choose a product that you recently purchased. Did you purchase the product because it has time, place, form, and/or possession utility? Explain your answer.

THINK CRITICALLY

1. How is marketing related to economics? What are three economic factors that directly influence marketing? Provide an example of each factor.

2. Discuss an economic choice you made recently. How did the choice you made relate to needs, wants, and scarcity?

3. Isabel would like to open a motorcycle repair shop in an empty garage at her mother's limousine service. Give examples of how she might need to use the four types of resources to do so. Will she need to use all four types to start her business?

4. Explain the law of supply and the law of demand. How do you think they relate to each other?

MAKE ACADEMIC CONNECTIONS

5. **SOCIAL STUDIES** Everyone makes purchases based on economic utility, whether they know it or not. Talk to three of your friends or family members and ask them about their most recent purchases. Ask them what influenced them to purchase the particular product they did. Based on their answers, determine which economic utilities the product provided for them. Create a PowerPoint presentation that shows who you talked to, what their purchases were, what questions you asked, and which economic utilities were provided.

6. **ECONOMIC HISTORY** Use the Internet or your local library to research the Great Depression. How did the concept of scarcity and the laws of supply and demand contribute to the economic troubles of that era? Develop an oral presentation to report your findings to the class.

Business Development

Goals

- Discuss business and its place in the economy
- Understand business cycles and other economic conditions
- Recognize challenges businesses will face in the future

Key Terms

- business
- profit maximization
- economic conditions
- prosperity
- recession
- recovery
- globalization
- technology

The World of Business

You go to the mall to buy new clothes for school. You visit the salon to get a haircut. At the pharmacy, you buy shampoo and deodorant. You stop at the bank to open a savings account.

Retail stores, hair salons, pharmacies, and banks are all businesses. Some sell products; others provide services. Some may be small, like the locally owned hair salon. Others may be large, like the multi-chain pharmacy.

Why should you examine business in more detail? You visit businesses often, and you will likely be employed by a business or perhaps start your own business at some point in your career. Learning business basics also can help you understand your own role as a consumer. You can recognize how marketing affects you. You also can see how you might market yourself to employers in the future.

Business Defined

An organization that uses labor, capital, land, and entrepreneurship to produce goods and services at a profit is a **business**. A successful business will have to take risks and make a profit. A good business will contribute to the community.

marketing matters

Lawrence Freeman has a part-time job after school as a cashier at a small pharmacy. Because he reads the advertisements in the Sunday newspaper, he knows that his company's prices are higher than the prices at the national pharmacy chains. His pharmacy does not advertise in the newspaper, but it does have an ad in the phone book. Lawrence likes his boss and would like to think of ways to help the pharmacy get more business. What suggestions could Lawrence make about how to increase business? How can Lawrence approach his boss without offending him or her?

©Nicholas Sutcliffe 2009/Used under license from Shutterstock.com

careerbuilder®

What Are Green-Collar Jobs?
Industries for the Future

By Kate Lorenz, CareerBuilder.com editor
Copyright 2009 CareerBuilder, LLC. - Reprinted with permission.

Recently, we've heard a lot about green-collar business initiatives and jobs, or jobs created by a shift to a more energy-conscious, energy-efficient society.

Many major political players are all talking about the green-collar movement and pledging the creation millions of new jobs, job training for current and future workers, and the identification of green industries of the future.

President Barack Obama—"We've also got to do more to create the green jobs that are jobs of the future. My energy plan will put $150 billion over 10 years into establishing a green energy sector that will create up to 5 million new jobs over the next two decades."

Republican Sen. John McCain—"We have the opportunity to apply America's technological supremacy to capture the export markets for advanced energy technologies, reaping the capital investment and good jobs it will provide."

This stronger focus on energy diversity and efficiency means more jobs: opportunities in sustainable energy sources like wind and solar, ethanol production, green building, hazardous waste removal, recycling and consumer goods; jobs in research and development, construction, manufacturing, technology, operations and sales.

Perhaps one of the greatest strides in this movement is the Green Jobs Act, part of the 2007 energy bill, which Congress passed and former President Bush signed in late 2007.

"This innovative proposal—green-jobs—will make $125 million a year available across the country to begin training workers for jobs in the clean energy sector," remarked Rep. John Tierney, D-Mass., who co-wrote the Green Jobs Act. "Thirty-five thousand people per year can benefit from vocational education that will provide for them secure employment in this country."

The availability of green-collar jobs will cross boards of workers at all skill levels, says Jerome Ringo, president of the Apollo Alliance, which promotes clean energy and energy efficiency policies and initiatives. "Whether your field is technical, you're a skilled or unskilled worker, you were laid off . . . the economic benefits from green jobs spread from the highly educated to the noneducated."

The act also provides funding for green-collar training particularly targeted to individuals in need of updated skills; military veterans; unemployed individuals; individuals seeking employment pathways out of poverty; and formerly incarcerated, nonviolent offenders.

continued on page 41

According to the act, energy efficiency and renewable energy industries covered under the term "green collar" include:

- energy-efficient building, construction and retrofits;
- renewable electric power;
- energy-efficient and advanced drivetrain vehicles;
- biofuels;
- deconstruction and materials use;
- energy efficiency assessment industry serving the residential, commercial or industrial sectors; and
- manufacturers that produce sustainable products using environmentally sustainable processes and materials.

"New technologies require new skills," said Rachel Gragg, federal policy director for The Workforce Alliance. "Adopting clean energy practices is critical to our nation's well-being, but these efforts won't succeed if we don't invest in the people who will actually do this work. We need people to install millions of solar panels, build and maintain alternative energy plants, make buildings more energy efficient, and maintain and repair hybrid vehicles."

Here are just some of the green areas employers will be hiring for in the coming years:

- Hybrid car manufacturing
- Energy retrofitting
- Food production using organic and/or sustainably grown agricultural products
- Furniture making from environmentally certified and recycled wood
- Green building
- Waste composting
- Hauling and reuse of construction and demolition materials and debris
- Hazardous materials cleanup
- Green landscaping
- Manufacturing of green products (like wind turbine blades and solar panels)
- Reuse and production of products made from recycled, nontoxic materials
- Solar installation and maintenance
- Retrofitting to increase water efficiency and conservation
- Whole home performance (i.e., heating, ventilating and air conditioning; attic insulation; weatherization; etc.)

com-mu-ni-cate

Marketers often present information in the forms of charts and graphs. Evaluate your own spending in five categories. Then create a chart or graph to show the percentage of your budget you spend in each category.

Taking a Risk A business owner takes risks when operating a business. A risk is a possibility for loss. Economic risks are risks based on changes in business conditions, such as increased competition, new government regulations, and changes in consumer preferences. Other risks include

You have worked hard on a construction site all summer. At the end of the summer, your boss gives you a $1,000 bonus and asks you to return to work next summer. You want to put your money into a savings account. If the interest rate is 8.25%, compounded yearly, approximately how long will it take for your money to double? Round to the nearest year.

SOLUTION

The formula for simple interest is $I = PRT$, where I is the interest you want to earn, P is the principal you're starting with, R is the interest rate, and T is time (in years). Express the interest rate as a decimal (0.825).

$$I = PRT$$
$$1,000 = 1,000 \times 0.0825 \times T$$
$$1,000 = 82.5T$$
$$1,000 \div 82.5 = T$$
$$12.12 = T \qquad \text{Your money will double in 12 years.}$$

$I = \$1,000$ because you want your money to double, or to earn interest equal to the principal. If you want your money to triple, I would be $2,000.

natural risks, such as a storm that destroys a warehouse or store, and human risks, such as dishonesty in the form of customer or employee shoplifting. As businesspeople consider new business opportunities, they have to evaluate the possible risks and plan how to overcome them.

Making a Profit Profits provide an incentive for operating a business. The ability to operate a business and make a profit helps contribute to the continued stability and success of our market economy. Businesses generally strive to make the most money in sales of products with the lowest expenses possible; this is called **profit maximization**.

Businesses are better able to make a profit when they understand consumers' needs and wants. Marketing helps businesses understand those needs and wants. If consumers do not know about a product or where it is sold, they certainly cannot buy it. Consumers probably won't buy a product if they cannot afford it or don't see the value of purchasing it. If consumers don't buy the product, the business will not make a profit. And without a reasonable level of profit, the business cannot operate! It is all interconnected, which is why economics is considered to be a *social* science.

Contributing to Society Businesses are expected to be good citizens, pay taxes, and contribute to causes that are important to the community. For instance, many businesses contribute money and resources to charitable organizations. Businesses are also expected to consider their employees by providing fair wages, reasonable job security, and opportunities for growth. Businesses that want to succeed in the long run should also provide value by producing high-quality products and selling them at a fair price.

Corporate Sustainability Sustainability—meeting today's needs without compromising financial, human, or natural resources for tomorrow—has emerged as an influential corporate strategy. Rather than focusing only on profits, this strategy requires that organizations balance their economic goals with social and environmental goals. It is a proactive, or forward-thinking, strategy. An organization plans to meet its current goals and the current needs of its stakeholders without compromising its ability to meet future needs and goals as well. Stakeholders are those who have a stake in the firm, such as shareholders, employees, clients, and the communities in which the organization has an impact.

Workshop

In small groups, discuss advantages and disadvantages of a company's commitment to a corporate sustainability strategy.

Check > Point

List the three types of risks faced by businesses, and provide an example of each type.

Business and the Economy

Economic conditions are economic factors that influence consumer buying power and marketing strategies. These factors include the business cycle, inflation, resource availability, and income.

Business Cycle The business cycle includes periods of prosperity, recession, and recovery in the economy. **Prosperity** is a time of higher incomes, increased production, and lower unemployment for employees.

Recession is a time of increasing unemployment, when consumers decrease their spending and businesses have fewer opportunities to sell their products. Economic **recovery** occurs when employment and business opportunities begin to increase again and consumers start spending more money.

Job opportunities abound during periods of prosperity. People who have sought-after skills may find that they are in great demand, receiving numerous offers of employment. People who are less skilled will also find positions available. During recession, even highly skilled workers may have trouble finding jobs that match their skills and meet their earning expectations.

Inflation Inflation refers to a continued rise in the price of products. Prices rise and fall at various times, but during an inflationary period, the effects of rising prices outweigh falling prices. Customers have to spend more on purchases; as a result, they cannot buy as much with their money.

Income Income is the amount of money earned from labor or the sale of products and services. The amount of income that individuals and businesses earn affects how much they can afford to spend and the types of products they buy. Businesses monitor income levels to assess opportunities for market development. During a time of prosperity, for example, many individuals earn more and spend more. Businesses recognize this prosperity

Did You Know?

Changes in the American population will have a great effect in the workplace over the next 20 years. The size of the work force may increase as little as 16 percent, compared with 50 percent from 1980 to 2000. The share of workers with post-high-school education will also decline from today's rates. The number of workers born in America from ages 25 to 54 will not grow at all.

diversity in the workplace

Empowering People Through Work

Goodwill Industries International is a network of 208 community-based, independent organizations that serves people with workplace disadvantages and disabilities by providing job training and employment services, as well as job placement opportunities and post-employment support. With locations in the United States, Canada, and 22 other countries, Goodwill helps people overcome barriers to employment and become independent, tax-paying members of their communities.

Goodwill agencies work closely with business and government to create career training and employment programs that reflect the needs of the community and local employers and anticipate labor market trends. Services include Employee Matching, Customized Skills Training, Workplace Accommodation, and Temporary Service. Many local Goodwill agencies` also consult with employers on hiring individuals with disabilities or inform them of special funding opportunities and tax benefits that may be available. Goodwill Industries also operates both in-house and community-based contracts for a wide variety of businesses and government clients.

and develop and market products and services that consumers will spend their extra income on.

Resource Availability The availability of resources is another important economic condition. When resources are readily available, their prices decrease. When resources are scarce, their prices increase. Do you ever notice gasoline prices? When there is plenty of oil, the price to fill up a gas tank is much lower than when the oil supply is scarce.

Check Point

What happens during a recession?

The Future of Business

Businesses will face many challenges in the new century, including globalization, technology, quality, and diversity.

Globalization **Globalization** means that products, services, labor, technology, and capital can move easily between businesses and countries all over the world. Businesses with a global perspective are able to consider new international marketing opportunities. A good that is bought in the United States but produced abroad is an *import*. Goods produced in this country and sold abroad are called *exports*.

Technology **Technology** continues to change rapidly, and businesses must adapt to new technologies to remain competitive. High-tech businesses must continue to develop new products. Businesses that use technology must be aware of advances that can affect their operations.

The Internet and e-commerce have changed the way some businesses operate by making products available directly to consumers. Businesses that use e-commerce technology must update their capabilities with new technology, while high-tech businesses that provide e-commerce capabilities continue to research more effective, efficient solutions.

Quality Consumers buy products with the expectation that the products will work as promised. In providing value to consumers, businesses must focus on offering quality goods and services. In the late twentieth century, American businesses faced stiff competition from foreign companies, many of which sold high-quality products at very competitive prices.

As an employee, you will be expected to perform your duties effectively and contribute to organizational quality, whether you work on a production line, in the payroll department, or in customer service.

Diversity The composition of the workforce is changing and will continue to affect U.S. businesses. Issues such as age, race, and gender cannot be ignored. For example, businesses that strive to attract and retain female employees will have a larger pool of potential employees.

Many businesses work with government agencies and high schools and colleges to promote opportunities for people of all cultural groups, ages, and genders to further their educations. The business community benefits from having a larger pool of well-trained employees, which can help businesses maintain a competitive advantage.

The Job Market and You

As you develop a career direction and plan to enter the job market, understanding economic conditions can help you make decisions. Use sources such as the *Occupational Outlook Handbook* web site to learn more about current employment and the job outlook for career fields that interest you.

If Carlota were interested in a marketing career, she would learn from the *Occupational Outlook Handbook* that in a recent year, managers in advertising, marketing, promotions, public relations, and sales held about 583,000 jobs. She would also learn that employment in these areas is expected to grow about as fast as average, increasing 12 percent between 2006 and 2016. Because of this expected growth, Carlota could estimate that demand for individuals trained in these areas will grow and that she should consider these fields.

Why do you think so many businesses want to recruit more women and minority employees?

2.2 Assessment

THINK CRITICALLY

1. What are some ways businesses can increase their profits?

2. Why do you think so many businesses contribute to charitable organizations? In what other ways do businesses contribute to their communities?

3. Which business cycle is the American economy currently in? What economic and political events contributed to this current state?

4. Why must high-tech companies continue to update their technology?

5. Explain how globalization might affect the American market for silver jewelry.

MAKE ACADEMIC CONNECTIONS

6. **HISTORY** Research the economic history of your state. What are some contributions that different cultures have made to the economy? Choose a particular contribution, and write a short story incorporating the information you learned. Create a setting, characters, and a plot that will give your readers a sense of the contribution you have chosen.

7. **ANALYSIS** You may have tried good versions and bad versions of frozen yogurt, socks, or water skis. Why do you think many businesses believe it is good business to produce high-quality products? Why do some businesses choose to produce inferior products?

Management and Leadership

Goals

- Explain management functions
- Understand the development of management over time, including different management styles

Key Terms

- management
- planning
- organizing
- leading
- controlling
- top manager
- middle manager
- first-line manager
- scientific management
- administrative management
- human resources model
- management science
- operations management
- systems theory
- contingency theory

The Functions of Management

Have you ever chaired a committee, planned an event, or scheduled a party for a friend? Do you act as captain of a sports team or squad, hold office for your school's student government, or represent your class or school in an outside organization? Even if you have never officially held the title of "manager," you have probably acted as a manager at school, work, or even home. If you have organized, controlled, planned, or led others, you have performed managerial functions. Understanding management and the responsibilities of managers will help you not only as an employee, but also in successfully managing your job search.

Photodisc/Getty Images

Management means using people, material resources, and technology to get an organization's work done. To do this, managers perform four main functions: planning, organizing, leading, and controlling.

marketing matters

Simone loves to shop at Wild Foods. The prices are good, the location is convenient, and the produce is high quality. After Simone checked out last week, she noticed that she had been charged more for apricots than the advertised price. When she took her receipt to the store manager, the manager apologized and refunded Simone's money completely. How was the store manager doing marketing for the grocery store? Can you think of a time when a manager's negative reaction affected the way you felt about a business? Describe the incident.

The military and the church provided examples for early management theory. They even provided some terms we commonly associate with management, such as *strategy* and *mission*.

Planning means determining in advance what needs to be done. Managers set goals and make decisions that affect the operation of the business. As the manager of your job search, you will set goals for completing your portfolio and for preparing job search materials, such as your resume. You will also make decisions about the content of your portfolio and the companies you would like to contact.

Organizing refers to how work is arranged and how resources are grouped. For example, most businesses are organized into departments based on similar functions, such as marketing, accounting, and human resources. You should organize your job search and career development in a way that allows you to accomplish your planned goals.

Leading involves getting people to work together to accomplish the shared objectives of a business. A manager might motivate her team to complete a project ahead of schedule, exceeding a deadline and saving the company money. You might work together with your teacher, guidance counselor, or parents to lead a "team" that can help you with your job search or college planning.

Controlling refers to monitoring the progress of a business to make sure its goals are met. A package delivery company's management team might use a computer system to monitor the percentage of packages received by customers the next day because that is one of the business's goals. You might control your job search by using a weekly planner to keep track of your activities for the week, checking off each one as you complete it.

Managerial Roles

Managers perform various roles within an organization. A manager's *interpersonal role* involves interacting with others, communicating with employees, and coordinating with other departments in the organization. For example, if a project has a fast-approaching deadline, the manager may be responsible for making sure the team and supporting people in the organization are doing all that needs to be done to finish the work on time.

The *informational role* of a manager involves gathering relevant information and making it available to employees. Perhaps a company plans to hold a workshop on designing multimedia presentations. A good manager informs those employees who might benefit from the workshop.

When a manager makes decisions, such as allocating resources and hiring employees, he or she is performing a *decisional role*.

Digital Vision/Getty Images

Levels of Management

Larger businesses have different types of managers, depending on the function and role that a job requires. Businesses also have various management levels that correspond to their work responsibilities.

Top managers look at the "big picture" and plan the overall, long-term direction of an organization. A top manager makes decisions about such issues as what steps to take when merging with another organization, how much money to invest in research, and where to build a new facility. Top managers are usually the senior executives in a company: chief executive officers (CEOs), chief financial officers (CFOs), presidents, and vice presidents.

Photodisc/Getty Images

Middle managers implement the plans and decisions made by the top managers. They have a narrower focus than top managers, considering months rather than years when planning their activities. They may be responsible for accomplishing plans and coordinating the activities of lower-level managers. They have titles such as marketing manager, plant manager, and regional manager.

First-line managers manage the day-to-day operations of an organization, including supervising employees. They have a specific, narrow focus and must ensure that work is done on time. Because of this, they tend to spend most of their time overseeing employees. They have titles such as office manager, shift supervisor, and store manager. Most new management employees are first-line managers.

Check Point

Assume you manage an office supply store. Give an example of each of the four basic functions of management (planning, organizing, leading, controlling) as they relate to the start of the new school year.

Management Evolution and Styles

Management was transformed into a distinct field with the transition to an industrialized society. Instead of owners managing their family farms and small businesses, managers were needed to manage many aspects of the big businesses created during industrialization. Today, management continues to evolve. Technology has changed production processes, the way information is processed and stored, and the way employees communicate. As companies adapt to the changing needs of the marketplace, adaptive management approaches lead companies to success.

Classical Perspective

The classical perspective emerged out of the Industrial Revolution in the late nineteenth and early twentieth centuries, as machinery changed the way work was done. The classical perspective includes scientific management and administrative management. Many people thought that effective

Photodisc/Getty Images

organizations should run like machines. Great economic expansion occurred in the United States, but employees were not always treated well by businesses.

Scientific management focused on management as a science centered on production and worker efficiency. Frederick Taylor, who wrote *The Principles of Scientific Management* in 1913, believed that the performance of individual workers could be improved if managers followed four steps. He believed managers should:

- Break the job down into small pieces and develop a science, or best way, to do each element of the job
- Select and train the most qualified workers
- Supervise workers to ensure they follow the proper procedures
- Continue to plan the work, establishing a level of pay and performance

Taylor's methods increased efficiency and provided more objective standards for workers. However, some workers felt it was a strategy for businesses to hire fewer workers and get more work out of each individual.

Administrative management focused on managing the whole organization for efficiency and effectiveness. The management functions of planning, organizing, leading, and controlling were identified by Henri Fayol, a French industrialist. Fayol also developed principles for effective

NETBookmark

Access **www.cengage.com/school/marketing/yourself** and click on the link for Chapter 2. You will be directed to several business and investor information sites that you can use to research a company before an interview. Choose a company you would like to work for and research it using one of the web sites. Write a fact sheet about the company that you could take to an interview.

management, including the division of work, authority, discipline, and initiative. Max Weber, a German sociologist, explained the concept of bureaucracy, which refers to specific rules called standard operating procedures, and levels of authority in organizations.

Behavioral Perspective

While the classical perspective portrayed organizations as similar to machines, the behavioral perspective that emerged out of the Great Depression of the 1930s focused on the *behaviors* of individuals in the workplace and the ways managers could effectively motivate employees. Instead of being viewed as tools, workers were viewed as resources that could benefit their organizations. Mary Parker Follett, an early management theorist, suggested that workers know the best way to improve their jobs and should be involved in job analysis. The behavioral perspective studied employee motivation.

The *human relations movement* stressed the importance of relationships in organizations. Managers' concern for workers would help workers feel more satisfied with their jobs and with the organizations for which they worked. Increased satisfaction would then lead to improved performance. The **human resources model** values the individual employee by focusing on how businesses can encourage communication and participation by workers.

Quantitative Perspective

The quantitative perspective, which emerged after World War II, focused on techniques such as mathematical models for management. Managers applied the mathematical approaches they used during the war to businesses in areas such as decision making and planning. **Management science** uses mathematical models and computer simulations to represent systems or processes within organizations. Simulations provide realistic information that can guide decision making, such as how many repair persons should be on call or how they should be sent out to handle repairs.

Operations management, a form of management science, focuses on all aspects of production, such as managing inventory and planning shipping routes.

Contemporary Perspectives

Contemporary perspectives recognize that there is no single right way to manage an organization. The classical, behavioral, and quantitative perspectives all influence the contemporary perspectives.

Systems theory considers the organization as a system with four basic elements:

- Inputs from the environment (external resources)
- Transformation (conversion of inputs into products)
- Outputs (finished products)
- Feedback about the process

Contingency theory suggests that managers must respond to the environment. Because a manager's behavior and decisions are based on unique situations, the contingency theory suggests that there is no single correct way to manage an organization.

Management Styles

As management evolved, theories relating to management styles evolved as well. Douglas McGregor, a key figure in the human relations movement, defined Theory X and Theory Y. William Ouchi, who researched culture and management in America and Japan, proposed Theory Z:

- **Theory X** Managers assume that people dislike work. Therefore, people will try to avoid it and must be coerced or controlled into working. Theory X managers also believe that people prefer to be directed in their work-related activities, don't want to take responsibility, and lack ambition. Theory X managers have a negative view of employees.

Photodisc/Getty Images

- **Theory Y** Managers assume that people do not inherently dislike work but view it as a part of life. They believe that if people are committed to organizational objectives, they will be motivated and self-directed to reach them. According to Theory Y, most people will seek and accept responsibility. People are bright and creative, but most organizations do not fully utilize their potential. Theory Y managers have a more positive view of employees.

- **Theory Z** Managers assume that people can be committed and focused and can work together effectively. They stress long-term employment, work groups, and a focus on the organization. Theory Z managers view employees very positively.

Leadership

Many leaders can manage, but can managers lead? While management may be a formal role, leadership can occur at any level of an organization. Good leaders possess certain qualities, or traits, including decisiveness, ability to motivate, courage, adaptability, competence, charisma, and willingness to accept responsibility.

Consider this example. Bria is a sales associate at a local retailer. During a severe storm, the power goes out. The store manager is at lunch, so Bria responds by assembling employees and directing them to various store areas to assist customers. She then makes an announcement to comfort concerned customers. While Bria is not the store manager, she certainly acted as a leader in this situation.

Leaders influence others and bring about action because they possess power. The five main types of leadership power are:

- **Legitimate power** Others believe the leader has the right, or authority, to lead. This may be based on title (manager, president, owner).

- **Expert power** Others believe the leader has expert knowledge or skills in a particular area (doctor, computer programmer, professor).

- **Referent power** Others identify with and want to be like the leader (athlete, celebrity, politician).

- **Reward power** A leader is able to offer rewards, such as raises, promotions, or other incentives (manager, owner, instructor).

- **Coercive power** A leader has the ability to impose a penalty, such as firing an employee. Coercive power can be used unethically, and for leaders who abuse this type of power, it often results in low employee morale.

Check > Point

How did managers of the classical perspective view workers? Discuss the implications of this perspective.

2.3 Assessment

THINK CRITICALLY

1. Why is it important for managers to organize? Give an example of a situation in which a manager's organizational activity is important.

2. The data entry department has made several major mistakes in the last month. The data entry personnel believe that it is because a top manager has not told them about several price changes that should have been entered into the computer system. The middle manager is responsible for solving the problem. How might the middle manager use all three managerial roles (interpersonal, informational, decisional) to solve the problem?

3. How do marketers affect the relationship between supply and demand?

4. How do you think job satisfaction was changed by the shift from the classical perspective to the behavioral perspective? How was it changed by the shift from the behavioral perspective to the quantitative perspective?

MAKE ACADEMIC CONNECTIONS

5. **PROBLEM SOLVING** Denise and Margarita are first-line managers at a baked goods outlet. They are also friends outside of work. Their middle manager told them that their coworkers feel awkward and intimidated because Denise and Margarita "never talk to anyone else unless they have to." What would you advise?

6. **GRAPHIC DESIGN** Design an illustration or cartoon that depicts the responsibilities of each of the three levels of management.

VOCABULARY BUILDER

Choose the term that best fits the definition. Write the letter of the answer in the space provided. Some terms may not be used.

_____ 1. A belief that there are clear and scientific ways to manage organizations and individuals

_____ 2. Unfulfilled consumer desires

_____ 3. Items necessary to produce goods and services, including physical capital, such as buildings, machines, and tools

_____ 4. Manager who focuses on the "big picture" and plans the overall, long-term direction of an organization

_____ 5. Belief that managers focus on the organization and long-term employment and assume people are committed and can work together effectively

_____ 6. Business cycle characterized by higher incomes, increased production, and lower unemployment rates

_____ 7. Manages day-to-day operations, including employee supervision

_____ 8. Anything required to live

_____ 9. When businesses make the most money and spend the least

_____ 10. Physical products, such as shoelaces and refrigerators

_____ 11. The economic condition caused by unlimited needs and wants and limited resources to fill those needs and wants

a. capital
b. first-line manager
c. goods
d. human capital
e. income
f. inflation
g. need
h. profit maximization
i. prosperity
j. recession
k. recovery
l. scarcity
m. scientific management
n. services
o. Theory Z
p. top manager
q. wants

REVIEW CONCEPTS

www.cengage.com/school/marketing/yourself

12. List and explain the four factors of production, or resources.

13. Briefly describe the evolution of management.

14. What are the four economic utilities? What does each involve?

15. What are three roles a manager has? What activities are involved in each role?

16. If a manager attends a meeting with managers from other departments, and then shares this information at a staff meeting with employees, what managerial role is he or she performing?

17. Explain the relationship between supply and market price.

18. Explain the relationship between demand and market price.

19. What level of manager would be responsible for giving an employee a performance review?

20. Compare and contrast the classical perspective on management with the behavioral perspective.

21. What are some examples of economic risk?

22. Is quality something you are responsible for as an employee? Explain.

23. List the five types of leadership power and provide an example of each.

24. Do you think management is a science? Why or why not? Explain your answer.

APPLY WHAT YOU LEARNED

25. When Ferdinand's manager tells him that he is making some mistakes on order forms, Ferdinand is embarrassed and angry. But Ferdinand's best friend, Marty, tells him that his manager is doing a good job and that Ferdinand should be thankful rather than angry. Is Marty right? Why or why not? Why is it important for managers to perform the *controlling* function?

26. How do supply and demand affect the employment market, including salaries?

27. Do you have a job? Can you identify what management style your manager uses? If you don't have a job, talk to a parent or grandparent. What kind of managers does he or she deal with? Compare that management style to the management style of a teacher or another person.

28. Anna Nordquist is going to buy her parents a flat-panel computer monitor for their anniversary. She shops around at different Internet sites and narrows it down to two choices: one on a major electronic retailer's web site and one on a popular auction site. The one from the retailer is of lesser quality and will cost $300 plus $15 to ship from the warehouse in Missouri. The one on the auction is of higher quality, will cost $200, and will be shipped directly from the factory overseas for $50. If Anna purchases the second monitor, from what future-thinking business trends is she benefiting?

29. Nike's line of Air Jordan shoes has been very popular. Explain how referent power impacts the sales and success of Air Jordans.

MAKE ACADEMIC CONNECTIONS

30. **TECHNOLOGY** Look at the web sites of five multinational companies. What kind of community involvement do these businesses have? If you admire what a company is doing, send them an encouraging e-mail. If you have a suggestion for how a company can contribute to society, send an e-mail.

31. **GEOGRAPHY** Go to your local supermarket or home goods store and identify items from 10 different countries. Then look at a map and note where those different countries are located. Can you think of some of the benefits of global business?

32. **ETHICS** Are there any reasons why treating human beings as machines is unethical? What are they? Why do you think that management has moved beyond this approach?

33. **ORAL HISTORY** The business world was very different 50 years ago. Perhaps you have a grandfather or an uncle or family friend who made a living selling door-to-door. Find someone who had a career in business, marketing, or sales at least 40 years ago. Interview that person and report your findings in a written report. Or, produce an audio piece.

34. **SOCIAL STUDIES** In the United States, workplace diversity is supported by legislation.

   - The **Equal Pay Act** of 1963 states that employers must base pay rates on skill, effort, and responsibility, regardless of gender.
   - The **Civil Rights Act** of 1964 prohibits employment discrimination because of race, gender, national origin, or religion.

- The **Age Discrimination in Employment Act of 1967** prohibits employment discrimination against people ages 40 and older.
- The **Americans with Disabilities Act of 1990** prohibits employment discrimination based on mental and physical disabilities and requires that employers not only hire, but also accommodate, persons with disabilities.

Use the Internet to research one of these Acts. For example, search for recent court cases that have involved workplace discrimination. In the future, how could the companies involved better implement diversity efforts to prevent employee dissatisfaction and lawsuits?

If you are interested in the rights of workers with disabilities, go to the web site of the U.S. Department of Labor's Office of Disability Employment Policy and search on "ADA." Read one of the articles about dispelling myths about the Americans with Disabilities Act, or read about the New Freedom Initiative.

Prepare an oral report or a PowerPoint presentation about the most interesting or unexpected things you learned through your research.

Small Business Management Team Event

The BPA Small Business Management Team Event involves a 90-minute test and a 10-minute oral presentation followed by five  minutes of questions from the judges. A team of two to four members must present a solution for the following management case study. Your team may use one laptop/ notebook computer, posters, flip charts, or graphs for the presentation.

CASE U.S. financial institutions have suffered major negative publicity from bad loan decisions and financial bailouts (taxpayer dollars) from the federal government. Your management team for a stable bank must develop a marketing strategy and promotion to maintain the confidence of your community. Your team will be evaluated for delegation of responsibilities, demonstration of teamwork, demonstration of a working knowledge of business management concepts, demonstration of critical thinking skills to make decisions, and demonstration of self-esteem and integrity for team management. Your presentation must convince the judge to choose your bank for management of their finances.

"The restaurant offered a great deal. You could get a free breakfast if you visited on Friday. My neighbor heard about it on the radio, and I saw an ad during the Super Bowl. Then it was in the local paper, and the evening news even talked about this promotion. When I went to the website, an announcement for the free breakfast was the first thing I saw."

"I was excited to see that the new video game was out. The television ad said it was available at the electronics store, and that it's on sale until Monday. Everyone at school has been talking about it, and my friends and I can't wait to play it! I just hope the store has enough in stock so it doesn't sell out before I get there."

Have you ever wondered how organizations coordinate their promotional efforts, decide which products to develop and market, determine selling prices, and get customers excited about them? Marketing campaigns often include messaging across many channels, including broadcast advertising, public relations, and online efforts. Marketing managers develop an organization's marketing strategies, often with the help of other employees, outside agencies, or consultants.

Employment Outlook

An average rate of employment growth is expected.

Job Titles

- Marketing Manager
- Sales and Marketing Manager
- Creative Director
- Chief Marketing Officer

Needed Skills

- A bachelor's degree usually is required, and an MBA often is recommended, especially for career advancement opportunities.
- The ability to work with many different people, coordinate efforts, and maintain effective relationships is essential.
- Creativity, strong communication skills, interpersonal skills, and analytic skills are needed.
- The ability to meet deadlines and handle stressful situations is important.

What's It Like to Work in Marketing Management?

Kelsey arrives early to prepare for her morning staff meeting at 7:30 A.M. As Marketing Manager for a gaming company, she meets weekly with the marketing coordinators and supervisors to make sure she is aware of any developments that might impact marketing. Before heading in to the meeting, she scans the sales reports, reviews the marketing communication plan for the upcoming new game launch, and pulls up the online news reports that mention her company.

Representatives from sales, IT, finance, and product development are in the meeting. Kelsey watches a brief demo of the new game, and discusses the latest headlines that mention the game. She responds to requests for additional sales support, gets verification on the launch date, and reviews a proposed change to the promotional materials.

Later in the day she meets with the Creative Director of the agency responsible for developing the promotional materials for the product launch to finalize the details. She responds to media requests for interviews and keeps up with the latest buzz about the new product. She also works with her staff to prepare for the official launch event and review progress on an interactive online gaming experience set to debut on launch day.

What About You?

Would you like to use information from many areas of an organization, as well as scan the external environment to help an organization manage its marketing efforts?

Chapter 3

Develop Your Product

3.1 Self-Awareness

3.2 Values and Goals

3.3 Features and Benefits

CAREERS IN MARKETING

American Airlines Center

Opened in 2001, American Airlines Center in Dallas, Texas, is home to the Dallas Mavericks NBA team and Dallas Stars NHL team. The unique design of this facility allows for a smooth transition from basketball games to hockey games, and even for use as a concert hall.

The Premium Sales Associate is responsible for creating revenue for suite and club seats and related products for this entertainment venue. The Associate generates sales leads, sells accounts, and provides customer service and follow-up to build and maintain long-term relationships with clients.

The position requires a college degree, sales experience, strong communication skills, and excellent product knowledge. Candidates should have proven business development experience, problem-solving and analytic ability, and an understanding of customer relationship management.

Think *Critically*

1. For a position such as this, what does product knowledge involve?
2. Why do you think it is important for someone in this position to focus on long-term client relationships?

Photodisc/Getty Images

PORTFOLIO BUILDER PROJECT
Interests, Values, and Careers

Project Objectives

The focus of Chapter 3 is evaluating the strengths of you as a product, or "Product Me." Who are you? What do you like to do? What are you good at? Do you like to work with lots of people or just a few? What is important to you? Where do you want to be in ten years? What can you offer a potential employer? These are important questions. In this project you will:

- Assess your personal and academic interests
- Identify which values shape your behaviors, actions, and goals
- Determine whether interests are features or benefits of "Product Me"

This project will help you assess yourself so you can choose a job that's good for you and good for an employer.

Getting Started

Read through the Project Process below. Using the Portfolio Builder CD, print the five assessment worksheets for Chapter 3. Use a pencil to fill in each form the first time.

Project Process

Part 1 Lesson 3.1 Complete the Personal Interests Worksheet. In the "What are my interests?" column, list school and personal activities you enjoy. In the second column, rate how important this interest is to you; this will help you better understand what you value so you can set priorities and spend your time and energy appropriately.

Part 2 Lesson 3.2 Complete the Personal Values Worksheet and the Personal Qualities Worksheet.

Part 3 Lesson 3.3 Complete the Basic Skills Worksheet and the Workplace Preferences Worksheet.

Project Wrap-Up

Consider what you learned about yourself from this project. Were you surprised by anything you discovered? Do you now feel more inclined toward a certain career or work environment? Write a short essay about your personality and priorities.

style-photographs/iStockphoto.com

Self-Awareness

Goals
- Analyze your personality and interests
- Define a method for self-improvement

Key Terms
- self-aware

Understanding You

Are you a risk-taker who enjoys living on the edge? Maybe you're an achiever who likes to make things happen. Perhaps your compassion and concern for others motivate you.

Who are you? It seems like a simple question, but it isn't. As a human being, you are a complex mixture of attributes. Some attributes can't be changed, such as age, gender, and ethnicity. But you also have attributes that can be changed, such as interests, talents, and experiences. When asked who you are, you might respond, "I'm Amy, a 17-year-old middle class female." To another, you might say, "I'm Amy, an Asian-American high school student." You can describe yourself in different ways, including physically, socially, emotionally, and economically.

Marketers provide products, or market offerings, to meet the needs and wants of customers. A product can encompass many things. When you think of a product, you might think of a tangible physical product, like a notebook computer, or a service, such as car repair. It also can encompass people, places, and ideas. To develop a product strategy, a marketer should have a clear understanding of what actually is being offered.

Just as a marketer must understand the product to more effectively offer it to a market, you must understand yourself to more effectively market yourself. Being **self-aware** means understanding the various factors that shape your personality. Self-awareness can help you in many areas of your life.

- Your personal relationships are better when you understand your own personality. For example, you might make friends more easily when you know that you are more comfortable meeting people one on one rather than in large groups.

marketing matters

Luis Lopez, a high school senior, is unsure of his future. He has gone to the career center at school for an assessment. How can his interests, as well as his likes and dislikes, help him select a career path?

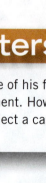

geotrac/iStockphoto.com

- Self-awareness is also important in the workplace. As you prepare for further education and your future career, self-awareness will help you make choices that are compatible with your personality, resulting in a more satisfying career and better business relationships.

- Understanding yourself will also help you sell yourself to employers. You will be able to market your best qualities and match them with the needs of the employer.

Recognizing your personality traits and your interests are two of the most important steps in developing self-awareness.

Personality Traits

Some personality traits are obvious. For instance, people can see that you are a caring person by your expressions and mannerisms. Other traits are not as obvious. Your strong problem-solving abilities may not be visible until someone gets to know you well.

Your personality is a large part of what makes you a unique individual. It includes your mental, emotional, and social characteristics. Do you have a pleasing personality? That may depend on the situation. If you are social and outgoing, your personality may be an advantage in a sales position. However, it may not work as well in a computer programming position that requires you to spend many hours working alone.

No matter where you work, personality creates the most diversity. If you know your strengths and weaknesses, and respect those factors in others, you'll be able to get along with most people and confidently market yourself at work or anywhere else.

Getting to Know Me Part of maturing is getting to know who you are. As you continue or complete your education and head into the world

Photodisc/Getty Images

Workshop

Go to **www.cengage.com/school/marketing/yourself** and click on the link in Chapter 3 to the personality test. Complete the test and then click on the trait description link and read about the MBTI® traits. Divide into small groups and discuss how you can identify the personality types of others at school and in the workplace.

of work, you will be a more valuable employee if you have an accurate picture of yourself. No employer wants to find out after hiring you as a middle school coach that you prefer to be around adults and do not have any leadership skills.

Career counselors have a variety of tools they can use to help you test your skills and personality. One common instrument used to identify personality traits is the Myers-Briggs Type Indicator (MBTI®). Created by two American women, Katharine Briggs and Isabel Briggs Myers, the MBTI® is

The MBTI® at Work

The MBTI® can help you learn what really makes you "tick" and in what types of work situations you'd be most successful. You can also learn how to manage your personality when relating with other people in any situation. After you determine your personality type, many good books about both topics can help you further your understanding. From the book *Do What You Are* by Barbara Barron-Tieger and Paul Tieger, here are sample lists of suggested work paths for two personality types:

INTJ (Introvert, Intuitive, Thinker, Judger)	ESFP (Extravert, Sensor, Feeler, Perceiver)
People of this type tend to be: autonomous, aloof, and intellectual; imaginative, innovative, and unique; critical, analytical, and logical; intellectually curious, driven to learn and increase their competence and knowledge; socially cautious and reserved; organized and definitive.	People of this type tend to be: warm, gregarious, and playful; impulsive, curious, and talkative; sensitive, caring, and gentle; social and unpredictable with a great zeal for life; active, responsive, and highly aware of the physical world.
The most important thing to INTJs is their independence and being able to live according to their own standards.	The most important thing to ESFPs is freedom to be spontaneous, have fun, and enjoy the company of others.
Intellectual property attorney News analyst Design engineer Biomedical researcher Network integration specialist Software developer Psychiatrist Cardiologist Freelance writer Inventor Media planner Chief Financial Officer Webmaster Architect Desktop publishing specialist	Early childhood education teacher Dental assistant Physical therapist Home health social worker Public relations specialist Radiological technician Occupational therapist Travel agent / tour operator Promoter Actor Veterinarian Special events coordinator Occupational therapist Marine biologist Sales: sports equipment

*Myers-Briggs Type Indicator and MBTI are registered trademarks of Consulting Psychologists Press.

based on the work of Swiss psychologist Carl Jung. After completing a short multiple-choice test, your four-letter personality type is determined. This instrument is popular in organizations that do personality testing as part of the hiring process and for team building activities. The table on page 64 describes two very different personality types in the context of the workplace.

The qualities tested by the MBTI® are the four vital personality differences of Introversion-Extraversion, Intuition-Sensing, Feeling-Thinking, and Perceiving-Judging. These terms in the MBTI® are used differently than you might use them every day, so you need to pay careful attention to the descriptions before applying them to yourself or others.

Your MBTI® type will stay consistent throughout most of your life, but you may lean toward other types as your life circumstances change. In each of these pairs, we all have a preference for which variable is most natural for us, but we also all have the ability to use the other variable if necessary. There are 16 personality types defined from the combination of these four trait sets.

Introversion-Extraversion (I or E) You've probably heard people described as introverts or extraverts before. Other people often define us using this personality preference. This trait can also help you define how you communicate and in what workplaces you would be most successful.

In the MBTI®, introverts are not necessarily quiet wallflowers who dislike groups, and extraverts are not always loud centers of attention. Instead, the MBTI® uses this quality to describe how you direct your energy and attention. Introverts are energized by their inner world and ideas. Extraverts find energy through people and external events.

Intuition-Sensing (N or S) This personality trait explains how you learn and receive information. Sensors usually focus on the here-and-now, facts, and details. Intuitors lean toward the future, possibilities, and theories.

Feeling-Thinking (F or T) Whether you're a Feeler or a Thinker, this trait shows how you make decisions. Feelers make them based on how the decision would affect other people. Thinkers are more objective and may seem impersonal when they make decisions.

Perceiving-Judging (P or J) This personality difference reveals how you approach life. Perceivers are more spontaneous and flexible. Judgers tend to follow rules and structure better.

If you're interested in learning more about yourself using the MBTI®, your school guidance counselor may be able to give you this test. He or she may also be able to help you to use the MBTI® as a career-finding tool and to understand yourself and others better.

Interests

Your interests are activities you enjoy. Your preference for group or individual activities, your likes and dislikes, active or passive activities, leadership ability, and communication style are all reflected by your interests.

Consider Rick, who works as a supervisor with a construction company. Rick's job often requires that he work outdoors, give direction to others, and coordinate schedules. He must report to work early, often before 7:00 A.M. When the alarm goes off each morning at 5:30 A.M., Rick

Did You Know?

You may be defined by a certain personality type, but how you act on these types is highly individualized. Below are some examples of four personality types:

ENTPs: Thomas Edison, Tom Hanks

INFJs: Mother Teresa of Calcutta, Oprah Winfrey

ESFJs: Danny Glover, Nancy Kerrigan

ISTPs: Tom Cruise, Clint Eastwood

Photodisc/Getty Images

hits the snooze button. He is often tired and dreads spending another day on the job. He can be unpleasant to others, including his family, and sometimes complains about work, his home, and his life.

In his free time, Rick reads adventure novels and tinkers with his computer. He enjoys the satisfaction of home improvement projects and designed and built an addition for his house. He prefers to spend his time alone or with his wife and daughter. He plans activities with a few close friends, but does not usually socialize in large groups.

Based on Rick's interests, you can see why he is unhappy with his current position. He is not an early riser and engages in more solitary activities. Even though his carpentry skills may have led to his current construction job, he prefers to apply his skills in a hands-on way—not leading a team of builders. But the time and energy Rick has spent at his current job is not a total loss: He can still use his skills and experience while better suiting his personality in another position. He might be happier and more successful as an interior designer who consults with homeowners or subcontracts through others. He could work with small groups or individuals, and his workdays might include working alone on design or research or periodically meeting onsite with clients or business associates.

Your interests provide clues to the activities and the environment you most enjoy. It is important to choose a career that follows these interests. If you love working with kids and enjoy sports, you might consider a career as a physical education teacher or coach. If you are a self-motivated person who enjoys meeting new people and traveling, you might consider sales. If a particular job does not sound appealing to you, trust your instincts and avoid choosing a career that will make you unhappy.

Check Point

What are two important steps for individual self-awareness?

Self-Improvement

Your personality and interests are very important in choosing a career path. Now that you have become more self-aware, think about some areas where you could use improvement. If you enjoy working independently but are interested in a career that requires more collaboration, you might want to expose yourself to more group-effort activities. If you tend to act on your emotions, be conscious of this when working with people who are more objective and logical. Don't take their seeming coolness personally. Change does not often happen overnight, so you need to plan your change strategy. The following steps will help you.

- Recognize and define the characteristic to be changed. Be specific.

- Establish a strategy for this change. Put together an action plan outlining the steps you are going to take to effect this change.

- Practice this strategy actively. The more effort you put into it, the better the results are likely to be.

- Evaluate your success. If your strategy works, good for you. If you experience difficulty, revisit your action plan and adjust it as necessary.

Notice how Rick goes about this process: He has decided that in order to be happier at his job, he needs to make some improvements in his personality and wants to become more outgoing and social. He knows that even if he changes careers, he will have to work with others. He recognizes a specific characteristic that he wants to change.

To be more outgoing and approachable, Rick creates an action plan. He decides to make small talk with coworkers and join them at lunch. He also plans one activity each week with someone outside his family. Rick begins sitting with coworkers during lunch and over time becomes friendly with a few people. He learns that Tomas is married and has a young daughter. He invites Tomas and his family for dinner.

Rick is pleased with himself for making an effort to socialize, so he rewards himself with a new adventure novel that he has been wanting to read. He also realizes that because he is often tired at work, it is more difficult to be friendly and pleasant and to find time for one additional activity each week. He decides to adjust his action plan to an outside activity every other week and to go to bed each night by 11 p.m.

Telling others about your plan may be helpful, especially if you are the type of person who needs help following through with plans. You may get support from those you tell, which will help you with your efforts. What is most important is that you actively work on the change. If you decide to keep your plans for change to yourself, you will need to reward yourself and praise yourself for the small achievements along the way. You should also mentally congratulate yourself for each step you make in the new direction.

Psychologists have determined that it takes about 21 days of *consistent action* toward a change for it to become a permanent part of your life.

Record your progress on a calendar and set interim goals and rewards on a weekly basis. As you make it through each day, cross it out on the calendar so you can immediately see how far you've progressed.

Check Point

List three things you can do to help your self-improvement action be successful.

3.1 Assessment

THINK CRITICALLY

1. What is self-awareness and why is it important?

2. Compare and contrast extraverts and introverts.

3. Why would it be helpful to have someone who knows you well describe your personality?

4. What are some specific areas of your personality you might want to improve? What are some steps you can take?

MAKE ACADEMIC CONNECTIONS

5. **PROBLEM SOLVING** Choose one personality trait that you would like to change. Use the process outlined in the text to develop a strategy for change. For two weeks, keep a journal tracking your progress. In your first entry, name the personality trait you plan to change and explain the strategy you've developed. In each additional entry, discuss what, if any, progress you've made. In your final entry, analyze the results of your strategy: Were you able to change the personality trait? Which parts of the strategy were helpful? Which were not?

6. **RESEARCH** Interview people who work in an industry that interests you. Ask them what personality traits helped shaped their job decisions. How does having these traits help them succeed in their jobs? How does it make their jobs challenging? How do they meet these challenges? After your interviews, think of different jobs in the same industry that might be good fits for your personality type. What jobs might be suitable for other types? Using notes you made during your interviews, report your results in an oral presentation to your class.

Values and Goals

Goals
- Understand values that are important to you
- Recognize the benefits of setting goals

Key Terms
- values
- terminal values
- instrumental values
- inclusion
- goals
- ABC goals

Charting Your Course

Think about what your life might be like in five years, in ten years, and in fifteen years. What will you be doing? How will you be living? Will you be satisfied with your life? If you're having difficulty responding, perhaps you need to think about your values and goals. Values refer to the way you live your life—the things that are important to you. Goals are what you want to do with your life. Planning your goals based on your values can help you achieve success.

In marketing, little is left to chance. Every detail of a product is planned and documented: the color of the package, the text on the label, the media that will advertise the product, the customers, the size of the product in ads, and much more. Marketers chart a course for product success, just as you should chart a course for career success.

What Do You Value?

Your **values** are the things most important to you. They affect your choices and your behavior. Values are often influenced by your society or culture. For instance, in the United States *individualism* tends to be valued over the group, while in most Asian nations, the group is valued over the individual.

Values can be terminal or instrumental. **Terminal values** are an end in themselves. They relate to states of existence. You might value a comfortable life, for example. **Instrumental values** refer to behaviors such as

marketing matters

During a visit to the career center at her college, Martina is asked to list her values and outline her goals for the future. She writes that her mother is the most important person and role model in her life, that she enjoys school, and that she wants to work in a fulfilling job. How can Martina be more specific about her values and goals? How can these values and goals guide her career choice?

Rubberball Productions/Getty Images

honesty or perseverance. Instrumental values help you to obtain the terminal values. If you value a comfortable life, you may rely on values of hard work and thrift to help you gain that comfort.

Some values are commonly held in the United States. Many can be traced directly to the Declaration of Independence: "We hold these truths to be self-evident, that all men are created equal, that they are endowed by their Creator with certain unalienable rights, that among these are Life, Liberty, and the pursuit of Happiness." Freedom, individualism, equality, education, and inclusion are key American values.

Freedom Freedom, or liberty, is a value on which this country was founded. The First Amendment to the Constitution grants various freedoms, such as freedom of speech, freedom of religion, freedom of the press, and freedom of assembly. One freedom you have as an American is the freedom to choose your career path.

Individualism Americans tend to think of themselves as individuals first and as members of groups (family, ethnicity, class, employer) second. Much of the Bill of Rights (the first 10 amendments of the Constitution) deals with individual rights, such as the right to bear arms, the right to trial by jury, and the right to be secure from unreasonable search and seizure. Individuals can own businesses and reap the rewards, including wealth, if they are successful. Another example of individualism is your right not to be harassed by others in the workplace.

Equality Equality refers to equality of opportunity. All people should have a chance to succeed based on their efforts. This principle is the

NETBookmark

Online self-assessments can be a helpful starting point for understanding how your skills and interests may point to career choices. To complete an online self-assessment, access **www.cengage.com/school/marketing/yourself** and click on the link for Chapter 3 to be directed to several self-assessment sites. After completing an assessment, provide a one-page review about it. State which assessment site you accessed, the information it provided about you, and how you can use this information to plan your job search.

basis of the American Dream, although over the years, certain groups in the United States, such as women and people of color, have had to fight for their rights. Equality in the workplace means, for example, that qualified candidates should have equal opportunity for consideration when a new position or promotion is available.

While some say that the United States is a melting pot, it is probably more accurately described as a "salad bowl" because the many diverse cultures of individuals don't merge into one. Instead, each culture keeps some of its uniqueness, and differing cultures that define the United States complement each other as they are included in the "salad bowl" of America.

Education The United States places a high priority on education. In most states, children are required to attend school until they are at least 16 years old. *All* children are entitled to a free and appropriate education.

The U.S. Secretary of Labor's Commission on Achieving Necessary Skills (SCANS) reported, "A strong back, the willingness to work, and a high school diploma were once all that was necessary to make a start in America. They are no longer. A well-developed mind, a continued willingness to learn, and the ability to put knowledge to work are the new keys to the future of our young people, the success of our business, and the economic well-being of the nation." Employees need more than just a desire to work hard. They need aptitude and a capacity to learn and use knowledge.

A high percentage of students in the United States choose to continue their education beyond high school. A college education is a requirement for careers such as law, medicine, and teaching. Some careers, such as construction and retail, may not specifically require advanced education, but salaries and promotions may be affected by a degree.

Inclusion **Inclusion** involves respecting and valuing the uniqueness of others. Rather than focusing on differences, unique qualities are acknowledged and appreciated. In the workplace, inclusion often is connected to diversity. For example, an organization that values inclusion likely will create a culture in which people with different skills, perspectives, and cultures are not only considered for positions, but, once hired, are welcomed and appreciated.

The Power of Values

Values can empower people to be responsible and accountable. If you value your family, for example, you will work to ensure their security and well-being. If you value diversity, you will be open-minded in your dealings with others. When you believe you are responsible for your actions, you are more likely to be responsible for your family, career, and community.

Louis Harris & Associates conducted a survey of college freshman, entitled "Generation 2001," for Northwestern Mutual Life Insurance Company and found that parents, family, religion, generosity, honesty, and integrity were important values to this group.

com-mu-ni-cate

Create a flyer that depicts and describes the five American values mentioned in this chapter: freedom, individualism, equality, education, and inclusion.

- 90 percent agree that helping others is more important than helping oneself
- More than 90 percent plan to eventually marry and have children
- 89 percent have faith in a higher power
- 73 percent have volunteered with schools, charities, and churches

As you evaluate your own values, think about what is really important to you. What makes you happy? What gives you a sense of purpose and meaning? Your values are the guiding principles of your life. Although they may change a little as you grow older, in general they remain consistent.

Activity: Prioritizing Values

Listed below are commonly held values. Review this list, making note of those values that are important to you. Next, prioritize the values you have determined to be important into columns A, B, and C on a sheet of paper. Your A list should include those values that are absolutely essential to you. You could not have a satisfying life without them. The B list should include important values. These values enhance your life and provide meaning. Your C list should include those values that are somewhat important, but not as much so as the values on your B list.

Achievement	Diversity	Hard work	Opportunity
Ambition	Effort	Helping others	Optimism
Appreciation	Empathy	Honesty	Organization
Caring	Efficiency	Hope	Patience
Civility	Equality	Humility	Perseverance
Commitment	Ethics	Humor	Persistence
Common sense	Exciting life	Inclusion	Problem solving
Compassion	Faith	Initiative	Respect
Consistency	Family	Inner harmony	Responsibility
Cooperation	Flexibility	Integrity	Self-sufficiency
Courage	Forgiveness	Learning	Service
Courtesy	Freedom	Listening	Sharing
Curiosity	Friendship	Love	Thrift
Dependability	Gratitude	Loyalty	Tolerance
Determination	Happiness	National security	Trust

Check Point

How do you think your family would rank the key American values—freedom, individuality, equality, education, and inclusion—in order of importance? How do you rank them? Explain your answer.

Setting ABC Goals

Understanding values helps you set goals. **Goals** are the things you want to accomplish. It is easier to accomplish goals if they are meaningful and important to you. For example, if you are writing an essay about friendship but don't value friendship, it will be difficult for to you to finish the essay. If you have deep friendships that play a significant role in your life, you likely will write a thoughtful and meaningful essay.

When thinking about your education and future career, do you have a direction? Do you know what type of college you want to attend? Do you have a career goal in mind? Do you know what level of education is required to achieve that career goal?

Goals aren't simply wishes. You may wish to live forever or to pass chemistry without attending class or doing the homework. However, these wishes are not goals because you can't really do anything to make them happen.

Goals may be classified in many ways, such as *personal* or *professional*. Personal goals relate to you as an individual. They can include such areas as your attitude, education, family, and health. A personal goal might be "I will develop patience in dealing with my sister" or "I will earn my high school diploma."

Juanmonino/iStockphoto.com

Professional goals relate to your career. Consider this example: "I will attain a job in advertising that allows me to be creative. I will use my creativity to develop award-winning ads in anticipation of a position as Creative Director."

Setting formal goals may seem difficult, however, using ABC goals can make the process easier and more successful. **ABC goals** are goals that are *actionable*, *bounded*, and *compelling*.

Actionable Actionable goals are goals that can be acted upon. They are behavior-related and are realistic because, as you plan a way to achieve them, you validate your ability to attain the goal.

Bounded Bounded goals are measurable. They are specific enough that you can measure progress toward achieving them. You can develop a time frame for achieving these goals based on your actionable plan.

Compelling Compelling goals compel, or force, you to action. Goals must truly be important to you so you want to work toward achieving them. Often other people such as parents, friends, or teachers, might set goals for you. If the goals do not represent things you are passionate about, you may not be compelled to work toward them.

Did You Know?

"If you don't know what you want, you will probably never get it." Oliver Wendell Holmes had the right idea about setting goals.

Mikaila has the goal of getting an A in her economics class. Is this an ABC goal? Let's take a look.

- Is the goal *actionable*? Yes, it is. Mikaila can do her homework and class assignments in order to reach her goal. The more she succeeds in her class and homework, the more capable she is of reaching her goal.

- Is the goal *bounded*? Absolutely—Mikaila can check her progress by speaking weekly with her teacher about her grade. She can plan ahead to give herself a few extra weeks to do any extra assignments.

- Is the goal *compelling*? For Mikaila, it is: She has always loved economics. She has an aunt who is an economics professor at a local university, and Mikaila is interested in studying business and economics when she goes to college. She knows that her success in this class will be important for getting into the college of her choice.

Do It

Businesses put their strategies for success on paper, and so should you. Writing your goals down makes them tangible and provides a visual cue for action. It's important not to set your goals too high, or you may become discouraged and lose motivation, but don't set them too low either, or you won't be compelled to achieve them. Goals should require some effort on your part, but ultimately they should be achievable. The following process can help you start setting goals:

- **Determine your ABC goals** Write down your goals.

- **Develop a strategy** Your plan for meeting each goal should include specific steps of manageable tasks. Mikaila didn't just hope she'd pass economics. She made time each night to do her homework, did all her class assignments, scheduled her research ahead of time, and talked to her teacher every Friday.

- **Consider possible roadblocks** What obstacles might you encounter that would make accomplishing your goals more difficult? Mikaila knows that her family is going on a week-long trip in November. Will this get in the way of her schoolwork?

- **Develop alternatives**   If you meet an obstacle, how will you handle it? Mikaila decides to talk to her teacher and get the assignments ahead of time so she can read before she leaves and while she is gone. She also asks her teacher to e-mail her if the schedule or assignments change.

- **Do it**   Now that you have written goals and a strategy, display them and begin taking action. You may want to tell others about your goals so that they can hold you accountable. For example, if you have a goal of being on time for student council meetings, tell a friend on student council. The friend might help by reminding you about meetings.

- **Revisit your goals**   Review your goals and document what actions you have taken toward achieving them. If more than a week goes by without any tangible results, reevaluate the goal; you may discover it is not an ABC goal.

marketing math connection

The Americans with Disabilities Act of 1990 defines disability as a "substantial limitation in a major life activity." In 2005, the United States Census Bureau published a study about Americans with disabilities. This bar chart shows the percentage of the 2005 population in each age group that was disabled. The total population of the United States that year was 291.1 million people.

Disability Prevalence by Age: 2005

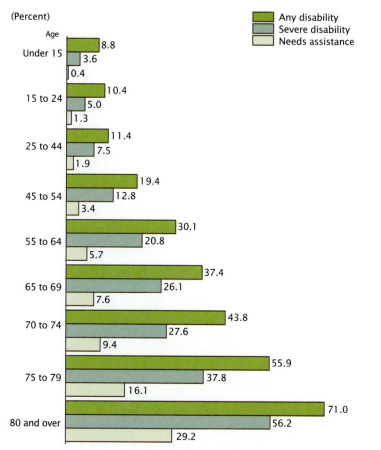

Source: U.S. Census Bureau, Survey of Income and Program Participation, June–September 2005.

1. In 2005, there were approximately 42,300,000 Americans between the ages of 15 and 24. How many Americans in that age group had a severe disability?

2. In 2005, 54.4 million people had some type of disability. What percentage of the total population had a disability?

SOLUTION

1. 42,300,000 × 0.053 = 2,241,900
2. 54,400,000 ÷ 291,100,000 = 0.187 = 18.7 percent

Goals aren't written in stone. You decide them, and you can change them. Sometimes goals change as a result of a life change, such as a birth or death of a family member or friend, or the loss of a job. They may also change as a result of your changing personality and interests. Think about some of the things you wanted to do when you were in elementary school. Do those same goals apply now?

Check Point

How does understanding your personal values help you set good goals?

3.2 Assessment

THINK CRITICALLY

1. How does writing down your goals help you achieve them?

2. List three examples of bounded goals. Circle the part of each goal that makes it bounded.

3. Write down one of your goals. List and explain the values supporting this goal.

4. Have you ever experienced a situation that supported your goals but conflicted with your values? Why did the situation create a conflict? How did you modify the situation or your goals to better support your values?

MAKE ACADEMIC CONNECTIONS

5. **LANGUAGE ARTS** Obtain a book of quotations from your school or community library. Write your favorite quotes about goals and values on index cards (one quote per card). Add a few blank cards to the stack for any additional quotes you may find. Punch holes in the top of the cards, and fasten them with ribbon or twine to create an inspirational flip chart for your locker or desk at home.

6. **SOCIAL STUDIES** Find a recent newspaper or Internet article about a situation in which individual or group values conflicted with the values of society, an organization, or even themselves. What values were compromised, and how? Write an article reporting the facts of the situation, or, write a letter to the editor responding to the article you found and the conflict of values it described.

INTERNET

@

Features and Benefits

Goals

- Discuss the role of features and benefits in the marketing industry
- Explain how you can use your features and benefits to market yourself in the workplace

Key Terms

- features
- benefits
- benefit selling
- accomplishment
- skill
- basic skills
- workplace competencies
- job-related skills

Features and Benefits in Marketing

When customers make any purchase, they consider a product's features and benefits to determine what to buy. **Features** are the factual characteristics of a product. The most basic feature of a product is its intended use. The intended use of a car, for example, is transportation. Physical features might include its color, a stereo system, air bags, air conditioning, and price. Perhaps your grandfather hires a cleaning service occasionally. The cleaning service's intended use is the cleaning of your grandfather's house. The features of a cleaning service might include three people to clean, provision of cleaning products, and a vacuum cleaner.

Benefits are the advantages a customer gets from buying a product. Benefits answer the question, "What's in it for me?" People often make purchases based on the benefits. For instance, Jose may need a car for transportation, so he *could* purchase any model that runs. He decides to purchase a model that gets very good gas mileage because he wants a car that is affordable. The benefit offered by the car of his choice is affordability. He can afford to drive it after buying it because he has calculated that he can afford the cost of gasoline. The benefits of the cleaning service at your grandfather's house might include a clean house, prompt and complete service, and a happy grandfather.

Marketers develop promotional messages that will persuade consumers to think positively about a product. They do this through

marketing matters

Martina's career counselor asked Martina to list her skills and accomplishments. Martina writes that she works well with others, knows how to use a computer, and has factory experience and good telephone skills. How can she demonstrate these skills? Did Martina list any accomplishments?

Photodisc/Getty Images

Stockbyte/Getty Images

factors such as the product's packaging and specific features and benefits that satisfy a customer's needs. Understanding the needs of a customer aids marketers in determining the features that should be included in a product. It also helps them establish which benefits the customer is really buying.

Marketing the Benefits Consumers don't just buy products. They buy what the products can *do* for them. Your grandfather's cleaning service means that he can spend the day fishing with you instead of cleaning his house. When a marketer promotes products by considering the needs and wants of the customer, the practice is called **benefit selling**.

In your job search, you will be "selling" your features (skills), benefits, and accomplishments. Understanding the needs and wants of employers will help you match these features, benefits, and accomplishments to their needs.

Check ⟩ Point

Explain the difference between features and benefits.

Skills, Accomplishments, and Benefits

When employers hire employees, they make a purchase (pay a salary) to obtain the skills individuals have to offer. Employees' skills are their *features*. When features are utilized well, the results are called **accomplishments**. Employers like to know that individuals have used their features successfully in the past. And, because employers are trying to satisfy their needs and wants, they hire individuals whose features and accomplishments will provide *benefits* to the organization.

Chuan-Li is interested in a position in public relations. He has a college degree in English, good writing and grammar skills, and strong organizational skills. These are Chuan-Li's features. Last year he interned at a community newspaper and organized volunteers in the company to participate in a community rebuilding project, which was a huge success. He also started a weekly column for teenagers. The successful community rebuilding project and teenage news column are Chuan-Li's accomplishments. As Chuan-Li interviews for the public relations job, he will link his skills and accomplishments to the needs and wants of the company to show the benefits he can provide.

Know Your Skills

Many advertisements for employment include a list of skills that candidates should possess. A **skill** is a proficiency or ability developed through training or experience. To determine the positions you are most qualified for, you must recognize the skills you possess and learn which skills are valued by employers. Three skill types include:

- **Basic skills** are skills that are important for life, not just work. These skills include reading, writing, speaking, basic math, problem solving, creative thinking, and self-management. Many people take these skills for granted, but they are critical for success in life.

- **Workplace competencies** are skills that effective workers possess and most employers desire. Workplace competencies are known as *soft skills*. Soft skills include teamwork, communication skills (oral, written, and electronic), time management, problem solving, ability to work as part of a team, attitude, adaptability, and the ability to work with diverse individuals. Skills like teamwork and communication are important in a small business *and* in a Fortune 500 company.

- **Job-related skills** are skills that are specific to a position, occupation,

Digital Vision/Getty Images

Workshop

Think about what it takes to be a great employee. Brainstorm some skills that great employees possess. Share your list with your classmates.

diversity in the workplace

The Multicultural Economy

Buying power, or *disposable income*, refers to the income an individual or group has available to spend on goods and services after paying taxes. If you were a marketer, how would you use the following statistics about predicted changes in buying power in the years 2007–2012?

- The African-American, Asian-American, Native-American, and Hispanic markets will grow faster than the white market.

- The African-American population will grow by 6.7 percent, and its buying power will increase by 34.2 percent.

- Asian Americans' buying power will increase by 45.9 percent. By 2012, 16.2 million Americans will claim Asian ancestry.

- The Native-American population will grow by 8.2 percent, and its buying power will increase by 35.6 percent.

- The Hispanic population will grow by 15.3 percent, and its buying power will increase by 46.3 percent.

"The Multicultural Economy, 2007." Selig Center for Economic Growth, Terry College of Business, The University of Georgia. Reprinted by permission.

careerbuilder®

Are You Employable?

Excerpted from *Career Building: Your Total Handbook for Finding a Job and Making It Work*, the Editors at CareerBuilder.com

Copyright 2009 CareerBuilder, LLC. - Reprinted with permission.

Here's the bottom line: You have to get a job, you have to go to work and someday, you'll probably have to change jobs. CAREER BUILDING: Your Total Handbook for Finding a Job and Making It Work *(Collins Business) is a one-stop guide for navigating all those times in your career.*

For some people, "If it ain't broke, don't fix it" is a guiding principle. And if you've found one job, you can certainly find another. You know all you need to know about job hunting, right?

If you find your job hunt isn't giving you anything but a stress headache, maybe it's time for a refresher. Ask yourself these questions:

Is my résumé targeted?

Just because you're applying for multiple jobs, don't assume the same résumé works for every position. Each job posting will stress different qualities over others, so rework each résumé to highlight the experience and skills that correspond to that particular employer. Your résumé will prove not only that you're qualified for the job but that you also pay attention to detail.

Am I networking?

We've said it once; we'll say it again—networking is crucial. Think about this: There is only one of you and there are thousands of job openings. The more people know you're looking for a job, the better your chances of finding one are. You can never be sure who will know of an available position. Networking can also connect you to a hiring manager, directly or indirectly, giving you the edge over other candidates.

Do I know something about the companies I'm applying to?

"Tell me what you know about the company" or "Why would you fit in well here?" have become staple interview questions, so don't be caught off guard. Shrugging your shoulders and saying, "I don't know" isn't going to score you points. Look at the company's Web site and read press releases and newspaper articles to see what's going on with your prospective future boss. In addition to preparing for the interview, you'll learn whether the company and its culture are a right fit for you.

Am I targeting my job search?

Sending out several résumés is key to finding a job, but you also need to be selective about the jobs to which you're applying. While you don't need to possess every single skill listed on a posting, you should at least

continued on page 81

be qualified for the position and prove that you have transferable skills. Your targeted résumé will help prove you're a serious candidate and have the right qualifications for the position. If you're spending time applying for jobs you're not qualified for, you're wasting valuable time you could be devoting to a position that's a better fit. If you recognize where your strengths lie and what transferable skills you possess, you'll see better results than if you apply to any posting you come across.

Has someone else evaluated my résumé and interview technique?

Feedback is critical to job hunting. Ask someone else to read your résumé and review it as if they were hiring for the job. Friends or colleagues can provide objective points of view to help you revise your résumé.

Your interview skills need the same attention. Are your answers succinct or too short? Thorough or rambling? What you think you're saying isn't necessarily what others hear, so find this out now rather than in the interview. If you don't think that a colleague or friend can offer constructive feedback, make an appointment with an interview coach.

How am I presenting myself?

Employers are assessing your presentation before you even show up for an interview. Your e-mails and phone conversations with hiring managers or recruiters should also send a professional message. Don't send emails written in all capital letters or using three exclamation points—it's bad netiquette in personal correspondence, but it's even worse in business. Put the same thought into your outgoing voice mail message. Don't try to be funny by playing 30 seconds of your favorite song or talking with a mouthful of food. Hiring managers might hang up instead of ask you to call them back. Give a normal, casual greeting, or use one of the preprogrammed options that come with most accounts.

If a recruiter calls you, don't try to hold a conversation with your TV blaring in the background or your child screaming on your lap. If you're asked whether it's a good time to talk, you can be honest and say you're in the middle of something. Then ask if he or she can call you back in 15 minutes or find another day that's convenient for both of you. You'll be prepared to answer all the recruiter's questions and won't be distracted.

Your goal is to find a better job than you had, right? So you have to conduct a better search this time around. Put the effort in and you'll see the results.

or industry. You may be trained to balance ledgers, write press releases, perform advertising research, calculate profits, and so on. In each job you hold, you will learn some job-related skills. You should appreciate these skills because they are a *benefit* to you. When you leave that job, those skills go with you.

Employers want to hire the right person for the job. They try to match your job-related skills with their specific needs, your workplace competencies and foundation skills with their general needs, and your personality with the climate of the organization.

Acknowledge Your Accomplishments

In addition to a strong understanding of your skills (features), you need to convince an employer that you can be an effective employee. A list of skills will probably not be enough to make you stand out from other potential employees. You need to show that you can add value to the employer's organization. One way to do this is by emphasizing your accomplishments.

As you learned earlier in this lesson, an *accomplishment* is something that has been successfully completed. When you turn your skills into action, the successful result is an accomplishment. What have you accomplished

with the skills you possess? Rather than stating, "I have strong organizational skills," Chuan-Li might tell of his organizational skills through something he has *accomplished*. He could say, "I planned and organized an employee community volunteer project during my internship. It involved coordinating the schedules of 35 employees, and we had an 85 percent attendance rate at the picnic."

Photodisc/Getty Images

Promote the Benefits

You can also show your potential value to an employer by stressing the benefits you may bring to the organization. A benefit statement shows how your accomplishments will specifically benefit an employer. An employer knows that Chuan-Li has a demonstrated skill. The employer may be wondering how this can benefit the organization, so Chuan-Li can add a benefit statement: "My ability to organize and coordinate means that I can effectively contribute to your public relations events and work as a member of a project team."

Using your skills, accomplishments, and benefits will help you to better understand your abilities and see how an employer might evaluate your potential for success. This information, along with consideration of your values and goals, will help you consider career options, develop an effective resume and job search letters, as well as prepare to interview successfully.

Check > Point

How are accomplishments and benefit statements used?

THINK CRITICALLY

1. Explain benefit selling. How can it be useful in the job search process?

2. Compare and contrast workplace competencies and job-related skills.

3. Why do employers want employees to have basic skills?

4. Which do you think is more important to employers: accomplishments or experience?

5. What are three features and three benefits that describe you as product?

MAKE ACADEMIC CONNECTIONS

6. **COMMUNICATION** Locate an advertisement that uses a benefit selling strategy. Prepare a five-minute presentation to outline your findings to your class.

7. **SOCIAL STUDIES** Many jobs have a marketing aspect, even if they are not in the marketing field. Talk to five people in your family and neighborhood who are not employed in the marketing field. Do any of their job responsibilities include aspects of marketing? Give an oral presentation to report your findings to the rest of your class.

8. **MANAGEMENT TRAINING** Use the Internet to locate the mission/vision statement of a company that interests you. Fold a sheet of paper vertically in half. In the left-hand column, write *Values* and list the values found in the statement. In the right-hand column, write *Examples* and list examples of how a job candidate could demonstrate to an interviewer how he or she has acted on these values.

INTERNET
@

VOCABULARY BUILDER

Choose the term that best fits the definition. Write the letter of the answer in the space provided. Some terms may not be used.

_____ 1. Respecting and valuing the uniqueness of others

_____ 2. Things you want to accomplish

_____ 3. The advantages a customer gets from buying the product

_____ 4. When a marketer promotes products by considering the needs and wants of the customer

_____ 5. Something that has been successfully completed

_____ 6. Skills of effective workers, such as teamwork and communication

_____ 7. A proficiency or ability developed through training or experience

_____ 8. The characteristics of a product

_____ 9. The things most important to you

_____ 10. Understanding the various factors that shape your personality

_____ 11. Values that are an end in themselves

a. accomplishment

b. benefits

c. benefit selling

d. features

e. goals

f. inclusion

g. self-aware

h. skill

i. terminal values

j. values

k. workplace competencies

REVIEW CONCEPTS
www.cengage.com/school/marketing/yourself

12. List five career options that an extravert might consider and five that an introvert might consider.

13. Why might it be valuable to know what other people think of your skills?

14. What are ABC goals?

15. Briefly describe the five key American values discussed in this class.

16. Explain how goals differ from wishes.

17. Identify some reasons that goals might change.

18. What are features? How do they relate to skills?

19. Describe benefit selling in your career development.

20. Why might organizations use personality testing with potential employees?

21. How can self-awareness help individuals plan a career strategy?

22. How can understanding values help you set goals?

23. Think of a job or career that you may be interested in pursuing. What are the basic skills, workplace competencies, and job-related skills you would need for that job or career?

24. Melissa knows that she is skilled with computers. She worked with her science teacher to develop a program for keeping track of science projects, including student name, year completed, and project description. Use benefit selling to write an accomplishment/benefit statement for Melissa.

25. Ang-Li always seems to be running late. A junior in high school, he is often a few minutes late for morning classes, and often arrives late for his part-time job after school at the movie theater. He recognizes that he needs to change his behavior. Put together a sample action plan for Ang-Li.

26. Rosa is one of the most active students in her senior class. Friendly and outgoing, she serves as president of the student government, coordinator of the student volunteer group, as well as a language tutor. She enjoys working with others, and is always ready to help with projects and give advice. What are some positions that might suit Rosa's personality and interests?

MAKE ACADEMIC CONNECTIONS

27. COMMUNICATION Create a flip chart or PowerPoint presentation describing your change strategy for self-improvement of a characteristic you would like to change.

28. ART/DESIGN Create a drawing, brochure, mobile, or sculpture that represents your interests, values, and goals. Use a variety of materials. Share your final masterpiece with the class.

29. LANGUAGE ARTS/FINE ART Visit www.cengage.com/school/ marketing/yourself and click on the link for Chapter 3. Visit the Foundation for a Better Life web site and click on Values in the top menu, then select one value from the bottom list to further explore. Write your own values story based on your understanding of your selected value. Or, click on the Billboards link to view values and billboard advertising. Select a value and create a billboard using a photo of someone you know and text describing how they live by this value.

INTERNET

30. COMMUNICATION Daragh, a software sales representative, recently took the MBTI® and found he is an INFJ. He is concerned that he is one of the introverted personality types because he thinks of himself as being good with people, and his sales record is outstanding. What other qualities of an INFJ would round out Daragh's personality and sales success? Work with a partner to create a list of five qualities. Present your ideas to the class.

31. TECHNOLOGY AND COMMUNICATION Visit www.cengage.com/school/marketing/yourself and click on the link for Chapter 3. Visit the recommended web site and read the opinions of employees at a company that interests you. Did you find any negative feedback? In a job interview situation you could clarify such feedback in a positive manner by asking about the general subject area (without asking directly if the information is true). For example, if you find a comment that says pay increases are unfair and random, you could ask about the company's salary review calendar and policy. Locate two negative comments on the web site and write a positive question for each that you could pose to an interviewer to get more information.

Sports and Entertainment Marketing Team Decision Making

You and a partner have been given the challenge of designing a promotional strategy for a seven-day state fair that has experienced declining attendance during the past five years.

Declining attendance has been attributed to admission prices, entertainment, and competition from similar events. You have the responsibility of creating a theme for the fair. Your responsibility also includes determining a wide array of entertainment for each day of the fair and designing unique promotions to attract special target markets (for example, senior citizens, children, and baby boomers) for different days of the fair.

You have 30 minutes to devise your plans for the state fair, using a management decision-making strategy. Be sure to outline your strategy because you will be given 10 minutes to present the information.

The judge/class/businessperson will have five minutes to ask questions about your plan of action.

Chapter 3 Assessment

Be an Effective Listener

When you are in school, how do you spend most of your time? While you may not realize it, you are probably spending most of your time listening. You might be listening in class, in the hallways between classes, or during a school-sponsored event in the auditorium. Listening is not often taught in schools, but if you assume listening is automatic, you might take it for granted.

Hearing vs. Listening

While some people use the terms interchangeably, hearing is not the same as listening. Hearing can be a passive activity. It is a physiological process in which your brain interprets sound that has been reflected from your eardrum. Listening involves more than just hearing. It is a process that involves receiving, attending, interpreting, and responding. This process often is called active listening.

Preparing to Listen

Listening is a complex activity which requires preparation. You need to prepare both your body and your mind to listen. As you prepare to listen, minimize the distractions that might prevent you from focusing on the speaker.

Attending

Rather than passively accepting information, become an active listener. Focus on the present rather than thinking about what you might say in response. Look at the speaker. Don't just listen to the words being said, but also observe the signs of nonverbal communication. If you are talking or thinking about what you want to say next, you are not effectively listening.

Interpreting

Listening involves more than just your sense of hearing. It often involves sight, such as with nonverbal communication. You interpret by assigning meaning to what you hear. For example, when you hear a teacher say, "What do you think?" at the end of a lecture while making eye contact, smiling, and raising his voice near the end of the phrase, you might interpret this to mean that the teacher is interested in your thoughts about the lecture. Conversely, if the teacher repeated the same phrase while rolling his eyes, smirking, and dropping his voice near the end of the phrase, you might interpret this as sarcasm rather than an authentic question.

Responding and Reflecting

Contemplate the message through reflection. Reflecting sometimes is referred to as paraphrasing the message. Your reaction to the message is your response. You might respond nonverbally, for example, by clapping at the end of a great presentation. You might respond verbally by asking a follow-up question.

Develop Your Skill

Listening can be improved with practice. Watch and listen to a nightly news report. Before it begins, prepare to listen by physically and mentally being present, as well as removing distractions. While you are listening, don't answer the phone, listen to music, or text your friends.

After listening to the broadcast, write down one company that was mentioned and list three points that were made about the company during the broadcast. To check your listening, visit the news broadcast's website and watch or read the report. Did you correctly list the information?

Chapter 4

Product Promotion: Your Self-Presentation

4.1 A Positive Attitude

4.2 Professional Behavior

4.3 First Impressions

CAREERS IN MARKETING

Apple Computer

After exploding on the personal computer scene with the Macintosh, Apple continued to develop and market innovative technology options. Its iPod and iTunes products revolutionized the music industry, and with iPhone, it made a splash in the cell phone market.

A Product Marketing Manager at Apple is involved in market research, product design, sales, and even finance, supporting Apple's goal to provide the ultimate customer experience. In the rapidly evolving technology industry, the Product Marketing Manager must be flexible, adaptable, and open to change.

Apple seeks candidates that can inspire others and build strong teams. They look for people who are creative, customer-focused, and innovative, who have a strong educational background; excellent communication, leadership, and decision-making skills; and a focus on building a world-class brand.

Polka Dot Images/Jupiter Images

Think *Critically*

1. Knowing that Apple is interested in candidates with the skills and qualities described above, how might a candidate make a strong first impression?

2. Why are qualities such as flexibility and adaptability important in this industry?

Project Objectives

The first entry in your portfolio should be a letter of introduction. This letter presents you and your work to the people who will review your portfolio. Your letter should be both personal and informative. In this project, you will:

- Determine traits, skills, and goals that will interest your potential employers.
- Identify work samples that best reflect your abilities and experience.
- Write a clear, concise, and error-free letter of introduction and learn how to update it as you expand your portfolio.

Getting Started

Read through the Project Process below. Print the sample letter of introduction for Chapter 4.

- Review the worksheets you completed in Chapter 3, focusing on your interests, skills, and accomplishments.
- Gather any work samples you've collected.

Project Process

Part 1 Lesson 4.1 Analyze your completed worksheets, paying particular attention to your Basic Skills Worksheet. Review the information in Chapter 3 about features and benefits. Which of your interests, skills, and accomplishments might be most beneficial to potential employers?

Part 2 Lesson 4.2 Review the work samples you've collected for your portfolio. Which items best demonstrate a positive attitude and reflect the pride you take in your work? Which items will make a favorable first impression on potential employers? Choose one sample to highlight in your letter of introduction.

Part 3 Lesson 4.3 Study the sample letter of introduction you printed from the Portfolio Builder CD. Write your own letter, including a description of yourself (for example, your personal and career goals, strengths, and important achievements), an explanation of the work sample you've chosen to highlight, and an interpretation of how your portfolio accurately reflects your interests, skills, and accomplishments.

Project Wrap-Up

You will write many versions of your letter of introduction as you expand your portfolio. For example, you may decide to highlight a different work sample, your career goals may change, or you may need to change your interpretation of your portfolio as you add or remove contents. Always remember to triple-check your letter for errors in spelling, grammar, and punctuation.

© Dean Mitchell, 2009/Used under license from Shutterstock.com

A Positive Attitude

Goals
- Explain the importance of a positive attitude
- Describe the role self-confidence plays in the workplace

Key Terms
- attitude
- social marketing
- self-esteem
- self-confidence
- arrogance

Packaging: Keeping Your Attitude Positive

Most people have, at one time or another, purchased a product they may or may not have needed based on the appeal of the packaging. Packaging does not only contain and protect a product; it also *promotes* the product to potential buyers. Marketers take packaging seriously because it can provide a competitive advantage for a product that differentiates it from similar products. Packaging affects buyers' attitudes and opinions of a product, which means that it can also affect their decision to purchase the product.

Have you ever returned to a particular checkout lane at the supermarket because the clerk was friendlier and more helpful than the other clerks? Whether she knows it or not, her "packaging" has attracted you. Like everyone else, you project your attitude and appearance outwardly. Your attitude and appearance can be considered your packaging. These characteristics affect how others view you.

The way you package, or present, yourself to potential employers and other interviewers can affect their ability to differentiate you from other candidates, and it can affect their decision to select you.

"Perception is reality" is a common saying in marketing. The way a customer perceives a product, even if that perception is incorrect, can affect the decision whether or not to purchase that product. According to research, in less than one second, people react positively or negatively to the products, people, and places they encounter. They may not even be aware of it. Promotional

marketing matters

Selina Ambrose has taken a job working in an assembly line. She notices that many of the employees complain about the work, the supervisors, and the company. Some of the complaints are legitimate, but many of them aren't. What can Selina do to keep a positive attitude in the workplace?

© Monkey Business Images, 2009/Used under license from Shutterstock.com campaigns are designed because the appropriate message delivered in an appropriate way can influence attitude, and attitude influences behavior.

Similarly, the way others perceive *you* determines how they react to you. Their perception is shaped in part by *your* attitude. Your **attitude** is the way you think or feel about something. You can maintain your own positive packaging in the workplace by:

- Knowing how attitude influences behavior
- Controlling your negative attitudes
- Developing a positive attitude

Influencing Behavior

Marketers can "sell" attitudes. **Social marketing** is marketing that encourages or discourages certain behaviors by attempting to influence attitudes that affect behavior. Examples of social marketing campaigns include campaigns promoting cancer screenings, quitting smoking, and drug abuse prevention. These campaigns are designed to influence attitudes about these issues, which may affect behavior.

In the workplace, attitudes—both negative and positive—can affect everyone's behavior. If you display a negative attitude, such as frequently coming to work late, acting irresponsibly, being dishonest, lying, complaining, or ignoring directions, managers may behave in a negative manner toward you by failing to promote you, watching you carefully throughout the day, reprimanding you for small mistakes, or, possibly even firing you. Your coworkers may not want to work with you because your attitude is dragging a project down. However, if you display a positive attitude by working hard, offering to help your coworkers, asking for advice when you need it, telling the truth, and behaving fairly, you will affect those around you. They will probably treat you with respect and work harder when they work with you. Do not underestimate the power your attitude can have on the people around you.

Controlling Negative Attitudes

When faced with a difficult situation, people often respond with a "fight or flight" response. This means they either try to fight back or run away from the situation by avoiding it or refusing to deal with it. As you are completing this lesson in class, for example, let's assume that your instructor has just announced that a five-page research paper on

aldra/iStockphoto.com

Workshop

List five qualities a negative person has. Compare those with the corresponding positive attributes. Which is easier to have: a positive or a negative attitude?

Did You Know?

When executives were asked what upsets them most about employees, almost all mentioned issues related to attitude. The top three answers: dishonesty and lying; irresponsibility and taking care of personal business at work; and arrogance, egotism, and an aggressive attitude.

stress at school with a detailed and properly formatted bibliography is due on Friday. How do you feel? Is your attitude positive?

Perhaps you feel that the assignment is unfair and you begin arguing with the teacher. You are reacting based on your "fight" mechanism. Your classmate decides that she just doesn't want to deal with the assignment, so she puts it out of her mind and does not complete it. She is responding through "flight." Both responses are inappropriate.

If you can maintain a positive attitude, you might instead discuss the requirements of the assignment in more detail with your teacher, and you would complete the assignment because you would understand that it was important to your learning process. Similar situations may happen on the job. You may be expected to meet tight deadlines, complete several projects at the same time, cover for a coworker who is out, or handle last minute demands from clients.

What kind of attitude will you display in these situations? If you have a negative attitude, your whining and complaining will not impress managers and coworkers and may reflect negatively on your performance evaluation because you will not appear to be a team player. Refusing to complete a task may result in loss of promotion opportunities or even job loss. Begin now to take control of your attitude, and plan to be a motivated employee and positive person. Don't play the blame game by trying to hold others responsible for difficulties you may experience. Instead, work on your attitude, striving to view each challenge from a more positive perspective.

Just how important is your attitude? As you can see in the chart below, it's the number one factor in hiring decisions.

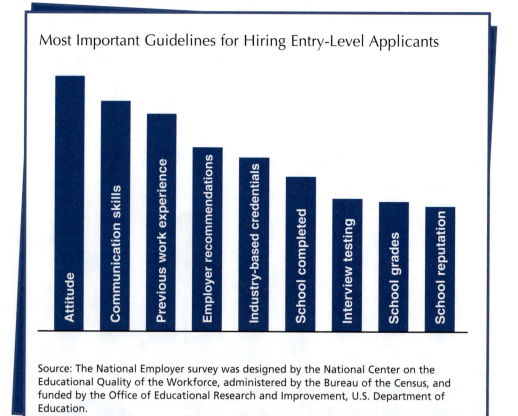

Most Important Guidelines for Hiring Entry-Level Applicants

Attitude · Communication skills · Previous work experience · Employer recommendations · Industry-based credentials · School completed · Interview testing · School grades · School reputation

Source: The National Employer survey was designed by the National Center on the Educational Quality of the Workforce, administered by the Bureau of the Census, and funded by the Office of Educational Research and Improvement, U.S. Department of Education.

diversity in the workplace

Workers with Disabilities

For people who have disabilities, finding a job can be difficult. However, since the invention of new technologies and legal interventions by Congress, it has become easier for those with disabilities to acquire and enjoy a job.

According to the U.S. government, more than 54 million Americans are disabled, meaning they have a physical or mental impairment that substantially limits one or more major life activities. The Americans with Disabilities Act of 1990 requires employers not only to give each person a fair opportunity for hire, but to also provide accommodations to make it possible for people with disabilities to do their jobs.

Elevators, ramps, and handrails are only a few of the accommodations that employers can offer workers with disabilities. Employees who can't use a keyboard can now use voice recognition software or switch devices controlled by head, mouth, or eye movements. Those with visual impairments benefit from Braille printers or optical scanners that allow them to read electronic documents, check e-mail, and surf the Web.

Source: Business Week Online

Developing a Positive Attitude

According to the National Center on the Educational Quality of the Workforce, attitude is the most important factor in hiring entry-level candidates. Generally, a positive attitude leads to appropriate, beneficial behavior. A negative attitude may have the opposite effect. While your attitude can be influenced by your peers, you definitely have control over it. Surrounding yourself with positive people can help you maintain a positive attitude, but generally others don't change your attitude—*you* do.

Education Education can assist in changing attitudes. Research has found that by being exposed to new experiences and practices, you can adapt your behaviors and change your attitudes. This means that you can learn to be more positive. Exposing yourself to others who are positive or even reading a book about how to be more positive can improve your attitude. Think about the people you know, such as friends or coworkers, who are consistently positive. Observe their behavior, and perhaps even ask them how they keep a positive outlook in spite of difficulties they may face.

Positive Thinking Are you an optimist or a pessimist? An optimist feels confident and positive, believing that things will work out, while a pessimist tends to take a gloomy, negative view of life. Your mind is very powerful, and you can train it to respond optimistically to your thoughts. Thinking positively and visualizing your success can help you achieve your goals and develop a positive attitude. View a negative situation as a challenge, and work to turn it into a positive situation.

Positive Self-Talk Focus on talking to yourself to motivate yourself, recognize your accomplishments, and remind yourself of your strengths. Give yourself compliments, encouragement, and balance. Instead of thinking that you are a failure because you left your math book at home, remind yourself that no one is perfect and that you strive to be organized and responsible.

Positive Body Language When Darnell gets up to make a speech, he crosses his arms and looks down as he speaks. Does his body language communicate a positive attitude? Your body can speak louder than your voice sometimes. Be careful that your body language doesn't say something you don't want it to say. To avoid negative body language:

- Stand up straight when speaking.

- Look other people in the eye and smile.

- Listen carefully to others.

- Monitor yourself for annoying habits, such as checking your watch frequently or glancing around the room while someone is speaking to you.

Positive Communication Your ability to communicate well is an important factor in the impression that you make on others. Do you use slang terms or derogatory language? Do you have difficulty communicating your ideas clearly? When you talk to people, your tone of voice and word choice communicate your image and your message. Individuals who speak in a polite, well-mannered way tend to be taken more seriously and shown more respect. The ability to clearly articulate your goals, thoughts, and ideas will serve you well in the workplace.

Positive Work Habits Sometimes you do not feel positive on the inside. But there are times when the best way to feel positive is to behave positively anyway. This is especially true at work. Developing positive work habits can help you behave in a positive way even when you don't feel like it. Think about how the following work habits can help you.

- Be courteous to others by arriving on time, completing your tasks, and helping others when they need it.

- Do not argue about issues that are not important. It's okay to give in to other people sometimes.

- Accept blame when things go wrong, rather than blaming others.
- Volunteer for unwanted tasks.

Each of these work habits will show your supervisor and coworkers that you are committed to your organization's success. People remember positive behavior and may be more likely to help you when you need it.

Check Point

Explain the importance of presenting a positive attitude in a job interview.

careerbuilder®

What Is Your Attitude Toward Work?

Anthony Balderrama, CareerBuilder.com writer
Copyright 2008 CareerBuilder, LLC.—Reprinted with permission.

Attitude counts for a lot. Just think of how often people's attitudes affect your perception of them. First impressions often come down to phrases such as, "He had the worst attitude" or, "She has the best attitude of anyone I've ever met."

When you walk into your workplace—whether it's a department store or hospital—what are you thinking? Do you feel excited because you love your job? Are you filled with dread because you hate your job?

Your attitude toward work might impact your career more than you realize.

The runway model

When models work the catwalk, they act as if the audience isn't there. The flashbulbs blind them, but their faces seem to say, "I don't have time to care about this crowd; I have a catwalk to strut down." They're on emotionless autopilot, if you will.

What works for models doesn't work for everyone ... in case that unsuccessful liquid diet you tried wasn't enough proof. A numb approach to work raises questions about your performance: Do you care about your job? Do you know what you're doing? How long will you stick around? Does anyone even want to interact with you?

Todd Dewett, associate professor of management at Wright State University in Dayton, Ohio, suggests these workers take a step back to look at their work in its appropriate context.

"All work is interdependent, yet most people have difficulty understanding where much of their work came from and where it will go—they don't see the connections in the larger process," he says. "The more someone understands how their work impacts others, the more they are likely to care." Dewett advises you to think of yourself as part of a team working toward a goal, not as an isolated cog in a machine. Look at the result of your hard work and maybe you can find a reason to care about your job, even if you don't love it.

The emotional teenager

Teenagers are nothing if not experts at looking at the cruel, torturous underbelly of life. A bad day when you're 15 years old isn't just a bad day; it's the worst day anyone has ever experienced in the history of human existence. Every phone call is a life-altering conversation of import no one can comprehend.

Hyperbolic workers aren't too different. They don't know how to put their workdays in perspective. Yes, some jobs are nightmares incarnate, but no job is nirvana, either. Difficult customers or incompetent bosses can mar the occasional day. Are you able to draw a distinction between a bad day and a bad situation?

continued on page 96

"It is possible to frame things mentally such that you see them as only short-term realities that can change over time. From this 'glass half-full' perspective, any single bad role or colleague is but a few frames in a long roll of film. The focus then shifts from obsessing on the current situation to designing a real plan of action to create a new and better future situation," Dewett says.

On the flip side, rather than make you appreciate your job more, a new perspective might make you realize you belong elsewhere. If you're conditioned to despise work every time the alarm rings, you could end up stuck at a job that's just wrong for you.

"If you do actually hate your job, you might not be in need [of] a job tweak, but rather a full-fledged job change or career change," Dewett suggests. "Having said that, even in the worst professional situations, for the open minded, there is a lot to learn about how you got there and what [likely exists] there that will help you avoid it completely in the future."

Pollyanna

The classic children's book "Pollyanna," which follows a girl whose philosophy to focus on the positive, is an admirable, if not impossible, model to follow. Yet, some workers' abilities to convey Pollyanna's unrelenting optimism astound others and can be detrimental to their own careers. The drawback to this work method is that you might find yourself out of the loop when it comes to how decisions are made, as they aren't always made in open discussions. Dewett cautions workers to pay attention to how decisions are made so that they can be aware of or participate in the process.

"People with overly rosy views (due to solid 'fit,' a great boss or colleagues or both) can be somewhat naïve politically," Dewett warns. "I would never advocate that a person with character and rosy glasses engage in too much political behavior, but you need to be aware of it." Don't sacrifice the love you have of your job. After all, many people would be thrilled to enjoy going to work in the morning. A balanced perspective is all you need.

"Love your job, love your company—but use your network so that you keep up to speed with the major political currents of the day as they might affect you and your work unit."

The transient

Perhaps more distracting than any other workplace attitude is that of the employee who never seems to set his or her bag down. For some workers, certain jobs are temporary. They never intend to stay long and they know something better is on the horizon, even if their employer is unaware of their agenda. While that approach might be appropriate in some circumstances— and you never want to assume that any job is the last one you'll take because you don't know what the future holds—don't live in that mentality.

For one thing, your boss and co-workers might get a sense of your fleeting mindset and treat you accordingly. If you never personalize your workspace or only talk about your future with the company in hypotheticals, they'll question your commitment. Do they want to give you a project or promote you if you seem to have one foot out the door already?

continued on page 97

For your own sake, allow yourself to consider the possibility that your job has a lot to offer. Even if you don't want to stay there forever, let your mind relax by accepting the fact that you can see yourself in that position a year or two from now. You'll be surprised how stressful always being on the move is. Plus, you might realize you were closing off opportunities for personal and career growth by keeping yourself primed to leave at any minute. If another job eventually comes your way, you can weigh the pros and cons of taking it—when you're faced with the decision, not because you're always looking for it.

Packaging: Self-Confidence

Self-confidence means knowing and understanding yourself and believing in your abilities. Self-confident people don't think they're perfect or feel that they know everything. That would be **arrogance**. Rather, self-confident people have a strong and accurate grasp of their skills. They know what they're good at and where they need support. They are proud of their accomplishments and grateful for what they have achieved.

Sometimes you may feel uncomfortable talking about your accomplishments and strengths. You don't want to brag and have others view you as egotistical or self-centered. But stating a fact related to your skills, strengths, or achievements isn't bragging—it's truth.

In your job search, self-confidence can give you the support you need to take risks in finding jobs. Once you've found a job, self-confidence is important to doing your job well and building on your successes.

Self-Esteem Leads to Self-Confidence

Believing in yourself and having confidence in your abilities means you have **self-esteem**. When you feel good about yourself, you project confidence. Your past experiences and relationships affect your self-esteem. The things you have done, as well as the people you have been exposed to, have helped build or diminish your self-esteem.

Your self-esteem is important because it affects every thing you do. Your choice of career, how you live your life, and how successful you are at achieving your goals will all be affected by how you feel about yourself.

When you have self-esteem, you feel important and valued. You are comfortable around others because you are comfortable with yourself. You are more concerned with how you see yourself than how others may judge you. You accept challenges because you feel confident that you can do the task.

Low self-esteem generally refers to personal insecurity, and insecurity often leads to uncertainty. When you have difficulty dealing with uncertainty, challenges look like problems, new acquaintances may be viewed suspiciously, and new situations are suspect. Most people feel insecure and uncertain at some point. If insecurity seems overwhelming, however, you may want to consider ways to feel better about yourself. One thing you can do is talk to a friend or relative who loves you and can help you deal truthfully with your low self-esteem. Sometimes it's necessary to go to a professional for help—don't be ashamed. When you work on building your self-esteem, you are working for your own future.

Building Self-Confidence

Self-confidence develops from positive self-esteem. Self-confident individuals appear poised and confident. They present themselves as mature, responsible people with goals to accomplish.

Your self-confidence will be reflected in your actions toward others. Consider these examples.

Jose is a "yes" person. He is constantly agreeing to help others with homework, studying, projects, and transportation to school events. In fact, he was 20 minutes late to dress rehearsal for the school play because he agreed to pick up two friends who lived in opposite directions. Jose is not able to set appropriate boundaries with people and often agrees to do things he doesn't really want to do because he is looking for acceptance and friendship. His self-confidence is low because he needs others to validate him worth.

Cindy, on the other hand, thinks mainly of herself. She often takes credit for the work of others, completes projects that attract attention from teachers and peers, and does not help others unless she somehow benefits. She does not derive satisfaction from helping others. Rather than being self-confident, Cindy might be considered arrogant.

From an employment perspective, individuals with positive self-esteem tend to be more effective employees. They are comfortable working with others because they are not threatened by others' ideas and input. They are self-assured in their ability to handle the job. They act reflectively, considering constructive alternatives and positive action.

Employees with low self-esteem sometimes feel that others are trying to take credit for their ideas and accomplishments. Consequently, they may not be effective team members. They may feel unsure of their ability to handle the job and may react to situations impulsively rather than thinking them though. They may act like Jose, taking on more than they can handle or feel comfortable with. This can cause stress as they struggle to complete everything they have taken responsibility for. Or they may behave like Cindy, seeking out only highly visible assignments and discrediting others. As coworkers become more aware of Cindy's behavior, they may refuse to help her and even try to avoid working with her.

As a positive employee, you will bring your healthy attitude and accurate self-confidence to the workplace. Your supervisor and coworkers will thank you.

Lesson 4.1 Assessment

THINK CRITICALLY

1. What does an individual's packaging consist of?

2. Explain the "fight or flight" response. Which do you react with most often?

3. List some ways that you communicate your attitude. Can you think of ways that you may convey a negative attitude? How can you change that?

4. List at least five things you can be self-confident about.

MAKE ACADEMIC CONNECTIONS

5. **RESEARCH** Find a newspaper, magazine, or online ad for one of your favorite retail stores. Look at the ad, and write down all the attitudes you think the ad is portraying. Show the ad to someone older or younger, and ask what attitudes he or she sees in the ad.

6. **COMMUNICATION** Is there a person at your home, school, or religious organization who always displays a positive attitude? Think about the effects of that behavior on you. Then write that person a card or letter thanking him or her for being positive.

Professional Behavior

Goals
- Understand the importance of getting along with coworkers, supervisors, and customers
- Explain the importance of ethics in the workplace

Key Terms
- cooperate
- ethics

Getting Along

Being cooperative is a key element of your long-term career success. When you **cooperate**, you work with others for mutual benefit. Cooperation is easy when you work with people you like and your workload is about right, but the picture changes when new coworkers or a new supervisor joins the team or when stress builds because deadlines aren't being met.

In today's organizations, people often work together in teams. They're expected to make decisions and achieve goals with little outside supervision. In this environment, everyone must get along.

What are some of the consequences of people not getting along in the workplace? You can probably think of several immediately, but the most likely consequence is conflict.

The way you handle your relationships, both in and out of the workplace, can have a major impact on your happiness and your fulfillment in life. The skills for getting along can be learned. Even if you're not expert at them now, you can learn to get along through understanding and practice.

Getting Along with Your Coworkers

From your first day on the job, you will be expected to work cooperatively with everyone in your organization. Start out by showing that you are approachable, friendly, and helpful. Whether you work in teams, units, or departments, you and your coworkers will need to be able to depend on each other.

marketing matters

Amir Doud has a coworker, Iris, who is always ill-tempered and loud-mouthed and is abusive sometimes. Amir wishes he could tell Iris to staple her mouth shut, since nothing positive ever comes out of it. But he knows that wouldn't be a constructive remark. How should Amir handle the situation instead?

Photodisc/Getty Images

Chances are, some of your coworkers will come from different cultural backgrounds. Realize that culture has a powerful influence on how people work, what they value, how they make decisions, and how they communicate. When people of different backgrounds work together, cultural misunderstandings can lead to conflict. If you don't know what a coworker means or why he or she is acting a certain way, ask questions to clarify. The better you and your colleagues understand each other, the better you'll work together.

To build positive relationships with your coworkers, follow these guidelines:

- Take time to listen. You'll learn more when you are listening than when you are talking.

- Show respect. Realize that different backgrounds and varied ways of looking at problems and situations lead to creative ideas.

- Communicate clearly. When others speak to you, let them finish without interrupting them. Nod and smile to show you're listening.

- Strive to be pleasant and positive. Don't whine or complain.

- Accept criticism as constructive, and try to learn from it.

- Don't criticize. When you offer corrective feedback, focus on the behavior, not the person.

- Avoid judging. Instead, try to understand others.

- Remember that your way of looking at things is not the only valid approach. Work to eliminate your prejudices and biases. Never express prejudice or bias at work.

- Get to know your coworkers on a personal basis.

- Praise and compliment your colleagues when they've done a good job. Don't take credit for their successes.

- Pitch in to help others.

- Work to resolve conflict that involves you as soon as you become aware of it. Try to find a solution that improves the situation for everyone, even if individual employees—including you—don't get exactly what they want.

Getting Along with Your Supervisor

Your relationship with your supervisor may be your most important relationship at work. Because your supervisor recommends you for promotions and can address your needs and requests, he or she can help you advance in the company—or possibly prevent your advancement.

Developing a relationship with your boss can be difficult, however. If your boss acts distracted or irritable, you may wonder if you have done something wrong. If he or she is a poor communicator, you may find it hard to develop a relationship.

Workshop

Pay attention to how you interact with your friends and how you interact with your supervisors or teachers. Is there a difference in your interaction styles?

In most cases, you will be able to gain your boss's attention and respect if you follow these guidelines:

- Learn what your boss expects you to do and do it well.

- Don't disturb your boss with problems that you can resolve. If you bring a problem to your boss's attention, have a solution ready to offer.

- Don't complain about your coworkers. Try to work things out.

- Watch others, and follow their lead. If no one knocks at your boss's door when it's closed, that's a sure sign that you shouldn't interrupt. If your coworkers stop in to see your boss when the door is open, you probably can too.

- Don't bring your personal problems to work or let personal problems interfere with your ability to get to work. Show that you're reliable.

- Respect your boss's time. People in supervisory positions are busy.

- Don't make your boss have to guess what you want. Communicate clearly and directly.

- Finish your projects. Give your boss materials that are complete and accurate so that no additional work has to be done.

- Don't waste time. Your hard work will make your boss look good, and he or she will take notice.

- Organize your thoughts before approaching your boss.

- Don't give insincere compliments. Show appreciation and admiration when it is due.

- Respect your boss's authority. If you dislike some of his or her actions or behaviors, focus on the things you can respect. Never go above your boss's head without his or her permission. That's a quick way to destroy any relationship you've built.

- Don't take every harsh reply or unfriendly action personally. If you haven't done anything to deserve the action, most likely your boss is reacting to something else.

Getting Along with Customers

Whether you work directly with customers or support the employees who do, the customer is the reason your job exists. Without customers, your company would have to close its doors. It's the customers who pay your salary by purchasing the services or products of your organization.

Customers are your company's greatest asset, and you'll be expected to provide every customer with the best service, whether or not customer service is a job responsibility listed on your job description. Always greet customers with a positive, upbeat attitude. Treat the customer like he or she is right, even if you think the customer is wrong. Smile and show that you're approachable. Be respectful, and try to meet the customers' needs. Getting along with customers is vital to your company's success. It's an area where every employee makes a difference.

Barriers to Communication

Many organizations realize that improved internal communication is a key to better employee performance and increased productivity. Common barriers to successful communication in an organization include:

- **Closed communication climate** In a closed environment, employees receive little organizational news. Such a climate acts as a powerful communication barrier.

- **Top-heavy organizational structure** Long lines of communication result when an organization has a top-heavy, multilevel structure. Each layer of management creates a roadblock to efficient communication.

- **Filtering** Filtering refers to the process of shaping, shortening, or lengthening messages as they travel through the communication network.

- **Lack of trust** Employees who distrust managers because they feel they are being tricked, manipulated, criticized, or treated impersonally are not likely to communicate openly.

- **Rivalry** Employees competing for recognition and advancement may misrepresent or conceal information from one another and from management.

- **Power and status** Many bosses are afraid to reveal difficulties, losses, or conditions that make them look weak. Subordinates avoid disclosing information about lack of progress, frustrations, or disagreements.

    Here are some specific ways organizations can reduce communication barriers.

- **Encourage an open environment for interaction and feedback** Communication barriers are greatly reduced when managers seek employee feedback.

- **Flatten the organizational structure** Businesses today are streamlining their operations and eliminating layers of management, thus shortening lines of communication. Information flows more naturally and problems get solved faster. Because messages travel shorter distances, less distortion occurs.

- **Promote communication among peer groups** Communication builds bonds among employees, boosts morale, decreases turnover, and enriches the organization through the exchange of ideas.

Image Source Black/Jupiter Images

- **Establish rumor-control centers**   Some large organizations use telephone or voice mail rumor-control systems to deal with inaccurate rumors. Employees can inquire anonymously about rumors at a central office.

- **Provide ample information through formal channels**   Recognizing the power of internal communication in today's competitive markets, increasing numbers of managers are talking candidly with employees, encouraging them to contribute ideas.

Check Point

List two guidelines for getting along that could apply to coworkers, supervisors, and customers.

Acting Ethically

We learn what is right and wrong at a young age by watching and listening to our parents, teachers, religious leaders, and other adults. From their words and actions, they teach us to work hard, treat other people fairly and kindly, and stand by our word. They teach the importance of honesty and getting work done on time.

"All I really needed to know, I learned in kindergarten," claims bestselling author Robert Fulghum. He means that we learn as youth a set of values that will guide our behavior for many years—at home, at work, everywhere. This set of moral values is called **ethics**.

As you grow older, the lessons you have learned about right and wrong become your conscience, or inner voice. If you listen to it, very often you will know the right thing to do.

Good ethics are reflected in values such as honesty, dependability, hard work, sincerity, respect, caring, punctuality, fairness, trust, kindness, and loyalty. Employees who display these values are chosen for important projects and assignments, because their supervisors trust their work ethics and know they will give their best effort.

Following Ethical Guidelines

The values you learn as a child form the foundation for your decisions about how to act at work, but additional ethical guidelines must also direct your actions in the workplace. These rules cover activities that are specific to your job, such as conflicts of interest, giving and receiving gifts, documenting time worked, confidentiality, being accountable for your actions, personal use of the Internet and e-mail, and others. You'll face ethical questions every day in your job, no matter if you are just starting out or are a senior-level manager.

Ethical guidelines, which are often called codes of conduct or professional standards, exist for different industries, professions, and companies. For example:

- The American Counseling Association has a Code of Conduct for mental health counselors, which is updated regularly.

- The American Chemical Society publishes the Chemist's Code of Conduct.

- The Food and Agricultural Organization of the United Nations has several codes of conduct, such as one for the use and distribution of pesticides.

- The Hippocratic Oath and the American Medical Association's Code of ethics guide the conduct of medical professionals.

- Law enforcement officials, university professors, and researchers also must abide by codes of conduct for their professions.

Most of the country's major corporations have codes of conduct. If your company has one, read it thoroughly and follow it to the letter. Your organization may also offer ethics training, where you can learn the behaviors required by your company. The company may have an ethics officer, who can provide guidance, or an ethics hotline, where experienced staff members help employees resolve ethical questions.

Making the Right Choice

Making the right choice is easy when one behavior is clearly right and one behavior is clearly wrong, such as the actions in the table on page 106. But sometimes, you will have to make a decision between two behaviors that you consider to be right. For example, suppose you see a coworker who is a friend of yours take money from the cash register and put it in her pocket. She notices you looking and asks you not to say anything, because she can't afford to lose her job. You must decide between supporting a friend and telling the truth, both of which are positive values. Or, suppose a coworker tells you to install defective screws into a product because the client needs the product immediately and there's no time to get replacement screws. Do you get the product to the customer on time, or do you insist on quality?

NETBookmark

The full text of various codes of ethics from professional organizations, companies, government departments, and schools and universities can be found online. Access the text's web site through **www.cengage.com/school/marketing/yourself** and click on Chapter 4. You will be directed to web sites for various codes of conduct. Access and compare three codes of conduct from three different professional categories listed on this web site. How are they similar? How do they differ?

Actions that are clearly right	Actions that are clearly wrong
• Listing only work expenses on expense reports	• Charging for non-work-related activities
• Using company supplies for work only	• Taking company supplies for personal use
• Taking only authorized time off, and not abusing sick-day policies	• Calling in sick when you are healthy

Here is a framework that may help you resolve such ethical dilemmas:

● **Step 1** Listen to your conscience or your instincts about the situation.

● **Step 2** Pay attention to the phrases you speak or hear. Comments such as "Just this once," "Let's not tell anyone," and "Just don't tell me about it. I'd rather not know" are indications of unethical conduct.

● **Step 3** Determine exactly what the issue is, then check your organization's and profession's ethical codes of conduct. Is the issue addressed?

● **Step 4** Think how you would feel if your actions were reported on the news or printed in the paper. Would you be pleased or ashamed?

● **Step 5** List alternative actions and their consequences. How might your actions affect you or your company? How would they reflect on you?

● **Step 6** Discuss the problem with your supervisor or your company's ethics officers. These people can steer you down the ethical path.

Check Point

How can having a code of conduct benefit a company?

THINK CRITICALLY

1. Think of two consequences, other than conflict, of people not getting along in the workplace.

2. Why is it important to respect your coworkers' various cultures?

3. You think Roger isn't pulling his weight at the bakery. He's supposed to get the bagels made by 7 a.m., but he's been working too slowly and the bagel bins are often empty. You don't like having to tell customers that you're out of bagels, and you begin to blame Roger. "I'm sorry," you tell your customers. "One of our bakers hasn't been doing his job. We're going to have to do something about this." How do you think customers would react to your news? What might be a better approach to take?

4. Your friend asks you to print his research paper at work because his printer is not working. He gives you the paper for the printer. Would you do it? Why or why not? What other action could you take?

MAKE ACADEMIC CONNECTIONS

5. **PROBLEM SOLVING** Work with a classmate to find solutions to the following problem: You have a coworker, Jawaharlal, who is known for socializing. What should you say when he invites himself into your office and sits down to chat? Create a skit that depicts your solution, and act it out in front of the class.

6. **DIVERSITY** Do ethics differ among cultures? Research the answer to this question at your local library, on the Internet, or by talking to at least five people from different cultures. Write a report that details your research methods and the results you found.

First Impressions

Goals
- Recognize the importance of first impressions
- Discuss appropriate appearance in professional situations
- Understand how to make a good first impression on the telephone and the Internet

Key Terms
- primacy effect
- business casual
- body art

First Impressions Count

How do I look? Am I dressed appropriately? Am I making a good first impression? You should be asking yourself these questions if you are looking for a job. Just like the jar of peanut butter that gets noticed on the shelf because of its attractive label design, you can create more interest by attending to your appearance.

Your image influences others, and your appearance communicates many things, including your personality, self-esteem, professionalism, and confidence. Your appearance can also affect your attitude. When you feel comfortable with your appearance, you will project that attitude and can be more effective in accomplishing your goals.

Judge and Be Judged

Psychologists have spent a great deal of time studying impression formation, and they have learned that, regardless of how objective people try to be, they often make judgments based on limited, external information within the first few seconds of meeting someone. Also, remember that meeting someone doesn't always take place face to face; it can also occur by phone or by computer.

In the first few seconds of an encounter, how much do you know about a person's skills, personality, or work ethic? Very little, if anything. But your first impression, whether positive or negative, is based on what you see or experience during that brief introduction: the way she talks, the clothes he wears, and the resume sent by e-mail. With only a limited amount of information, you judge people. Scary, isn't it? The first time an interviewer meets you, perhaps with that initial handshake or the

marketing matters

Hank Huisman was hired as a part-time employee at a local discount retailer. In his position as a greeter, he wears a nametag, but not a uniform. He wants to appear professional and positive. What are some ways he can present himself?

Photodisc/Getty Images

introduction, he or she may have already decided your fate. That's why positive first impressions are so essential.

The Primacy Effect

The initial impression we make when meeting someone new also has a greater impact on his or her perception of us than later information, so we need that impression to be positive. This is known as the **primacy effect**. Negative information weighs more heavily, and negative impressions are less likely to change than positive impressions, even after contradictory information has been discovered. If someone you wish to impress thinks badly of you for coming to an appointment five minutes late, even if you have a very good reason, they may not change their negative perception. People like to be right, and they tend to maintain their beliefs, sometimes even after they have been proven incorrect.

This means that if you visit an employer in person to drop off a resume in the hope of securing an interview, but you arrive with faded jeans and greasy hair, no matter how superb your resume might be and how strong your skills appear, the employer may not want to interview you.

com·mu·ni·cate

Go to a mall or another public place. Take notes about how ten people are dressed and other aspects of their appearance. What do you believe these people are communicating about themselves by their appearance?

Check Point

Explain the primacy effect.

Workplace Appearances

When you take control of your image, you can affect the impressions that others form about you. You want an interviewer's first impression of you to be: "What a self-confident, well-groomed, professional candidate this is."

Hygiene and Grooming

Factors of hygiene and grooming may seem shallow, but they are not, as anyone knows who has ever worked alongside someone who smells unpleasant. Cleanliness is important, not only in terms of image, but also for your overall health and well-being. Bathe or shower daily, wash your hair regularly, brush your teeth at least twice each day, and wear deodorant. Men, keep your nails short and neat, and appear clean-shaven (facial hair is discouraged by some organizations). Women, makeup should be tasteful, and nails should be neat,

Workshop

How would you dress to meet the President of the United States? How would you dress to go to a movie with your friends? What impressions are you trying to convey with your appearance in these two situations?

and if polished, it should be conservative. Apply cologne or perfume sparingly. Hair should be neat, nicely styled, and preferably a natural-looking color.

Personal Appearance

Different organizations have different dress code policies, but you should always look professional. A professional look helps others see you as confident and responsible, and they may take you more seriously. Always dress well for an interview, even if you know the organization is informal. When you dress professionally, you are showing the interviewer that you respect the organization and will conduct yourself professionally.

Some organizations have a business casual dress policy. **Business casual** means dressing in a professional yet relaxed manner. Khakis and a polo-style shirt for men and pants with a sweater or blouse for women are examples of business casual dress. Whatever you wear, never push the limit on your appearance. Use your clothing to make a statement at home or on the weekend, but not at work.

Body art is another element of your personal appearance. Body art refers to tattoos and body piercing, and it has increased in popularity in recent years. Keep in mind the effect that body art may have on the impression you make on potential employers and their customers. Many employers will require you to cover tattoos or remove piercings while on the job. These suggestions are not made to stifle your creativity or self-expression. They are offered so that you make informed decisions.

Digital Vision/Getty Images

Check Point

Explain how "casual dress" could mean different things at different companies.

marketing math connection

Calculate how much a company will lose in one year if an employee takes the following items for his or her personal use every month.

2 pens	$0.76 each
1 pad of paper	$1.29 each
10 personal photocopies	$0.03 per copy
45 minutes of tardiness to work	$9.00 per hour
30 minutes extra at lunch	$9.00 per hour
60 minutes surfing the Web	$9.00 per hour

SOLUTION

Loss incurred per month for:

Pens	=	2 × $0.76	=	$1.52
Pads of paper	=	1 × $1.29	=	$1.29
Photocopies	=	10 × $0.03	=	$0.30
Tardiness	=	0.75 × $9.00	=	$6.75
Long lunches	=	0.50 × $9.00	=	$4.50
Web surfing	=	1 × $9.00	=	$9.00
				$23.36
				× 12
Total loss			=	$280.32

Telephone and Online Impressions

Companies use telephones and the Internet to send and receive information quickly. The better your ability to communicate using these tools, the better your chance of creating a good impression.

Telephone Impressions

Telephone conversations are used to establish a person-to-person connection. Understanding barriers to effective telephone communication and effective use of voicemail can help you use the telephone to its greatest advantage.

Telephone and Communication Barriers Telephone use creates unavoidable barriers to communication. First, the telephone takes away your ability to send and receive nonverbal messages. Therefore you must listen for vocal clues and be mindful of the signals you are sending with your voice. Next, when you are on the phone, you are unable to see who is speaking to you. Your hearing must be sharp to make up for this. If you listen carefully, you will be able to detect when voices are hesitant, fearful, or timid. Lastly, your telephone voice may sound different from the way you hear yourself. Put a little extra warmth in your voice when you speak on the telephone. Smile when speaking on the phone and it will show up in your voice.

Voicemail You may leave messages for a job contact who is unavailable when you call, or receive messages from potential employers. Be sure to consider your voicemail greeting. An inappropriate greeting that tries to be cute, uses characters from television or movies, or includes loud music can cost you an interview or job offer. Likewise, when you are leaving a voice mail message, be professional. Speak clearly, state the reason for your call, leave a callback number, and keep your message simple.

Online Impressions

Online communication, including e-mail and social networking, also is used in business and job-search communication. As with the telephone, understanding how to use these tools wisely can increase the effectiveness of your communication.

E-mail E-mail is used through the Internet and on cellular phones. When sending e-mail messages do not use shorthand or emoticons. Instead, format your e-mail messages the same way you would on hard copy. Be concise and use proper grammar and punctuation, a greeting, and a closing. Also be sure to give your contact information, including full name, address, phone number, and e-mail address. Creating a name-based e-mail account specifically for your job hunt and monitoring it regularly is an effective way to communicate with potential employers.

Social Media If you have a blog, FaceBook, MySpace, or LinkedIn account, you are participating in social networking. Social networking sites offer the opportunity to stay in touch with friends and family, share information, and promote yourself. They also offer the ability for anyone to learn about you, including potential employers.

Be sure to use the privacy options provided by most social media websites, and make certain your online activities are visible only to close friends and family. Be aware that what you post may be accessed by potential employers. Your words, photos, or videos may be used to determine whether or not you would make a good addition to their team.

Check ▶ Point

Why is it important to use the privacy options provided by most social media websites?

Lesson 4.3 Assessment

THINK CRITICALLY

1. Why are positive first impressions important?

2. Describe a time when someone made a positive first impression about you. Has that impression been accurate? Has that impression remained with you?

3. How can a professional appearance benefit you?

4. Dalia is interviewing for a desk clerk position at a local hotel. She knows that if she gets the job, she'll be wearing a uniform to work every day, so she wears jeans and t-shirt and sneakers to the interview. Did Dalia make a good choice? Why or why not?

5. How can you make a positive impression by telephone?

6. Maya uses a social networking site to post comments and information about herself as well as keep up with her friends and other groups in which she is interested. She sometimes uses vulgarity when she posts comments, and has some pictures posted that are not very complimentary. How do you think this would be viewed by a potential employer? What should she do?

MAKE ACADEMIC CONNECTIONS

7. **MARKETING/RESEARCH** Who are some of the leading makers of professional clothing and shoes for men and women? Research five companies and write a brief paragraph about how each company successfully markets itself to professionals. If possible, add pictures to your report to demonstrate what you are saying.

8. **SOCIAL STUDIES** Business casual in the workplace has increased in popularity over the last decade. In groups, research some employers who have adopted a business casual or partial business casual dress code and provide examples of what constitutes business casual according to their policies.

VOCABULARY BUILDER

Choose the term that best fits the definition. Write the letter of the answer in the space provided. Some terms may not be used.

_____ 1. How one feels or believes about something

_____ 2. Personal insecurities that lead to uncertainty

_____ 3. Encourages or discourages behaviors by attempting to influence attitudes

_____ 4. The initial impression one makes has a greater impact on another's perception of the individual

_____ 5. Includes tattoos and piercings

_____ 6. A person who takes a negative view of situations

_____ 7. Includes attitude and appearance, and can provide a competitive advantage

_____ 8. One's visual impression

_____ 9. Knowing and understanding yourself and your abilities

_____ 10. One who feels confident and positive, believing things will work out

_____ 11. A set of moral values that guides our behavior

_____ 12. The feeling that one is perfect or knows everything

_____ 13. A style of dress that is professional yet relaxed

a. appearance
b. arrogance
c. attitude
d. body art
e. business casual
f. ethics
g. hygiene
h. low self-esteem
i. optimist
j. packaging
k. pessimist
l. positive self-esteem
m. primacy effect
n. self-confidence
o. social marketing

REVIEW CONCEPTS

www.cengage.com/school/marketing/yourself

14. How can your packaging affect an employer's decision to hire you?

15. What is meant by the saying "perception is reality"?

16. Describe social marketing and give an example.

17. Why should you practice positive thinking? Name one way you can do this in your own life.

18. What is positive self-talk? Do you ever use positive self-talk? If so, think of a time it helped you and describe it. If not, think of a time when it would have helped.

19. Why are self-confident employees usually effective employees?

20. Why is it so important to get along with customers?

21. Why should you consider the primacy effect when job searching?

APPLY WHAT YOU LEARNED

22. Think about a time when a principal, teacher, supervisor, or parent demonstrated a negative attitude. Record the behaviors that were a clue to the person's attitude.

23. Bradley is a very shy person. During his first week at a computer software store, his coworkers were very friendly to him. He answered their questions quietly and looked at the floor, but did not start any conversation. By the end of the first week, his new coworkers were discussing him behind his back. Some thought he was rude. How have they judged Bradley according to his outward attitude? How can he begin to change their perception?

24. Think about each of the following characteristics: intimidation, jealousy, gossiping, superiority, defensiveness. Write one sentence about how each characteristic can hurt you in the workplace.

25. Reflect on several significant events in your life and write them down. Then think about how these events may have affected your self-esteem positively or negatively. Record that as well. You may still need to address some of these issues in order to increase your self-esteem. Your school may have a counselor, or you could ask you instructor for a suggestion about whom to talk to.

26. Provide an example of "fight or flight" as it relates to a situation you have been faced with.

27. You have just called a potential employer to follow up after an interview, and you were transferred to voicemail. Write out an example of an appropriate message you might leave.

28. Think about an e-mail you received from which you were not sure if the person sending it was happy, annoyed, angry, etc. How might you avoid this problem when sending e-mails?

MAKE ACADEMIC CONNECTIONS

29. **COMMUNICATION** Consider the first time you met someone new who later had a big impact in your life, perhaps a teacher, supervisor, or friend. Write a one to two page paper about your first impression and the application of the primacy effect.

30. **DESIGN** Prepare a storyboard or comic strip detailing the transformation from low self-esteem to positive self-esteem. Be creative. Use a character that you design to show this transformation.

31. **TECHNOLOGY** Visit an image planning/consulting site. Review the topics covered and develop three strategies for making positive changes.

32. **SOCIAL STUDIES/HISTORY/RESEARCH** Trace the history of costume and dress in six different countries around the world—one country from each populated continent. Create a timeline with pictures that show the development of the country's cultural dress.

Business Ethics

Every day individuals are faced with ethical issues in the business world and workplace. Business ethics involve choosing between right and wrong. Ethics are influenced by moral choices and values. Your team of two or three members will interview a business leader in the community to determine a current ethical dilemma in today's business world. Your group must present and defend your positions related to an ethical dilemma.

Two 4" × 6" note cards will be provided for each participant and may be used during the preparation and performance of the case. Information may be written on both sides of the note cards. No reference materials, visual aids, or electronic devices may be brought to or used during the preparation or performance. One member will introduce the team and describe the ethical situation. All team members must participate in the presentation. Teams have seven minutes to present the ethical dilemma. Following each presentation, judges will conduct a three-minute question-and-answer period.

"I saw the recycling bins all over town. The bins are there because of a new community initiative to recycle, which I read about in the local newspaper. I'm glad that officials are making it easy for citizens to participate and support the cause."

Did you ever wonder how an organization tells its story? Community affairs and community relations initiatives communicate an organization's goals and ideas to its customers, investors, government agencies, and members of the community. Public relations specialists work with the media to communicate information about the organization, its initiatives, its partners, and its business. They write press releases, arrange speaking engagements for officials, research, write and prepare press kits and annual reports, and speak on behalf of the organization. They also work closely with the media, and may be assisted by other employees, outside agencies, or consultants.

Employment Outlook

An above-average rate of employment growth is expected.

Job Titles

- Public Relations Specialist
- Community Relations Coordinator
- Outreach Coordinator
- Communications Specialist
- Community Affairs Director
- Media Specialist
- Press Secretary

Needed Skills

- A bachelor's degree usually is required, and accreditation is available through professional organizations.
- The ability to work with many different people, motivate others, and communicate effectively is essential.

- Creativity, initiative, and good judgment are needed.
- An outgoing personality, strong research skills, self-confidence, and the ability to handle stressful situations are important.

What's It Like to Work Community Relations?

Jamie puts the finishing touches on the township's annual report, calls the printer to discuss details about the finished report, and e-mails the files to the printer. He contacts the events manager to finalize plans for the annual community day festival. Then he takes a call from a television news reporter who wants to include a statement from the township manager in a story the station is completing for the evening broadcast.

The township is planning to launch a "go green" initiative, greening its operations and educating the public about energy conservation and preservation. Jamie hurries to a meeting with the township manager, several commissioners, and the director of a local environmental action group to plan a strategy for communicating the new initiative. After the meeting, Jamie works with the creative director and copywriter from the marketing agency the township has contracted to develop the messaging and materials that will be used to launch the "go green" initiative. He ensures that the township's story is presented clearly and effectively.

What About You?

What are some key considerations when working with the media and the public to share an organization's story and communicate its initiatives?

Chapter 5

Who Is Your Market?

5.1 Identify Market Segments

5.2 Research Your Target Market

5.3 Explore Opportunities

CAREERS IN MARKETING

PNC Financial Services Group

PNC Financial Services Group, with branches focused in 13 states and the District of Columbia, is the fifth largest bank by deposits in the United States. In addition to financial services, PNC is building its reputation for green building, work/life balance, and corporate social responsibility.

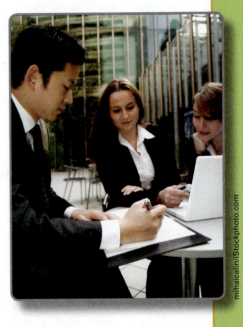

mihaicalin/iStockphoto.com

The Community Development Coordinator supports Community Development Banking at PNC. Targeted customers for this group include low- and moderate-income consumers and communities, community development corporations, non-profits, small businesses, and women and minority-owned enterprises. The Community Development Coordinator is responsible for compiling Community Development Banking reports, managing the information necessary for these reports, managing projects, coordinating meetings, and supporting the Managing Director.

The position requires a college degree, strong customer service skills, the ability to work with a diverse clientele, excellent computer skills, and strong communication skills. The candidate should be self-motivated, able to effectively multitask, have a high tolerance for stress, and require minimal direct supervision.

Think *Critically*

1. Why do you think this position requires someone who is able to work with a diverse clientele?

2. How can a candidate demonstrate that he or she is self-motivated and able to multitask?

PORTFOLIO BUILDER PROJECT
Involving Others in Your Portfolio

Project Objectives

The key to involving others in your portfolio is **networking**. Networking is actively making as many people as possible aware of your job search. In this project, you will:

- Create an extensive contact list of people you know.
- Compile a list of qualified references.
- Request letters of recommendation.

Getting Started

Read the Project Process below. Look at the resources on the Portfolio Builder CD.

- Study the sample contact list.
- Plan how to model your own list of references on the sample references list.
- Look over the sample letter of recommendation.

Project Process

Part 1 Lesson 5.1 Your network begins with personal contacts who link to others. List at least 25 people in your network and compare your list with your classmates' lists. Did their lists remind you of anyone you missed? Create a final list with contact information.

Part 2 Lesson 5.2 Identify three people, unrelated to you, who can vouch for the qualities that will make you a good employee. Contact these individuals and update them on your career plans. Ask for permission to use them as a reference. Write your reference list, with contact information, and place several copies in your portfolio.

Part 3 Lesson 5.3 Ask those three references for a letter of recommendation. Be sure to tell these individuals about any new skills you have as well as your target job objective. Display the letters in your portfolio.

Project Wrap-Up

Think about what your references wrote about you. Did they point out any job skills or personal assets you had previously overlooked? List any qualifications you could later incorporate into a resume or cover letter.

Creatas Jupiter Images

Identify Market Segments

Career Research

As you begin the journey of marketing yourself—feeling positive, self-confident, and self-aware—consider the importance of your destination. If your destination is a position with an organization, you need to determine what you're interested in doing and where you might like to work.

You can relate your search for employment to a marketer's search for customers. As marketers plan for successful product introductions, they use two strategies to find customers: segmenting and targeting. First, they identify **market segments**—components of a market that are made up of consumers with one or more similar characteristics. Then, they divide the market even further into their **target market**—a clearly identified portion of the market to which the company wants to appeal.

You can use these marketing strategies in your search for employment. Segment your market by dividing it into possible occupations (including specific college majors or degree or certificate programs) and industries. Then, identify your target market by collecting information about specific companies. Base your promotional messages, including your resume and cover letters, on this target market.

Segmenting

A market includes all the consumers a business would like to serve, but it is impossible for a business to serve all customers well. Therefore,

marketing matters

The Spotless Dishwasher Company recently noticed a decrease in sales. To reverse this trend, the company started advertising its new model, the 3000X, on a local television station. The ads air during the week from 3 P.M. to 5 P.M. and on Saturdays from 7 A.M. to 11 A.M. But after six months, sales have not improved. Why do you think the advertising campaign has been unsuccessful?

blue_iq/iStockphoto.com

marketers segment their markets into groups of consumers with common characteristics, such as needs and wants or previous purchase decisions. Similarly, you will segment your market into possible occupations and industries.

Career Self-Knowledge

A major part of determining your possible market segments is career self-knowledge. In Chapter 3, you worked through a self-assessment, looking at your personality and interests, considering your values, developing ABC goals, and analyzing skills and benefits. These exercises, coupled with your knowledge from Chapter 4 about attitude, behavior, and appearance, provide you with a strong basis for self-knowledge. And self-knowledge is the first step in determining your career possibilities.

Shanice wants to be an accountant. She has always liked math and enjoys completing tasks that require attention to detail. Her mom is an accountant, and during high school breaks, Shanice helps out at her mom's office. She plans to major in accounting in college. Because she has very specific goals, Shanice has identified only one market segment: accounting positions.

But not everyone has such specific plans. Roberto is unsure of his career future. His parents want him to attend college, but he does not have a clear idea of what he would like to do. Therefore, Roberto has numerous possible market segments.

Shanice chose accounting as a market segment based on her interests and skills, as well as her knowledge of what the career involves. Her self-knowledge directed her to this position. Roberto can also use factors such as his interests, values, goals, and skills as a basis for career choices to narrow his choices. He might consider using a self-assessment to help him determine the positions and industries that may be a good match for him.

Did You Know?

Several years ago, a dog food manufacturer conducted market research to identify the most profitable target market for a new type of dog food. Because dogs don't shop, they segmented dog owners into four groups, according to how they related to their dogs: dogs as grandchildren, dogs as children, dogs as companions, and dogs as dogs.

They decided to target the most lucrative segment, although it wasn't the largest group, and sell the food through pet stores. Which group did they target? Dogs as grandchildren.

Check > Point

Why is it important for marketers to segment their markets?

Possible Occupations

Using your self-knowledge to segment your market by possible occupations is an important step in identifying your target market. However, with more than 20,000 potential occupations, you may need some additional help in identifying occupations of interest to you. A school counselor may be able to help you review your self-assessment results. In addition, some useful sources of occupational information are described in this lesson.

Career Clusters

Sixteen career clusters were developed by the U.S. Office of Education to provide a focus for career-related learning and academic study. Each cluster includes occupations in a particular field that require similar skills and knowledge, and each cluster includes various career pathways. The sixteen career clusters are listed in the following table:

Agriculture, Food & Natural Resources	The production, processing, marketing, distribution, financing, and development of agricultural commodities and resources including food, fiber, wood products, natural resources, horticulture, and other plant and animal products/resources.
Architecture & Construction	Careers in designing, planning, managing, building and maintaining the built environment.
Arts, A/V Technology & Communications	Designing, producing, exhibiting, performing, writing, and publishing multimedia content including visual and performing arts and design, journalism, and entertainment services.
Business Management & Administration	Business Management and Administration careers encompass planning, organizing, directing and evaluating business functions essential to efficient and productive business operations. Business Management and Administration career opportunities are available in every sector of the economy.
Education & Training	Planning, managing and providing education and training services, and related learning support services.
Finance	Planning, services for financial and investment planning, banking, insurance, and business financial management.
Government & Public Administration	Executing governmental functions to include Governance; National Security; Foreign Service; Planning; Revenue and Taxation; Regulation; and Management and Administration at the local, state, and federal levels.
Health Science	Planning, managing, and providing therapeutic services, diagnostic services, health informatics, support services, and biotechnology research and development.
Hospitality & Tourism	Hospitality & Tourism encompasses the management, marketing and operations of restaurants and other foodservices, lodging, attractions, recreation events and travel related services.

Human Services	Preparing individuals for employment in career pathways that relate to families and human needs.
Information Technology	Building Linkages in IT Occupations Framework: For Entry Level, Technical, and Professional Careers Related to the Design, Development, Support and Management of Hardware, Software, Multimedia, and Systems Integration Services.
Law, Public Safety, Corrections & Security	Planning, managing, and providing legal, public safety, protective services and homeland security, including professional and technical support services.
Manufacturing	Planning, managing and performing the processing of materials into intermediate or final products and related professional and technical support activities such as production planning and control, maintenance and manufacturing/process engineering.
Marketing	Planning, managing, and performing marketing activities to reach organizational objectives.
Science, Technology, Engineering & Mathematics	Planning, managing, and providing scientific research and professional and technical services (e.g., physical science, social science, engineering) including laboratory and testing services, and research and development services.
Transportation, Distribution & Logistics	Planning, management, and movement of people, materials, and goods by road, pipeline, air, rail and water and related professional and technical support services such as transportation infrastructure planning and management, logistics services, mobile equipment and facility maintenance.

Source: The Career Clusters icons and definitions are being used with permission of the States' Career Clusters Initiative, 2009, www.careerclusters.org.

Occupational Outlook Handbook

Available through your counselor or local library, the *Occupational Outlook Handbook* is also accessible online. This government publication details 11 major industry clusters and more than 250 occupations. Information that can help you make career decisions, such as required education, earnings, and job outlook, is available through the web site. The U.S. Department of Labor's *Occupational Outlook Quarterly*, a periodical that reports on job market trends, is also available online.

Workshop

Divide into teams and write a description of a board game or a television game show based on the title "Fantasy Workplace." Include information about the criteria you used to define the ideal work-place, such as industry, occupation, job title, or other details such as work-ing hours, dress code, and benefits. Be prepared to explain your choices.

© Stephen Coburn, 2009/Used under license from Shutterstock.com

America's Career InfoNet and Jobweb

Sponsored by the U.S. Department of Labor and Jobweb, America's Career InfoNet, part of CareerOneStop, provides information about licensed occupations as well as general occupational information. The National Association of Colleges and Employers' Jobweb also provides occupation and industry information, including a list of the fastest-growing jobs in the United States.

Trade Publications

A variety of publications provide information on related occupations. Visit the library or conduct an Internet search to locate publications that focus on the occupations you are considering. For instance, if you are considering a photography career, you might browse *Editor & Publisher*, *Outdoor Photographer*, *Shutterbug*, *Photo Life*, and *Photo Resource Magazine*.

Occupation-Based Associations

WEDDLE's Association Directory provides a free search engine with access to thousands of trade associations in its database. Select an occupa-tional category, and a list of associations in that career field is provided. For example, a search for "sales/marketing" returns more than 100 associations. These associations can be great sources of career-related information about the occupations they represent.

Check Point

How can information about occupations help you identify your target market?

Possible Industries

An **industry** is a specific employment field—a branch or segment of the economy. As you did when you determined possible occupations, you can use your self-assessment to help you determine which industries to consider. Many types of industries exist, and you can use your self-knowledge to focus on specific segments that may be a good fit for you.

Industry Overview

There are systems for classifying industries, such as the North American Industrial Classification System (NAICS). For the most part, the NAICS has replaced the older Standard Industrial Classification (SIC) system, and is the standard for classifying business establishments. The NAICS classifies business establishments by economic activity. It allows business activity statistics to be compared more easily. It recognizes 350 new industries such as fiber optics, semiconductor machinery manufacturing, convenience stores, cable networks, satellite communications. It was developed jointly by the United States, Canada, and Mexico. The NAICS industry segments include Agriculture, Forestry, Fishing, and Hunting; Mining, Quarrying, and Oil and Gas Extraction; Utilities; Construction; Manufacturing; Wholesale Trade; Retail Trade; Transportation and Warehousing; Information; Finance and Insurance; Real Estate and Rental and Leasing; Professional, Scientific, and Technical Services; Management of Companies and Enterprises; Administrative and Support and Waste Management and Remediation Services; Educational Services; Health Care and Social Assistance; Arts, Entertainment, and Recreation; Accommodations and Food Service; Other Services (except Public Administration); and Public Administration.

Determining Possible Industries

Shanice has settled on a possible occupation: accounting. To improve her chances of career success and satisfaction, she should target industries that employ accountants, such as education, manufacturing, services, and agriculture. Shanice has volunteered in her community treasurer's office and in a local hospital. Based on her interests and these experiences, she decides to include government and healthcare industries in her possible market segments.

Review the list of possible occupations you developed and the NAICS list of industry segments and identify some industries you are interested in exploring. Refer to the *Occupational Outlook Handbook* or a similar source to learn as much as possible about these industry segments.

Check Point

What is the NAICS?

THINK CRITICALLY

1. Explain the two strategies marketers use to find customers.

2. How might trade publications help you learn about specific occupations?

3. Why do today's workers have more choices when selecting an occupation than earlier generations did?

MAKE ACADEMIC CONNECTIONS

4. **MARKET RESEARCH** Look back at the Did You Know box on page 121. Select a product or service and brainstorm three or four market segments for the product or service. Develop a "portrait" of each segment.

Product or service:			
Segment	Characteristics in relation to product	Other characteristics of the segment	Best way to reach this segment
Name:			
Name:			
Name:			
Name:			

5. **RESEARCH** To visit the *Occupational Outlook Handbook* and the NAICS web sites go to **www.cengage.com/ school/marketing/yourself** and follow the links for this chapter. Compare the *OOH's* 11 clusters to the NAICS segments. How are the two classification systems different? How do they overlap? Can you add any items to either list? Write a two-page paper that reports your results, including the answers to these questions.

INTERNET

@

Research Your Target Market

Goals
- Learn which aspects of a company to research
- Use external and internal sources in your research

Key Terms
- targeting
- publicly owned organization
- privately owned organization
- external information
- internal information
- annual report

What to Look For

Now that you have identified possible occupations and industries, you can begin determining your target market by researching specific organizations. Marketers conduct research to make informed decisions, which involves collecting relevant information about prospects. For example, a cereal manufacturer, after segmenting customers by common characteristics, might conduct research and learn that one of their identified segments includes children ages three to eight who like healthy cereal with activities on the outside of the box. Before changing the design of the box, the product manager might survey parents of children in this segment to learn more specific details that might affect box design.

Before contacting organizations, you should know as much as possible about them so you can tailor your promotional messages, including your resume, to their needs and wants. Your knowledge of an organization communicates your interest in it, as well as your desire to be a part of it.

In addition to collecting information about an organization's products and operations, you should also collect contact information. Search for names, mailing addresses, e-mail addresses, and phone numbers of people who work in or manage positions you are interested in.

marketing matters

Yi Han is interested in a copywriting job in the advertising industry. He has researched the occupation and the industry thoroughly. Two weeks ago, he applied for an open position at AdSource, a local advertising agency, and yesterday, a human resources employee called him to schedule an interview for later this week. What additional research should Yi do to prepare for the interview?

© jackhollingsworthcom, LLC, 2009/Used under license from Shutterstock.com

Targeting

Marketers carefully research a market before introducing a new product. They want to learn about potential customers, competitors, regulations, and anything else that might disrupt a successful product launch. They consider the results of this research and target messages to create awareness in the minds of the potential customers. When organizations seek out those who are most likely to buy their products and market directly to them, it is called **targeting**.

Photodisc/Getty Images

You can use targeting techniques in your job search. Research the companies in your possible market segments to determine which ones are most likely to hire you. Also, use your research to improve the effectiveness of your resumes and cover letters.

Researching Companies

To make informed and effective marketing decisions, marketers research three categories of information: business environment, marketing functions, and customers. You can adapt these categories to your search for information about organizations.

Business Environment Researching an organization's business environment involves learning industry information, such as any economic conditions, government regulations, changes in technology, or competition that might affect the organization. If you were considering employment at a manufacturing firm, for example, you would gather information about the size of the market it serves, its potential for growth, the kind of technology it commonly uses, and who its competitors are. You can find this information using the internal and external sources that are described later in this lesson.

Marketing Functions Compiling information about an organization's marketing functions will help you learn about the organization's relationship to its market. You will want to research elements such as:

- Products and services
- Prices of products and services, as well as salary information
- Place or distribution—where products and services are available or accessed
- Promotional strategies, such as advertising campaigns, use of a sales force, and recent publicity

diversity in the workplace

Multicultural Missteps

Research is a crucial step in the marketing process—especially for organizations that sell their products in other countries. Without a strong understanding of their international market, such companies will undoubtedly encounter, or even cause, cultural misunderstandings. These firms learned the hard way that only research can prevent a multicultural misstep.

- Liz Claiborne had to recall a line of jeans that featured sacred Muslim verses. The Council on American Islamic Relations expressed outrage that the verses were printed on the back pockets of the jeans, which meant that people who wore them would sit on the verses. In addition to recalling the jeans, Liz Claiborne agreed to conduct sensitivity training to prevent similar mistakes from happening in the future.

- After printing thousands of signs for a new Chinese market, Coca-Cola discovered that the way its name was rendered on the signs meant "female horse stuffed with wax" in some dialects. The company reprinted the signs using a phonetic equivalent that translates to "happiness in the mouth."

- Pepsi found that its slogan "Come alive with the Pepsi Generation" translated to "Pepsi will bring your ancestors back from the dead" in Taiwan.

- General Motors wondered why its Chevy Nova, which was selling spectacularly in the United States, had such dismal sales in South America. After research revealed that "No va" means "It won't go" in Spanish, it renamed the car Caribe.

Sources: AIESEC; DiversityInc.; Richard Bucher, *Diversity Consciousness* (Prentice-Hall, 2000)

Customers Marketers research *demographic* information, such as age, gender, and level of education; *psychographic* information, such as attitudes, needs and wants, and lifestyle; and *geographic* information, such as the ZIP codes where their customers live.

Consider the organization itself to be your customer and research information about its internal environment. Demographic information about an organization might include length of time in business, ownership information, and details about employment requirements (for example, education and experience levels). Psychographic information might include the organization's mission and vision, its attitude toward customers and employees, and its culture. Finally, an organization's geographic information might include its physical locations, or even its web site.

Check Point

Why do marketers perform research before introducing a product?

com-mu-ni-cate

Visit at least three small companies based in your community. Write a report comparing them. Include topics such as industry, products or services offered, target market, length of time in business, annual growth rate, marketing strategy, and the factors that make each company unique. Illustrate your findings with charts or other graphics.

Where to Look

Using the categories demographic, psychographic, and geographic, you can prepare to collect information that will help you in your job search. Many sources of information are available, often through your counselor's office or the library. Some sources are available free via the Internet, and some charge a fee for access.

Public or Private?

Before you begin to research an organization, consider its status: publicly or privately owned. **Publicly owned organizations** make shares of stock available for purchase on a stock exchange. They are required by law to provide certain types of information to shareholders, which simplifies your research. To determine if a company is publicly owned, check the following sources. You may access these web sites through **www.cengage.com/ school/marketing/yourself**.

- Stock listings in your local paper
- Investment research web sites, such as Big Charts
- Stock exchange web sites, such as the American Stock Exchange, NASDAQ, and the New York Stock Exchange

Privately owned organizations are organizations that do not offer shares of stock for public purchase. You may have more difficulty locating external information about these privately owned organizations, but be persistent.

Sources of External Information

External information is information made available outside of an organization. Sources of external information include:

- Directories, which compile information about organizations
- Indexes, which often provide fee-based information about organizations
- Chambers of commerce, which provide information about local organizations
- Trade publications, which profile or list organizations
- Newspapers, which can be searched for articles about specific organizations

Directories Directories can be effective sources of information for publicly, and some privately, owned organizations. They can be found in libraries' reference sections, and some can be found online. Helpful directories include:

- *Standard and Poor's Register of Corporations, Directors, and Executives*
- *Thomas Register of American Manufacturers*
- *Dun & Bradstreet Million Dollar Directory*

- Moody's Manuals
- *Cifar's Global Company Handbook*
- *Directory of Corporate Affiliations*

Indexes Indexes provide articles and general organizational information. Most indexes are fee-based and are available on the Internet or on CD-ROM. Check with your local library to find out which indexes it subscribes to. Helpful indexes include:

- ABI/Inform
- Business Periodicals Index
- Predicast's F&S Index

Chambers of Commerce Many cities and towns have chambers of commerce that provide regional information about the area and its organizations. You can request a relocation packet, which is usually available for free or for a small fee. To find chamber addresses and phone numbers, visit this textbook's web site at **www.cengage.com/school/marketing/yourself** and follow the links to this chapter, or consult the *World Chamber of Commerce Directory*.

Trade Publications In addition to providing industry information, trade publications publish articles or features about specific organizations. Many industry associations publish trade journals, which you may find at your local library.

Newspapers Newspapers can be good sources of articles about organizations. Use the links provided at **www.cengage.com/school/marketing/yourself** to find a list of newspapers online.

Sources of Internal Information

Internal information is information developed within an organization. Sources of internal information include:

- Annual reports
- Company web sites
- Informational interviews

Annual Reports Publicly owned organizations are required to provide stockholders with an **annual report**, a report that includes operational and financial information and describes what the business is currently doing and is planning to do. When reviewing an annual report, be sure to read the letter from the CEO near the beginning of the report. It generally provides an overview of the company's current situation as well as future direction.

Company Web Sites Company web sites often provide general information, such as location, management, and products and services. If you don't know the URL for a company site, enter the company's name into a search engine such as Google.

Workshop

Brainstorm a list of nouns and adjectives you would use to describe yourself to someone who has never met you. Consider your personality, physical characteristics, current job or student status, lifestyle, hobbies, and so on. What could a marketer learn from this list?

Informational Interviews *Informational interviews* are informal interviews with a person who works in the occupation or for an organization you are targeting. Informational interviews are not job interviews; they are opportunities to learn more about an occupation or an organization, including information that may be difficult to find otherwise, such as organizational culture or management's attitude toward employees.

Informational interviews can occur in person, by phone, or by e-mail. Phone or e-mail contact is particularly effective for long distance interviews. Regardless of the format, be clear about your reason for wanting the interview, be timely, have questions prepared, and send a thank-you letter. In addition to learning more about an occupation or organization, use the interview as an opportunity to network and make a valuable career contact.

Below are some standard questions to ask during an informational interview.

- How did you get started in this industry or field?
- How did you get started with this organization?
- What do you like about the position, industry, and organization? What do you dislike?
- What are some future goals and directions for this organization?
- What are some qualities that this organization looks for in employees?
- What can I do to prepare for a career in this industry?
- How does this organization normally hire people?
- What is a typical day like for you?
- What are your job responsibilities?
- What is the corporate culture like?
- Who are your customers?
- Who are your organization's main competitors?
- What distinguishes your organization from its main competitors?
- Is it possible to tour this organization?

Check Point

What is the difference between external and internal information? List two sources of each type of information.

THINK CRITICALLY

1. Explain the three categories of information that marketers research before making decisions.

2. How do publicly owned organizations and privately owned organizations differ?

3. List the five sources of external information and the three sources of internal information discussed in this lesson. Can you think of any other sources of company information?

4. How can a company's annual report help you learn more about that company?

MAKE ACADEMIC CONNECTIONS

5. **ANALYSIS** Identify employers you believe are ideal for you, and then find the best way to communicate your choices, and the reasons behind them, to the rest of the class. You can write a report, make a poster, record a radio feature, design an overhead or PowerPoint presentation, or choose another medium.

6. **COMPANY RESEARCH** Choose three companies you are interested in working for. Use a search engine to find each company's web site. If one of the companies does not have a web site, choose another one that does. Compare the web sites based on six to eight features of your choice, such as ease of navigation, graphics, and details about the company. Write a memo to your instructor in which you explain your criteria for comparison and describe your findings.

Explore Opportunities

Goals

- Identify methods for finding jobs
- Explain methods of contacting employers

Key Terms

- job bank
- resume bank
- human resources department
- cold call
- direct mailing
- mass mailing
- modified mass mailing

Searching for work

Lila has targeted pharmacy and training as positions of interest to her. She has identified healthcare and education as industry segments to consider. She has researched a number of organizations in those industries and feels confident that she has strong basic knowledge. Now she is ready to search for opportunities.

You found some companies you would like to work for. You have already targeted positions and industry segments. Now it's time to find positions. Positions become available as employees retire or move on to other positions or companies expand to create new opportunities.

Some job search methods are traditional, such as reading classified ads. Other methods rely on technology such as the Internet. Not all opportunities are advertised, so contacting employers directly and talking with people you know can help you uncover hidden jobs.

The Internet

The Internet contains a wealth of information for job seekers. According to one e-recruiting information site, more than 28 million jobs were posted

marketing matters

Renee Sokolov has been reading the classified ads for weeks and has sent resumes to more than 20 companies. She has only had two interviews, and neither company offered her a job. She's beginning to think she will never find a position in the marketing field. Renee's father tells her she should call his friend, the head of marketing for Central Bank, about a job. Do you think Renee should follow her father's advice? Why or why not? What else can Renee do to locate job openings?

Photodisc/Getty Images

on the Internet in 2000. The Internet can be used for many other aspects of the job search process, including:

- Locating information on industries, occupations, and organizations
- Finding job openings
- Posting your resume
- Contacting employers

Job Banks **Job banks** (also known as employment sites) are web sites that offer databases of available positions that can be searched by job title, location, keywords, and so on. Examples of job bank web sites include CareerBuilder, Monster, and HotJobs. Most job banks also offer **resume banks**, where job seekers can post their resumes to be viewed by recruiters and employers.

Corporate Web Sites Corporate web sites sometimes offer information about the companies' job openings. Not all company sites list job openings, but most do. Look for a link such as "Careers" or "Employment."

Niche Sites Niche sites specialize in jobs in particular industries or occupations. For example, if you are interested in working with a nonprofit organization, you might visit Idealist.org. If government jobs are your target, you can search for them at USAJOBS. See **www.cengage.com/school/marketing/yourself** for links to these web sites.

Virtual Career Fairs

Virtual career fairs utilize technology to help organizations stay relevant to job seekers who may be accustomed to using Internet searches and social media to find information and communicate with others. The entire process occurs online, making it easier for busy employers and job seekers to connect with each other. It also makes it easier for job seekers who are searching for international positions, or positions in other geographic areas. The National Association of Colleges and Employers (NACE) and JobWeb are among the organizations coordinating virtual career fairs.

Employers

After you research your target organizations, you may choose to contact some of them directly. According to the U.S. Bureau of Labor Statistics, 35 percent of job seekers obtained positions by applying directly to employers.

If your target organization is small, you may deal with the owner or president. If your target organization is larger, you may be directed to the **human resources department**. This department is generally not the hiring authority, but supports the hiring process by:

- Preparing materials, such as position descriptions
- Screening applicants by reviewing their qualifications
- Forwarding the resumes and cover letters of qualified applicants to the manager or hiring authority

Workshop

Do you agree or disagree with this quotation from Julie Griffin Levitt, a business consultant and author: "Employers trust recommendations from people they know more than from people they don't know."

- Scheduling interviews
- Helping new employees complete paperwork

Some job seekers send out information to organizations blindly—without researching the organization, making direct contacts, or knowing of specific openings. These blind mailings, which are not customized to meet an employer's needs and wants, usually are not effective.

Classified Ads

The "Help Wanted" ads in newspapers are a traditional source of job listings. Most papers have a classified section, including an expanded version in the Sunday edition. Classified ads should not be your only source of job leads. They often provide only vague information, and experts suggest that as few as 15% of positions are filled through the want ads. Some advertised openings may not be openings at all.

Despite the drawbacks, the classifieds can still be a useful research tool. If you are relocating, search the local newspaper for advertised positions. If you see appropriate openings on a regular basis, you can assume that a demand exists in your new location.

Similarly, you can use the classifieds to judge which industries have open positions. For example, John sees an ad for a community relations coordinator at a local bank. In addition to applying for the opening, John realizes that other banks probably have similar positions, so he adds banks to his list of industries.

Career/Placement Centers

School career or placement centers are in place to help students find jobs. Their staff members generally bring hiring organizations to the school for student interviews. These offices may also offer career counseling, assessments, and job search and career advice. While you should not rely on them to hand you a job, they can be great sources of career information and support.

Employment Agencies

Employment agencies are in the business of finding permanent or temporary assignments for job seekers. Some agencies are for-profit, charging a fee to either the organizations or the job seekers. Other agencies, such as state employment agencies, do not charge fees for job assistance. These agencies offer career assistance as well as job listings.

Networking

Your network consists of the people you know. It's like a web that allows messages to be communicated between people. Individuals are the basis of this web, and relationships form between them. These relationships produce *word-of-mouth* information—information gained from conversations between the individuals in the network.

Everyone you know—including your friends, relatives, teachers, and acquaintances—can be a source of job leads and career information.

You have probably heard the saying "It's not *what* you know; it's *who* you know." While *what* you know is important, *who* you know—especially someone with the right connections—can help you get your foot in the door. Your network should include:

- Family members
- Friends and neighbors
- Teachers, counselors, and coaches
- Former employers and coworkers
- People who attend your place of worship
- People who provide services, such as dentists and insurance agents
- Members of any athletic teams or organizations you belong to

As you build your network, use a "soft sell" approach in your conversations. Avoid demanding, high-pressure tactics to gather information. Listen well, and show appreciation for any assistance your contacts offer. Do not ask for a job. Instead, explain your interests and background and ask for suggestions, including position information, possible organizations, and names of others who may have useful information. Ask for permission to use your contact's name as a reference when contacting others. Be sure to follow up as necessary, including sending thank-you letters and keeping your contacts informed about how your job search is progressing.

Check Point

List three drawbacks to using classified ads to search for positions.

Contacting Employers

When you finish your research, you're ready to begin contacting employers. Common methods of employer contact include telephoning, e-mailing, cold calling by telephone or in person, and sending direct mail.

Telephoning

Telephoning is sometimes the most practical contact option. If an employer is located in another state, you may not be able to hop on a plane and visit, but you can pick up the telephone and have a one-to-one discussion.

Record Keeping You should keep a record of all telephone contacts with potential employers. Prepare "phone logs" for your organizer or use a spiral notebook to record the basic information about each employer you contact. Include space for the following information on your sheets.

careerbuilder®

Internet Tips and Tricks to Help You Land Your Next Job

By CareerBuilder.com

Copyright 2008 CareerBuilder, LLC.—Reprinted with permission.

There's a wealth of career information on the Internet, and these resources are just a mouse-click away for any job seeker.

But as comprehensive as sites like CareerBuilder.com are, there are other resources on the Internet you can use to land a new job. Here are a few tips and tricks to help maximize your job search on the Web.

1. Career assessment tests

Career assessment tests can be engaging and fun, and the results can give you important insight into your working style to help you find the best fit.

For example, CareerPath.com has a number of helpful career tests, including a color test that gauges your reaction to colors and suggests potential career paths based on the result. Take note of any keywords that appear in your test results and use them as search terms.

2. Network, network, network

Most career experts encourage job seekers to expand their networks. You can connect with other professionals via Web sites like BrightFuse and LinkedIn, and even a personal contact on Facebook can provide an important connection to an opportunity.

Alumni groups with an online presence can also be a great place to network, since the focus of those groups is their eagerness to connect with fellow graduates.

If you're not sure where to start, sign on to a networking site. Search for current or former co-workers and managers and invite them to join your network. Engage your network by sending messages and giving other users recommendations or kudos for the positive experience you had with them.

3. Research your prospective employer

If you're competing against other candidates with equally impressive skills, education and experience, you really need to break ahead of the pack. One way to do that is to know your prospective employer.

Start with the company's Web site; look in the "About Us," "Media" or "Press Room" sections. To be fully informed, you'll want to check out other sites with detailed information.

"Use online news sites to understand which companies are doing well or expanding," suggests Patrick Madsen, the director of professional career services at The Johns Hopkins Carey Business School. "Reading through articles and generally knowing where the world is going can open potential new doors and windows."

Madsen also suggests that job seekers research information sites like Hoover's, Vault.com or Careerbeam to learn about companies.

4. Person to person

Do an Internet search on yourself. A recent CareerBuilder.com survey found that one in four hiring managers are researching candidates online. If there's any information out there that could hurt your chances of being hired, you need to be aware of it.

Once you've landed an interview, you can also research the person you'll be talking to. Madsen recommends doing a simple Google search on the interviewer's name, as well as checking Facebook or LinkedIn to see if he has a profile there. The interviewer may also be featured on the company's Web site.

Mark Moran, founder and CEO of Dulcinea Media in New York City, says this step is vitally important. "I've interviewed perhaps 500 people in the last five years, and I can tell you most of them failed to get the job because they did not use the Internet to research me, the company or our industry."

5. Brave the cold

It's ideal to use sites like CareerBuilder.com to reply to job postings from employers actively seeking candidates in your field. But you can also use the Internet to do a "cold" search on companies that are in your field.

Career expert Chris Russell, the founder of the Secrets of the Job Hunt blog, recalls his initial job search. He researched companies in his area (none of which were actively hiring) and compiled a list of 80. From there, he identified a contact at each company. Russell launched his own "direct mail" campaign and soon had seven interviews. One of those companies hired him.

The twist to the story? Russell's job search was in the pre-Internet days of 1993. "The Internet would have made my campaign a much easier one if I had access to it back then. Today, there is so much information on the World Wide Web it can be daunting," he admits. "But if you know where to search, you can end your job hunt that much faster."

6. Back to basics

Some important basic tips to remember when using the Internet to land your new job:

- Make sure your e-mail address is professional; a handle like "party-guy2002" will give employers a negative perception of you before you've even started.

- Don't rely on spell check alone to capture any errors in e-mails, cover letters and résumés. The difference between the word "shift" and a common curse word is only one letter.

- Be sure to have text-only versions of any documents, so they can be easily sent or submitted to employers.

- Date of the initial call
- Employer's name and contact information
- Names and titles of the people you speak with
- Specific questions you want to ask and their answers
- Results of the call
- Follow-up reminder

Discussion Notes Some people are very comfortable speaking on the phone, while others may feel a little anxious. Preparation helps reduce anxiety, and your discussion notes will help you be prepared for your calls. Discussion notes are not the same as a script. Reading from a prepared script may sound fake and not spontaneous. Instead of planning out exactly what to say, put together notes you can refer to. Use an outline format to discourage yourself from reading verbatim. Discussion notes should include:

- **Name** Be sure to introduce yourself by name.
- **Purpose** Why are you calling? Keep it brief.
- **What's in it for them?** What can you offer employers? Use the skills-accomplishment-benefit statements you prepared in Chapter 3.
- **Action** What do you expect from the call? Do you expect an interview, information about the company, or a referral to someone else?
- **Courtesy** Be sure to thank the person for his or her time.

Phone Tips As you prepare to contact employers by phone, remember the importance of first impressions and the primacy effect: In the first few seconds of your phone conversation, an employer will form an opinion about you. Practice your phone conversation from your discussion notes, perhaps with a friend or family member. Build your confidence and enthusiasm so it comes across in your voice. Keep a mirror nearby, and watch your expressions as you speak. Smile and relax your muscles, which helps your voice sound positive.

E-Mailing

E-mailing is usually as efficient as and often more inexpensive than telephoning. Continue to keep track of contacts with record-keeping sheets, and use discussion notes to prepare your e-mails.

NETBookmark

E-mail will be an essential tool in your contacts with potential employers, as well as in your communications in the workplace after you're hired. To make sure you use this tool to your advantage, go to **www.cengage.com/school/marketing/yourself** and follow the links to the Net Bookmark for this chapter. After visiting several of the web sites, write a sample e-mail introducing yourself to a potential employer.

marketing math connection

The Danton Company surveyed 1,200 people about their new product, Silk Smooth soap. Based on the results in the table below, what percent of all respondents gave Silk Smooth soap a rating of better than average?

Ages	Product Rating				
	Excellent	Good	Average	Poor	Total
18–30	78	185	118	15	396
31–45	145	190	31	37	403
46–60	203	135	52	11	401
Totals	426	510	201	63	1,200

SOLUTION

Total, better than average rating = "Excellent" total + "Good" total
 = 426 + 510
 = 936

Percent, better than average rating = 936 ÷ Total respondents
 = 936 ÷ 1,200
 = 0.78
 = 78 percent

Because you will use your e-mail address for professional contacts, choose an appropriate one that is not offensive or immature. Be sure to check your e-mail account regularly.

Avoid using abbreviations in e-mail to professional contacts. Keep your messages brief, and always check for spelling and grammar errors. Finally, stay away from emoticons, such as smiley faces and winks. They may be cute, but they are inappropriate in professional correspondence.

Cold Calling

Unannounced phone calls or in-person visits are known as **cold calls**. If you are confident and assertive, you might try making unannounced in-person visits or phone calls to potential employers. In some industries—for example, retailing—cold calling may be effective. It also tends to be more effective at smaller companies, where you have a better chance of meeting a manager or supervisor. If you do choose to cold call employers, remember a few important points.

- Speak professionally on the phone, and dress professionally if you plan to visit in person. You can't predict the outcome of a cold call, and you may be interviewed on the spot, whether by phone or on site, so prepare as if you will be.

- Review your research on the organization.

- Review your discussion notes, and be sure to follow them.

- Keep record-keeping forms with you. Take a moment and write down names, and get business cards if you are on site. Following the cold call, record the information right away.

Direct Mailing

Direct mailing involves sending a marketing packet—a cover letter, a resume, and sometimes a sample sheet or references—to potential employers. Direct mailing can be a difficult way to reach your audience: According to some marketers, you should expect a response rate of only three to four percent, or three or four responses for every 100 packets you send. If you aren't able to reach an employer by phone, by e-mail, or in person, try mailing them a marketing packet. After sending a customized packet, wait a few days, usually no more than a week, and attempt to contact the employer again.

Some job seekers choose to use a **mass mailing** technique for their marketing packets: They prepare a stack of packets with basic resumes and cover letters and send them, unsolicited, to organizations that may or may not have openings. With a **modified mass mailing** you customize each cover letter with the name of a specific person.

Check Point

Describe a situation in which you might contact an employer by direct mail.

5.3 Assessment

THINK CRITICALLY

1. How can the Internet be used to locate employment opportunities?

2. Explain how to use a "soft sell" approach while building your network.

3. List and explain four ways to approach potential employers.

4. Describe networking.

MAKE ACADEMIC CONNECTIONS

5. **RESEARCH** Many recruiters recommend reading the career advice available on many job bank web sites. How useful is this material? Visit five job bank sites and read and rate the how-to information. Is the advice easy to read and understand? Did you learn anything new? Prepare an oral presentation to report your results.

INTERNET

VOCABULARY BUILDER

Choose the term that best fits the definition. Write the letter of the answer in the space provided. Some terms may not be used.

_____ 1. A specific employment field; a branch or segment of the economy

_____ 2. A clearly identified portion of the market to which a company wants to appeal

_____ 3. An organization that does not offer shares of stock for public purchase

_____ 4. A report that includes operational and financial information about an organization

_____ 5. A group of consumers with one or more similar characteristics

_____ 6. A site where job seekers can post their resumes to be viewed by recruiters and employers

_____ 7. Actively making as many people as possible aware of your job search

_____ 8. An organization that makes shares of stock available for purchase on a stock exchange

_____ 9. A site that offers a database of available positions

_____ 10. An unannounced phone call or in-person visit

a. annual report

b. cold call

c. direct mailing

d. external information

e. human resources department

f. industry

g. internal information

h. job bank

i. market segment

j. networking

k. privately owned organization

l. publicly owned organization

m. resume bank

n. target market

REVIEW CONCEPTS
www.cengage.com/school/marketing/yourself

11. How is a target market different from a market segment?

12. How can segmenting help you in your job search?

13. Explain what marketers focus on when they research an organization's business environment. What should you focus on when researching an organization's business environment during your job search?

14. What three types of customer information do marketers collect? Explain each type.

15. List and describe three sources of internal company information.

16. Explain the role of the human resources department in hiring.

17. What are niche sites? How can they help you in your job search?

18. What key information should be recorded on record-keeping sheets when contacting employers?

APPLY WHAT YOU LEARNED

19. Why should you research an organization's business environment, marketing functions, and customers?

20. How does a publicly owned organization differ from a privately owned organization?

21. How can you use networking to enhance your job search?

22. How might internal information be used when contacting an employer?

23. Why are discussion notes helpful when calling employers?

24. How should you prepare for making a cold call to employers?

MAKE ACADEMIC CONNECTIONS

25. **COMMUNICATION** Conduct research on e-mail etiquette. Write a two-page paper describing proper e-mail etiquette. Be sure to explain why this is an important topic for job seekers to understand.

26. **ART/DESIGN** Using the *Occupational Outlook Handbook* or the North American Industrial Classification System (NAICS) segments, create a poster showing your targeted positions and the industries where these positions may be found.

27. **LANGUAGE ARTS/FINE ART** Consider two occupations you are interested in. Visit the Weddles Association Directory web site by following the links to this chapter at **www.cengage.com/school/marketing/yourself** and find the associations related to these occupations. Use one of the "Quick Search" links on the home page. Of these lists, which do you think would be most helpful to you?

28. **SPECIAL-INTEREST SITES** Visit at least three of these sites and fill in the table below. Use an Internet browser or click on **www.cengage.com/school/marketing/yourself** to access the web sites.

Site	Target audience	Special features	Quality of information	Overall rating
The Black Collegian Online				
Job Accommodation Network				
Latpro.com				

Teens4hire				

Hospitality Services Management Team Decision Making

You and a partner are consultants for the hospitality industry. The industry is seeing trends toward fewer business meetings and conferences, more teleconferences, and less tourism due to an uncertain economy and heightened concern about U.S. security.

As a result, a major five-star hotel is concerned about its declining occupancy rate and has asked you to develop strategies to increase their business (occupancy rate). Hotel rates are $200 per night during the week, and special weekend rates are $120 per night. The hotel needs to maintain an average daily occupancy rate of 70 percent to make a profit.

You have 30 minutes to make decisions with your partner and plan your strategy for the hotel. Outline your strategy carefully because you will have only 10 minutes to present the information to the judge/class/businessperson. Your audience will have five minutes to ask you questions about your plan.

Evaluating Online Sources of Information

When you are writing a paper for a class or researching a company prior to an interview, how do you determine the sources of information you should use? Which sources are credible? Which sources contain valid, reliable information? As you gather information, it is important to assess the affiliation, credibility, and objectivity of the information, both for print and online sources.

When you access print sources, especially those available in an academic library, the librarians, academics, or other knowledgeable people have evaluated it. Online sources provide access to a variety of information, though this wealth of information has its limitations. It is relatively easy and inexpensive to make information available online, and it is therefore important for you to assess the affiliation and credibility of the information prior to citing it.

Affiliation

Assessing affiliation involves determining authorship and publisher. Consider the owner of the URL and the author of the particular piece you are reviewing. Is it a personal web page, an organization's page, or a news page? One tool that can help you to assess a web site is Alexa, which you can access by visiting www.cengage.com/school/marketing/yourself and clicking on the links for this activity. After entering the web site address on the "Site Info" link, Alexa will provide information regarding web traffic, where users are located (by country), demographics for the users, and site ownership information. Infomine and Librarians' Internet Index also provide details for information sources.

What is the author's background and level of expertise? Conducting a search on the author's name may help you to determine the background and credentials of the author. What about the publisher of the information? Is the information available through an academic journal or book that may have already undergone review prior to publishing? Is it part of an academic, scholarly, or news organization's web site? If the information is not part of these sites, what is the relationship between the site owner/publisher and the author? Is the site affiliation relevant to the information you are reviewing?

Credibility

Credibility involves authorship, as well as objectivity and verifiability. What background does the author or publisher bring to the information provided? The author's expertise or the publisher's knowledge or experience in the field related to the information can help you to evaluate the credibility of the information. What is the bias, or viewpoint, that the author or publisher might bring to the information? What is the context in which the author's work is presented? This may help you to determine if the information, for example, is presented as an opinion piece or editorial, which may not be objective, or a research study, which may possess objectivity. Is a bibliography available so you can further verify the information provided? You can further verify the information presented by researching some of the sources cited in the bibliography or reference list.

Develop Your Skill

Critically assessing online information sources can be very beneficial, both for school and for job searching. Do not use sources that cannot be verified, both for affiliation and credibility.

Select a company with which you would like to work. Conduct an online search for information about the company, including its size, market offerings, financial condition, and other important information that will help you in an interview. Develop a system of assessment for evaluating information sources based on affiliation and credibility, and then use this system to evaluate the sources you found. Your initial list of information sources may have been rather large, depending on the nature of the company you selected. What percentage of the information met your criteria for both affiliation and credibility? Of the sources that did not meet your criteria, what types of issues did you find?

Chapter 6

Strategy and Planning

6.1 Positioning Yourself

6.2 Your Personal Marketing Plan

6.3 Career Trends

CAREERS IN MARKETING

H. J. Heinz Company

The H. J. Heinz Company is a U.S.-based food company with a global reach, serving markets on five continents in 200 countries and employing more than 30,000 people. Now known for its iconic Heinz ketchup, the first product introduced by Henry J. Heinz was actually horseradish. In addition to its flagship Heinz brand, the company now offers a variety of brands, including Ore-Ida, Bagel Bites, Boston Market, T.G.I. Friday's and Weight Watchers frozen foods, and Classico sauces.

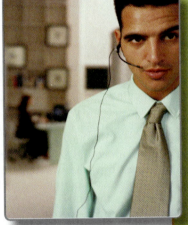

A Customer Service Administrator (CSA) at Heinz communicates with both internal and external customers on a daily basis, and optimizes satisfaction through error-free customer order processing and order invoicing. The ability to multitask is very important, as this person is responsible for processing customer orders, coordinating logistics including warehousing and transportation to ensure on-time deliveries, and coordinating pricing and promotions for customers and brokers.

A CSA should be able to build customer loyalty, contribute to the success of the team, be well organized, and possess excellent written and verbal communication skills. This position also requires a bachelor's degree and proficiency with computers, including knowledge of Word, Excel, and PowerPoint software.

Think *Critically*

1. This position involves communicating with both internal customers and external customers. Differentiate between these customer categories.

2. How does customer service contribute to the success of an organization?

Photodisc/Getty Images

PORTFOLIO BUILDER PROJECT
Your Self-Marketing Plan

Project Objectives

Can you identify a specific problem in your community or school? Are you qualified to solve the problem? How would you describe your goals for solving this problem? Answering questions such as these are part of developing a **marketing plan**—a written plan that addresses a current situation, identifies marketing strategy goals, and outlines how to reach those goals. In this project, you will:

- Identify marketing opportunities in your school or community.
- Understand the importance of creating a marketing plan.
- Develop a marketing action plan.

Getting Started

Read the Project Process below. Look at the resources on the Portfolio Builder CD.

- Compare the marketing plan to the marketing action plan. The marketing plan identifies the problem and states the larger goals. The marketing action plan outlines the specific actions to take to achieve the goals.
- Review the Portfolio Project worksheets for Chapter 3 on your own values and interests.

Project Process

Part 1   Lesson 6.1 Think about something that is missing from your community or school. Try to identify a problem that a product, organization, or service might solve. For ideas, interview a wide variety of people. Write a paragraph describing the problem you want to solve.

Part 2   Lesson 6.2 Develop and analyze your solution to the identified problem. Answer the following questions, developed by the Small Business Association (SBA): (1) Is this product or service in constant demand? (2) How many competitors provide the same product or service? (3) Can you effectively compete in price, quality, or delivery? Describe your main goal, and explain why you are qualified to solve the problem.

Part 3   Lesson 6.3 Write your marketing action plan. Divide your larger goal into smaller objectives, and list the steps to complete each one.

Project Wrap-Up

What did coming up with a product and developing a marketing plan teach you about marketing yourself? List the similarities and differences between marketing a product and marketing yourself to an employer.

© Opla, 2009/Used under license from Shutterstock.com

Positioning Yourself

Goals

- Define the term strategic marketing
- Identify positioning strategies

Key Terms

- marketing strategy
- marketing plan
- mission statement
- SWOT analysis
- common strengths
- distinctive competencies
- positioning
- differentiation
- perception

Strategic Marketing

Karen, Juanita, and Kai-Lee are about to hit the court with their basketball team. Kai-Lee wants to take a moment to stop and plan some strategic moves. Karen and Juanita just want to wing it. If Karen and Juanita ignore Kai-Lee's advice, they may or may not be successful. However, if they take a moment to plan a few strategic moves, they will increase their chances of winning.

Organizations develop *strategic plans* to help them coordinate activities, assess resource needs, and determine how to achieve their goals. Unlike teammates planning a win, though, they also take marketing concerns into account. When an organization recognizes the importance of marketing, the planning process becomes centered on customers' needs. These needs are identified, and a target market is researched before products are developed. An organization's strategic plan usually includes its mission statement, goals and objectives, and a review of its current situation which includes a SWOT analysis, an examination of the strengths, weaknesses, opportunities, and threats that may impact an organization.

marketing matters

Nick Suarez has what he thinks is a great idea for an in-line and ice skate exchange business. It would allow children and adults to trade in used and outgrown skates for skates they can use. After trading in their own equipment, they would get vouchers to use as credit toward used skates of their choice. When people buy skates, Nick would accept vouchers plus cash or cash alone. Nick's uncle will let him use the area in the back of his hardware store to start his business, but he wants Nick to show him a business plan and explain his marketing strategy first. What does Nick need to think about before starting his business? To whom should he market his business?

Photodisc/Getty Images

Getting the Big Picture

Developing a marketing strategy involves looking at the big picture and considering the marketplace itself. Consider the following questions:

- Where are we now?
- Where do we want to go?
- How can we get there?

A **marketing strategy** comes out of an organization's goals and mission statement and takes into account existing strengths, weaknesses, opportunities, and outside threats. A **marketing plan** describes how to implement the marketing strategy in specific ways.

Organizational Mission, Goals, and Objectives

An organization's goals grow out of its mission. Many organizations develop a written **mission statement**—a statement of purpose. A mission statement describes the fundamental nature of the organization, providing a view of what the organization is and what it wants to become. It answers the question "Why do we exist?" In a few sentences, it conveys the essence of the organization and its long-term identity. This identity, or understanding of purpose, provides direction to keep the organization on track.

The goals that grow out of a mission statement focus on the desired result. They can be short term (for immediate action) or long term (as far-reaching goals). Objectives are actions that will support the attainment of the goal. For each goal, the organization probably will have several objectives that are related to that goal.

Think of an umbrella. The umbrella's mission is to keep you dry. To do that, one goal might be for it to cover your head and upper body. For the umbrella to open and cover you, it needs spokes that open and expand the fabric. The spokes are like the objectives that support the goal. If the spokes are aligned with and connected to the fabric properly, the umbrella's goal will be achieved: It will open and cover you. When this happens and you are covered, it has fulfilled its mission to keep you dry. When an organization communicates a clearly defined mission, its employees understand where it is headed and can become more committed to supporting the organization's cause by focusing their day-to-day activities on overall goals.

Your Personal Mission Statement

How does this relate to you? In Chapter 3, you identified personal goals and values, and in Chapter 5 you determined your target career. You can use this information to develop a personal mission statement that will, much like an organization's mission statement, act as your statement of purpose. Shaped by your values, it should identify who you are, who you want to be, and what you want to do. Your mission statement can guide you as you consider your personal and professional goals. It also can provide long-term direction and a basis for action as you begin your job search. As you develop your mission statement, you should also perform a SWOT analysis.

What Is a SWOT Analysis?

A **SWOT analysis** is an analysis of an organization based on existing **S**trengths, **W**eaknesses, **O**pportunities, and **T**hreats. An evaluation and understanding of these factors can help an organization support its mission by:

- Focusing on *strengths*
- Correcting or eliminating *weaknesses*
- Promoting awareness of *opportunities*
- Dealing effectively with *threats*

Strengths and weaknesses tend to be internal, while opportunities and threats are external. As you learn about SWOT analysis, consider your own strengths and weaknesses, as well as the opportunities and threats you may encounter in your job search.

Strengths Strengths include skills and competencies. Organizations try to identify both **common strengths**—abilities shared by most firms in a given industry—and **distinctive competencies**—the things an organization does particularly well. For instance, most retail banks demonstrate common strengths in their ability to handle customer deposits, cash checks, and open accounts. If a bank also provides online banking that offers 24-hour access to accounts, allowing for online fund transfers, account balancing, bill paying, live chats with bank representatives, and loan services, it may have a distinctive competency.

You identified skills, accomplishments, and benefits in Chapter 3. These will likely be your strengths. Your distinctive competencies could be any qualifications you have that make you uniquely qualified for a job.

Weaknesses Weaknesses include skills or competencies that may be lacking or that do not support the mission. For example, a desktop publisher's weakness might be not adopting new software technology that is commonly used in the industry. Weaknesses can be converted to strengths, or the mission can be changed to accept the weakness. The desktop publisher can acquire the software and train people to use it, converting the weakness into a strength. One way to convert a personal weakness into a strength is to focus only on the positive aspects of a trait. For instance, your weakness might be perfectionism. Instead of thinking about how your perfectionist nature causes you to take longer to complete projects, you might think about it as proof of your attention to detail and ability to complete most tasks correctly the first time.

Opportunities Opportunities are favorable circumstances or advantageous times that foster increased performance. A medical equipment company may learn that Congress plans to pass legislation requiring the sterilization of certain types of medical waste. The company could speed up development of the sterilization equipment it has been working on to help hospitals meet the new regulations. This situation would be considered an opportunity because the company has the chance to benefit from outside circumstances that could increase its business.

Threats Threats are factors in the business environment that might hamper performance. For example, a new competitor entering the market could threaten a business. Awareness of this type of threat signals the business to develop strategies for dealing with the new competitor. The business could offer special promotions for new customers or provide an incentive for current customers. How do threats affect your personal marketing strategy? A projected hiring decline in your area of interest is a threat. To address it, you would need to broaden the scope of your job search by considering additional industries or occupations.

Check ▸ Point

Come up with one example for each SWOT category that applies to the employment market in your field of interest.

Positioning

Positioning involves creating distance between products in the marketplace in the minds of consumers who differentiate between the features and benefits of similar products. For instance, one restaurant may be positioned as a quick and inexpensive option, while another may be positioned as the healthier alternative.

Positioning creates **differentiation**—a focus on uniqueness, or the differences between a product and its competitors. Such distinctions help shape consumer perceptions. **Perceptions** refer to the images of a particular product that come to mind. If a friend mentions a brand of cereal, you might have a mental picture of that cereal, as well as an opinion about it.

Positioning affects products in a variety of ways.

- It affects the features and benefits that are derived from products.
- It affects price, in terms of a product's position as a low-cost, good value product, or a high-end premium product.
- It affects place, in terms of where products are available for purchase.
- It affects promotion, including where products are promoted and what media are used to promote them.

A product can't be all things to all people, so marketers intentionally influence what a product means to consumers by positioning. For example, if someone mentions a certain sports utility vehicle, you might form a perception of that make and model. Depending on the marketing position created for that vehicle, your perception might include ideas about safety,

Workshop

With a partner, analyze three types of hair gel or shampoo and describe how each one has tried to achieve a unique position in the marketplace.

ruggedness, adventure, independence, economy, quality, and so on. If *you* are properly positioned, "buyers" should be able to recognize your benefits.

Positioning Strategies

Positioning can be based on a number of factors, depending on how a company wants consumers to perceive its product. These factors include:

- **Features**   What does the product include? Laundry detergent A may be known for its fresh scent formula. Laundry detergent B may be known for its ability to keep colors bright.

- **Benefits**   What does the product really do for consumers? A household cleaner might be positioned as providing the benefit of more leisure time because of its versatility and strong cleaning powers.

- **Price/Quality**   Lower cost represents a better value, or, conversely, higher cost represents a high-end, luxury item.

- **User**   What type of person uses the product?

marketing math connection

Tina works 20 hours a week at a retail store for $8.50 an hour. She is also a full-time student and needs about 20 hours a week for homework and extracurricular activities. She is an honor roll student and hopes to obtain a scholarship to help pay for college.

In exchange for the privilege of driving her parents' car, Tina agrees to detail (wash, wax, vacuum, and touch up) the car. She usually spends about eight hours and $30.00 in supplies on this chore. The local detail shop charges $150.00 and can do it in two hours. Is it more expensive for Tina to detail the car herself or bring it into the shop? Given all the above factors, what "costs," in addition to money exchanged, might be considered as she makes this decision?

SOLUTION

Add Tina's lost wages to her expenses to determine the cost of detailing the car herself.

Lost wages = 8 hours × $8.50 = $68.00
Cost = $68.00 + $30.00 = $98.00

Therefore, Tina saves $52 by detailing the car herself.

Other costs to consider include lost time spent on homework or socializing. While Tina isn't "paid" to do her homework, her grade point average may directly affect how much money she can obtain for college. Tina may also feel it's worth paying a professional to do this job so she can spend time with her family and friends.

- **Use** How is the product actually used? Baking soda, for example, has been positioned as an odor remover.

Use these examples to write your own positioning statement. Think about the industries and organizations you will target. How do you want to appear? Effective research and targeting can help you position yourself in the most appropriate and effective manner.

Check Point

What does creating distance have to do with positioning? Explain how you can use positioning to market yourself to employers.

6.1 Assessment

THINK CRITICALLY

1. This lesson compares corporate marketing strategy to self-marketing strategy. Who is the customer in a self-marketing strategy? What aspects of this customer should job seekers focus on as they begin the process of self-marketing?

2. Why do organizations base their goals and marketing strategies on customers' needs?

3. Which should you develop first: a mission statement or a marketing plan? Explain.

4. Of the five product positioning factors listed in this lesson— *features*, *benefits*, *price/quality*, *user*, and *use*—which two best relate to your self-marketing strategy? Explain.

MAKE ACADEMIC CONNECTIONS

5. **SOCIAL STUDIES** People from other countries are often amazed by the vast number of products available in the United States. A grocery store in France might have five or six varieties of toothpaste on the shelf, while most stores in the U.S. have as many as twenty. Why do you think the U.S. has so many types of toothpaste? Do people in the U.S. have different needs for this product? How are some of the toothpaste brands and types within brands positioned? Write a one- to two-page report about this issue.

Your Personal Marketing Plan

Goals

- Understand the purpose of a marketing plan
- Develop the three parts of a personal marketing plan

Key Term

- marketing action plan

Develop a Marketing Plan

As you continue on your career journey, remember that your destination should be a place where you are strongly positioned to take advantage of opportunities. Your marketing plan serves as your road map. It guides you as you coordinate activities and helps you stay on track. As a road map, it provides a basis for making decisions and achieving your goals. A marketing plan is a written plan that addresses issues such as the current situation, marketing strategy goals, and the method or steps for reaching those goals.

According to the U.S. Small Business Administration (SBA), a marketing plan should answer the following questions.

- Is this product in constant demand?
- How many competitors provide the same product?
- Can you create a demand for your product?
- Can you effectively compete in price, quality, and delivery?

marketing matters

Everybody admires the aquarium at Anju Patankar's house. Her parents' friends often tell Anju that they would love to have such an aquarium, but they don't have the time to maintain it. Anju is thinking about starting an aquarium business—setting up and maintaining aquariums in other people's homes for a start-up fee and a monthly rate. Do casual remarks such as those made by her parents' friends assure Anju that there are enough committed customers for her services? What questions should Anju ask to develop a marketing plan for her product and services?

Photodisc/Getty Images

Creating Your Own Plan

As you work to develop your personal marketing plan, think about how you can meet employers' needs: How can your skills and distinctive competencies benefit employers? Careful planning and research will help you develop a successful plan. A marketing plan is not written in stone. Instead, it is flexible—based on both your changing interests and changes in the marketplace.

What You Need to Know

Marketing plans typically contain three main sections: market analysis, marketing strategy, and action plans. You will need an understanding of:

- Yourself
- Your target market, including positions, industries, and organizations
- The problem to be solved and the benefits you provide
- The marketplace, including trends and competitors

Check Point

Select two of the SBA questions on page 156 and explain how you can use them in your self-marketing plan.

The Three-Part Plan

Are you a planner or someone who likes to plunge into a project and see where it takes you? Have you ever ended up going so far in the wrong direction during a project that you didn't want to start over? Whatever your goals may be, it helps to plan ahead so you can avoid mistakes that cost time and money. On your career journey, you may take a few detours and wrong turns, but with a map to follow, you will increase your odds of traveling in the right direction. A plan for marketing yourself includes a market analysis, marketing strategy, and action plan. Developing your overall marketing plan is an important step in the career development process. It can provide the guidance you need to reach success.

Market Analysis

The market analysis includes:

- The development of a mission statement
- An examination of current markets
- A careful look at the competition
- A SWOT analysis

Workshop

Working in a small group, develop an idea for a free service that is needed in your school. Draft a mission statement describing the purpose of the service you selected.

Did You Know?

The person hired for a job is not always the one who is most qualified. The person selected is the one the employer believes is most qualified.

Complete Your Mission Statement Remember that the mission statement is a statement of purpose. You can use the personal mission statement you began to develop in Lesson 6.1.

Examine the Current Markets A review of current markets involves identifying the employers you plan to target and exploring their needs. What types of skills are they looking for? Do they want a seasoned professional for a certain position, or do they want someone they can train who will work for less money?

Photodisc/Getty Images

Eye the Competition

A review of the competition is essential in a marketing plan. You should learn about the admission requirements of the college you want to attend or the hiring practices of your targeted employer. What is the average ACT or SAT score for incoming freshman? How does the admissions department weigh different factors, such as class rank and test scores? Does the employer like to hire new people based on referrals from within the company? Is your competition likely to have better technical skills?

Use Your SWOT Analysis You can use the SWOT analysis you began earlier for your marketing plan. Refresh your memory by re-reading the descriptions of the SWOT categories on pages 152–153.

NETBookmark

Government and career information sites are great sources for learning about employment projections, industry trends, population, immigration, and education data. To access several of these sites, go to **www.cengage.com/school/marketing/yourself** and follow the links to this chapter. Think of two or three careers you are interested in pursuing. After visiting several of the web sites, write a brief paragraph about each of the careers. Use these sites to help you develop your marketing plan to learn about current markets and the employment outlook for your field of interest.

Marketing Strategy

Your marketing strategy will explain how marketing relates to your career development. After developing your personal mission statement, reviewing the market and competition, and preparing your SWOT analysis, you are then ready to plan your marketing strategy. It will identify:

- Your goals and expected outcomes
- A description of your target market
- Your own positioning statement

Digital Stock

Define Your Goals and Expected Outcome Your goals and expected outcomes should include your ABC goals from Chapter 3, as well as the expected outcome of your job search based on your goals. It is important to be specific while leaving room to grow and change.

Define Your Target Market In Chapter 5, you learned about market segments and targeting, and conducted research to select target industries, occupations, and companies. Consider any recent changes that may have affected your target markets, or any changes that will affect the market in the future.

Formulate Your Positioning Statement Review positioning on pages 153 and 154, and explain how you can differentiate yourself from the competition in the eyes of potential employers.

Planning for Action

Your **marketing action plan** is your detailed "to do" list. It is based on your personal marketing strategy and should include a list of planned activities or tasks, and explain how they activities should be completed and the dates by when they should be completed. For each goal, ask yourself what objectives you need to achieve to accomplish the goal. Plan the companies you will contact. How can you use your positioning statement to capture the interest of these potential employers? Breaking up larger jobs into smaller, manageable tasks will help you chip away at your goals and make them seem less overwhelming.

How is your overall marketing plan different from your marketing action plan?

6.2 Assessment

THINK CRITICALLY

1. One of the Small Business Administration's questions asks how you can create a demand for your service or product. Could this question apply to your self-marketing plan? If so, how?

2. A marketing plan is not written in stone. What factors do you think would cause you to change your marketing plan?

3. For your marketing strategy, how might a description of your target market change throughout your career?

4. In a SWOT analysis, how could opportunities be tied to networking?

MAKE ACADEMIC CONNECTIONS

5. **SCIENCE** Research a scientific innovation, such as microfiber, Velcro®, or artificial sweetener. Report on how one or more products that resulted from this innovation were marketed.

6. **GRAPHIC DESIGN** Create a poster outlining the market analysis for an idea that could lead to a small business. Include a mission statement, the needs of the current market, a look at the competition (including photos or illustrations, if available), and a SWOT analysis. Also include any diagrams that clarify your strategy.

7. **COMMUNICATIONS** Businesses market themselves to customers through advertising and other costly means. They also send out press releases that sometimes generate free publicity. Find an example of a press release and use it to write your own press release to announce your job search. In your press release, include personal information, special qualifications, and recent job-related activities. Make it exciting.

Career Trends

Goals
- Recognize job market trends
- Understand workplace and marketing trends

Key Terms
- environmental scanning
- market opportunity awareness
- labor force
- displaced workers

Job Market Trends

Have you ever bleached or put a hole in your jeans? Bought new eyeglass frames even though your prescription didn't change? Cut your hair to match a movie star's hair? Hunted through the mall for a sought-after electronic device or game? If so, then you have followed a marketplace trend.

You watch television shows and commercials, notice magazine ads, and are exposed to music and musicians, all the while being influenced by what you see. You visit the mall and are presented with displays, mannequins, and showcases promoting the latest fashions and styles. As you walk around your high school, you notice other students dressed in particular fashions and wearing new accessories and hairstyles. By taking all of this in, you are scanning the environment.

You may not realize it, but you scan the environment and become aware of market opportunities in a way that is similar to an organization striving to make sure its products do not become obsolete.

marketing matters

Emily Chung wants to become a clothing buyer for a major department store. She was excited about an upcoming training program offered at a local community college. Two of the courses were to be taught by a clothing buyer for her favorite store. After high school, she had hoped to enroll—until she read an article in the newspaper that said traditional department stores were in decline. Should Emily find a completely new career path? What areas would you tell Emily to explore that might lead to the discovery of similar work in her field of interest?

Photodisc/Getty Images

Environmental Scanning

Environmental scanning involves identifying important trends in the marketplace. For instance, the buying power of Asian Americans is projected to be $752 billion in 2013, an increase of 180 percent from 2000 to 2013 (according to the Selig Center for Economic Growth). Because of this trend, brokerage firms and many other industries are increasing their efforts to reach out to this valuable segment of the population.

Market Opportunity Awareness

As discussed in Lesson 6.1, an opportunity refers to a favorable circumstance or advantageous time. **Market opportunity awareness** involves an awareness of circumstances or timing that allows action toward a goal. Being on the cutting edge of a market opportunity can offer organizations the chance to reap big rewards—developing a customer base and making a profit. Microsoft took advantage of a market opportunity by licensing the DOS operating system when personal computers were first gaining popularity.

As a job seeker, you can scan the environment, looking for trends that may impact your career field, including positions of interest and targeted industries. You can also look for market opportunities that may put you on the cutting edge of an emerging profession or industry.

The Job Market

Both environmental scanning and market opportunity awareness can help you become more aware of trends in the job market. As you plan for your career, you will want to have access to information related to opportunities. According to the U.S. Bureau of Labor Statistics, job opportunities tend to arise from greater demands for services and products caused by increases in population. They may decrease, however, if the size of the labor force exceeds the demand. For example, if there is a large group of people trained to be commercial airline pilots, but air travel is down, job opportunities in this field will be scarce. In this instance and in many others, significant changes in industries also play a role.

Population

Population trends affect not only the demand for goods and services, but also the size of the labor force. For instance, a growing teenage population will increase the demand for post-secondary teachers.

The population of the United States is expected to grow by more than 9 percent, or 22 million people, by 2016. This growth includes increases in the number of older Americans (ages 55 to 64). Groups once considered minorities, such as Hispanics and Asians, are projected to grow at a faster rate than Caucasians in the United States.

This growth will result in an increase in consumers, who will purchase a variety of goods and services. This is projected to mean more demand for workers in various industries.

Labor Force

As the population grows, so does the potential size of the labor force. The **labor force** includes people who are working or looking for work. By 2016, the U.S. labor force is expected to grow by 8.5 percent, or nearly 13 million people. So in 2016, more than 164 million people in the United States will be working or looking for work.

The labor force will also become increasingly diverse. Groups such as Hispanics, Asians, African Americans, and women will continue to increase.

Many of the occupations with the strongest expected growth through 2016 require on-the-job training and do not require a bachelor's degree. These occupations include retail sales, customer service, health aides, and janitors. Fast-growth occupations requiring a bachelor's degree include network systems, data communications, and computer systems analysts, management analysts, elementary teachers, accountants, and computer software engineers.

Industries

The United States will continue to move toward a service-based economy, as about 80 percent of the U.S. economy is service-based. While growth in the service sector has slowed, the *Occupational Outlook Handbook* projects service-sector growth over the long-term. Three of every five new jobs will be in service-producing industries, with two-thirds in business, health, and social services. Overall, nearly 15 million new service-based jobs will be added by 2016.

com·mu·ni·cate

Interview someone with at least 15 years of experience in your field of interest. Ask this person how his or her job has changed over the years and also how he or she would prepare to enter the field in current times. Summarize the advice in a one-page report.

diversity in the workplace

Many organizations claim to value diversity, but how many achieve it at all levels of their organization? At the Comcast Corporation, a major cable and communications company, 40 percent of its regular workforce is minority and half is made up of women. In the category of "officials and managers," Comcast employs 25 percent minorities and 40 percent women, more than most companies.

Vice President David Cohen says his company's commitment to "greater racial, ethnic, and gender balance stems from both moral and business reason." He says, "If you do not have an environment that embraces diversity, you will be at serious disadvantage." Comcast believes it must tailor its services and marketing to reflect the demographic changes in the population. How better to do this than by employing a diverse workforce? Although Comcast still does not have the diversity it wants at top levels, it believes that the numerous programs currently in place will groom and identify individuals from its diverse workforce for future leadership positions.

Source: *Philadelphia Inquirer*, Sept. 25, 2002.

The professional and business services sector is expected to grow by more than 23 percent, adding more than 4 million new jobs by 2016. This includes positions in management, scientific and technical consulting, computer systems design, employment support, administrative support, and waste management and remediation. Jobs in education and health services will increase by more than 18 percent. These jobs include positions in hospitals, nursing and residential care facilities, and public and private educational services. Finance, insurance, and real estate employment will increase at a rate of more than 14 percent. Security and commodity brokers, insurance carriers, insurance agents and brokers, and real estate positions will be at the forefront of this growth.

Government employment is projected to increase by nearly 5 percent by 2016. The greatest growth will be in state and local governments.

Goods-producing industries, in contrast to service-producing industries, have remained relatively stagnant in recent years, with a 3 percent decline expected overall by 2016. However, increases in construction and pharmaceutical manufacturing are expected.

Occupations

The increase in service-sector industries will create demand for many different occupations. Among these, professional and related occupations are projected to increase by 17 percent. Much of this increase will come from a demand for computer and mathematical professionals, healthcare practitioners, and technical support occupations. Positions in education, organizational training, and library services will also grow.

The number of service workers, including those in food service and healthcare support, is expected to increase by nearly 17 percent. Employment in transportation, such as jobs for motor vehicle operators and material moving occupations, are projected to increase by about 5 percent.

Employment in management, business, and financial occupations should increase nearly 11 percent. Demand will increase for social and community service managers, gaming managers, financial analysts, and personal financial advisors.

Sales positions will increase nearly 8 percent. Maintenance occupations, such as automotive service technicians and telecommunications line install-

©Corbis

ers and repairers, will increase by more than 9 percent. Administrative support positions are expected to increase by about 7 percent, with customer service representatives seeing the most growth. The occupations with the largest expected increases in employment by 2016 include registered nurses, retail salespersons, and customer service representatives.

Evaluating trends, especially industry and occupation trends, can help you develop your marketing plan. Consider your career targets from Chapter 5. Are your positions of interest in growth areas? Are the industries you target expected to grow? If not, you will need to make sure you have the necessary skills and can provide definite benefits to an employer. Competition for available positions will likely be tough.

Check Point

In what sector of the economy will most jobs be added? List five examples of jobs in this sector.

Workplace and Marketing Trends

According to Elaine Chao, former United States Secretary of Labor, three main issues will shape the U.S. economy and quality of life: the skills gap, demographic destiny, and the future of the American workplace. As the workplace moves toward high-skilled, information-based industries, workers' skills must change and grow rapidly to keep up. Growing numbers of retirees and the increasingly diverse American population contribute to a demand for new ways of handling work.

How businesses market their products and services has also changed. The same factors listed earlier—a diverse population and growth in the retiree and youth age groups—combined with greater disposable incomes for some groups have led businesses to focus their marketing efforts. Examining how marketing has become more sophisticated in recent years can help you understand the importance of fine-tuning your own marketing strategy.

Workplace Trends

Today's workplace is much different from that of 30, 20, or even 10 years ago. Many of the changes that have occurred can be attributed to advances in technology and increasing involvement in the global marketplace.

Worker Mobility Today's employees often work for five to ten different organizations over the course of their careers. This trend affects retirement, pensions, and benefits. Knowledge of these and other trends can help you better plan for career success. Take responsibility for adapting and managing your career as your needs and your employers' needs change.

Workshop

Most of us are exposed to marketing efforts every day. List the three most recent examples of marketing information you received. How was the information delivered? How did you respond? Were you the appropriate target market for the material? If the marketing was ineffective, how could the marketer have improved it?

Focus on gaining skills you can apply to several closely related fields. Seek out new tasks and pursue on-the-job training to increase your skills.

The Virtual Office Offices are now in homes, hotel rooms, client offices, and anywhere else laptops can be plugged in and connected to traditional offices via the Internet. This trend may come as no surprise to people who have been exposed to computers all their lives. However, developing the specific technical skills and learning to be flexible will show an employer that you are comfortable working in a virtual office environment. If you have specific skills in this area, you may wish to feature them in your self-marketing plan.

Technology The times in which we live are both exciting and frustrating. As you read this, thousands of people are working to develop new uses for computers that will be ready in the near future. Many people think computers are taking away their jobs. What is actually occurring, though, is a shift in the job duties and skills needed to work in business and industry. When workers are replaced by computers, companies need to retrain the workers with skills in programming, operating, or repairing computer systems. **Displaced workers**, or workers who are unemployed because of changing job conditions, must adapt to the changing job market in order to stay employed.

Faster Work Pace By reducing traditional barriers such as time and distance, technology has sped up work demands and expectations. Everything from making major decisions to approving minor projects occurs more quickly, making it necessary for workers to respond faster. In the past, the time it took time for information to travel from one place to another created a buffer for employees. Now employers can reach workers on vacation, on a bus, or just about anywhere. Those entering the workforce need to be aware of these workplace pressures and be prepared to cope with them.

Team Focus Although the authority that upper management holds continues to be important, many organizations now emphasize teams rather than traditional hierarchical relationships. In the past, layers of workers reported to and waited for instruction from management. Now, the greater availability of information through e-mail and other technological advances aids communication and promotes the sharing of ideas and skills. Working on a team increases a worker's responsibilities and his or her role in decision-making. What does this mean for your career? The need for team leaders and team players who are adaptable problem solvers will be greater than ever.

Marketing Trends

Marketing has changed tremendously in the last few decades. It is much more precise in who it targets; it has increased in volume and variety; and it collects and uses information in increasingly sophisticated ways. A job seeker who is aware of marketing trends may be more creative and thorough in his or her self-marketing efforts.

Sophisticated Information Gathering Did you know that surveillance cameras at some stores are set up to record your shopping habits rather than to catch shoplifters? They document how people move in a store, what attracts them, and how much time they spend in a given area. Companies use this information to arrange displays and plan marketing within stores. "Frequent shopper cards" used at supermarkets and some other stores are another example of methods used to detect patterns in customer shopping habits.

Precision Targeting Have you noticed that different types of movies seem to be aimed at different types of people? It wasn't always this way. It used to be that an entire family went to a single screen theater to see whatever was offered. Now large multiplex cinemas offer something for everyone: movies marketed to women, urban youth movies, family films, teen flicks, and so on. A group of people going to the movies may choose to split up so different people can view their movie of choice. Marketing today takes the needs and interests of different groups into account and targets them.

Targeted Information Delivery People hear about products and services specifically geared to their own lifestyles while they are engaged in activities related to their interests. An entrant in a triathlon contest might receive a coupon from a sporting goods store. Catalog companies target addresses in the ZIP codes where they think potential customers live. Banner ads appear on web sites that potential customers might browse, and television commercials appear on shows watched by the target audience.

Innovative Sampling Businesses now provide more than just product samples, such as free packs of teeth-whitening gum. They also offer samples of an experience, such as trying out the latest iPod at an Apple retail store, or downloading a free song from a newly released CD. One way to let a company sample your potential as an employee is to complete an internship.

Social Media Marketing If you have visited web sites like MySpace or Facebook, you have accessed social media. Social media can serve as a marketing tool. Organizations can take advantage of the large numbers of visitors, or traffic, that frequent social media sites. By becoming popular on social media news sites, like Digg or del.icio.us, organizations can acquire links to its site and build their recognition and following.

Whether you find intensified marketing efforts intriguing or annoying, it pays to be aware of how marketing finds its way into your life. To many consumers, how and when something is presented is almost as important as what is presented. Consumers and employers recognize and respond to effective marketing. Sloppy, outdated techniques turn people off. Learning the tricks of the trade will not only make you a more savvy consumer, but also help you target your audience and display your qualifications to future employers in the best possible light.

Check Point

What does worker mobility mean? How do you think it will affect how you market yourself throughout your life?

careerbuilder®

Using the Right Keywords in Your Job Search

By Anthony Balderrama, CareerBuilder.com writer
Copyright 2009 CareerBuilder, LLC. - Reprinted with permission.

The right words make all the difference in life. Try asking "Wanna get hitched?" instead of "Will you marry me?" for proof.

Even in a job interview, you wouldn't say, "Hey, dude." You'd probably say, "Nice to meet you." And your résumé wouldn't include slang, either. You know all this. At least, I hope you do.

But the need for well-chosen words starts when you search job postings. From the job title to the list of requirements, knowing how to tweak your words to yield the best results is vital to getting your job hunt started off right.

Here are a few ways to make sure you're using the right keywords:

Be a copycat

In your résumé and interviews, you want to let your best qualities and unique point of view shine through. But to get to those stages, you first have to find the right job. That means you have to do something that's unacceptable in every other circumstance: plagiarize.

Go to an online job board and search for jobs that you think you're a great match for. Then study the language they use to perform your own searches. For example, if you find a listing for a project coordinator position that sounds ideal, you should apply for it, of course, and then pull out key phrases to search other jobs. If they use the phrase "method calibrations," plug that into the search field to see what other positions comes up. Employers might use different job titles or you might find other positions that are good fits but you didn't know they existed.

Don't get stuck on titles

When you have defined goals for your career and subsequently your salary, you can find yourself fixated on having a certain job title. Although your ambitions are admirable and beneficial to your career, don't forget that not all titles are created equal. Every company has its own culture and often its own lingo. One employer's vice president is another's senior associate. Search for the job title you want, but remember to dig deeper for other title ideas.

Look to the responsibilities and skills detailed in a job posting for a more accurate gauge of its duties. You'll still find the jobs you're looking for if you search by responsibility instead of title, except you'll be working backward. If, for example, you want a retail manager position, you should search for related terms, such as "supervisor" or "customer relations." Filter through the results to find good matches. You might find that you're a perfect fit for a "team leader" position that you wouldn't have otherwise found.

continued on page 169

Treat it like a search engine

When you're looking online for something that interests you -- say, a new apartment -- you suddenly become a master of the Internet query. You're trying different keywords, searching by ZIP code one moment and neighborhood nickname the next. If there's an available property in a two-mile radius, you'll find it. You know how to work a search engine without a second thought.

Take that mentality to your job search. One of the simplest ways to broaden or narrow your search is to use quotation marks. Searching for a phrase without quotation marks (i.e., dental assistant) will find you jobs with either word in the description. However, enclosing the entire phrase (i.e., "dental assistant") in quotes will only return jobs with those words together in that exact order. If you find your searches are returning too many hits or too few, play with quotes. You can also use the advanced-search options to tailor your searches or use other shortcuts, such as minus signs to exclude words from results.

6.3 Assessment

THINK CRITICALLY

1. Describe what could happen if a business neglected to scan its environment.

2. List specific ways you can increase your own market opportunity awareness.

3. How do you think an increase in the number of people ages 16 to 24 by 2016 will affect your own marketability?

4. Why have teams become more important in the workplace? What are the advantages and disadvantages of working on a team?

MAKE ACADEMIC CONNECTIONS

5. **CREATIVE WRITING** Write a science fiction story about someone working in an office in the year 2025. Describe how the organization is structured, the types of equipment, office furniture, and communication technology used, as well as any other details you think represent the trends of the future.

6. **DEBATE** Is marketing a nuisance? Or does it inform us about the products we want to use at just the right place and time? Choose a partner to debate these opposing points of view.

VOCABULARY BUILDER

Choose the term that best fits the definition. Write the letter of the answer in the space provided. Some terms may not be used.

_____ 1. An examination of an organization based on strengths, weaknesses, opportunities, and threats

_____ 2. The things companies or individuals do particularly well

_____ 3. The images of a particular product that come to mind

_____ 4. The knowledge of circumstances or timing that allows action toward a goal

_____ 5. An organization's statement of purpose

_____ 6. The larger strategy that emerges from an organization's goals and mission statement and takes into account marketplace concerns

_____ 7. A detailed "to do" list of planned activities and tasks

_____ 8. Identifying important trends in the marketplace

_____ 9. A written plan that describes how to implement the marketing strategy in specific ways

_____ 10. People who are working or looking for work

_____ 11. A focus on uniqueness, or the differences between a product and its competitors

_____ 12. Creating distance between products in the marketplace in the minds of consumers

a. common strengths
b. differentiation
c. displaced workers
d. distinctive competencies
e. environmental scanning
f. labor force
g. market opportunity awareness
h. marketing action plan
i. marketing plan
j. marketing strategy
k. mission statement
l. perceptions
m. positioning
n. SWOT analysis

REVIEW CONCEPTS

www.cengage.com/school/marketing/yourself

13. List and define the four parts of a SWOT analysis.

14. List and briefly explain five factors on which positioning can be based.

15. According to the Small Business Administration, what four questions should a marketing plan answer?

16. As you develop your personal marketing plan, what do you need to understand?

17. How does a market analysis differ from a marketing strategy?

18. In a market analysis that you do for yourself, what does an examination of current markets involve?

19. Who is the competition in a market analysis that you do for yourself?

20. When you write your own positioning statement, what should you focus on?

21. What can being on the cutting edge of a marketing opportunity offer an organization?

22. How can market opportunity awareness help job seekers?

23. As the U.S. population increases, which two age groups will grow at an even faster rate?

24. List and briefly describe four trends in marketing.

APPLY WHAT YOU LEARNED

25. Stefan and Carly both work at Carmine's Gourmet Deli making sandwiches and desserts. Stefan works quickly, making few mistakes. Customers and coworkers say he makes the best desserts. Carly spends a lot of time talking to coworkers and goofing off. When she is responsible for making the desserts, Stefan has to correct her mistakes. Carmine, the owner, plans to open two new stores and wants to hire Carly as a trainer. She works hard when Carmine is around, and he is impressed by her plan to enroll in a restaurant management program. What can Stefan do to market himself to his employer?

26. How do increases in population affect the growth of certain industries? How could population increases cause the employment rate to go up or down?

27. Opportunities and threats arise when the marketing environment changes because of outside events such as legislation, national and local events, entertainment trends, and media stories. What types of opportunities and threats would present themselves in a small community where a major motion picture is to be filmed? Describe how the filming might affect two types of people: restaurant owners and employed healthcare workers.

MAKE ACADEMIC CONNECTIONS

28. **SOCIOLOGY** Futurist Faith Popcorn makes a living predicting future trends and has written books on the subject. To read one of her recent books or visit her web site, go to **www.cengage.com/school/ marketing/yourself** and follow the links to this activity. Write a brief report about her latest predictions.

29. **SOCIAL STUDIES** Different marketing approaches work for different groups of people. Research the likes and dislikes of people in two different countries or regions of a country. Describe how you would market the same product differently to the two different groups of people.

30. **COMMUNICATIONS** Analyze at least five advertisements in magazines and newspapers. Figure out whom the information is marketed toward and how the product is positioned. Present your findings in a poster or flip chart presentation.

Global Marketing Team Event

Teams will develop a written international marketing plan that identifies the customer base. The participating team must demonstrate oral communication skills to market a new product. The written marketing plan must not exceed ten pages. Refer to bpa.org for the parts of marketing plan.

You are the Marketing Director for Golden Farms Vegetables. Your vegetable farm and food processing operation is located in Southern Texas. Your reasonably priced fresh vegetables are packaged and sold throughout the United States. The majority of your customers are wholesalers and supermarkets. Research indicates that the global economy offers numerous markets for your fresh vegetables. Your company recently has developed a unique packaging system that will ensure the delivery of fresh vegetables to international customers. This package meets all international standards, so the products are likely to clear other countries' customs, which are restrictions imposed on imported products.

Your presentation must explain your marketing plan for conducting business globally.

"This ad campaign is really creative! I love the use of animation and the cleverly drawn characters. This will really attract attention. I'm glad to see that the same characters and design elements are being used on all of the promotional materials for a more integrated, cohesive feel. This should really make an impact with customers!"

Have you ever noticed a creative advertisement and wondered how it came to be produced? Graphic designers develop visual solutions to address communication needs. They work with clients to find effective ways to communicate messages to customers using a variety of media. Many types of media are available, and graphic designers usually are familiar with everything from print, broadcast, and film to electronic and digital media. They prepare artwork and designs that visualize the message by working with print, computer programs, photography, animation, and sound. They may develop material for print, television, and radio ads; design magazine and newspaper layouts, packaging, signage, and displays; and create television and movie credits, multimedia presentations, and web pages.

Employment Outlook

An average rate of employment growth is expected.

Job Titles

- Graphic Artist
- Design Director
- Creative Director
- Desktop Publisher
- Art Director

Needed Skills

- A bachelor's degree usually is required, although an associate degree may be acceptable for technical positions.
- Computer software skills with software such as Photoshop, Illustrator, InDesign, and QuarkXpress.
- Able to synthesize information from multiple sources to produce images that meet specified needs.

What's It Like to Work in Graphic Design?

Jun-ying returns to the office after a business trip to Boston. She had been meeting with a client to finalize the presentation materials for its annual shareholder meeting, and the client wanted Jun-ying, the Senior Graphic Designer, as well as her firm's Creative Director, to meet with the team in person. Before she can drink her coffee, one of the graphic designers on her team stops by to remind her about a client presentation at 4 p.m. She needs to have the graphics files to the production team by noon if she wants the mock-ups ready for the presentation.

She finishes the graphics files and e-mails them to production, and then begins working on the new logo designs and graphics for a web development project with a one-week deadline. She meets with her staff during lunch, reviewing their projects and planning out design needs for the next few weeks. She also supervises the design interns working at the firm and assigns them to work on various design teams based on the needs of her staff.

After her working lunch, Jun-ying begins to craft a proposal for a potential new client who contacted her over the weekend by e-mail. She likes to send proposals out quickly so clients do not lose interest. She doesn't finish the proposal because she needs to leave for the 4 p.m. presentation. After the presentation, she takes the clients to dinner, knowing she will have to work at home to finish the proposal she started earlier in the day.

What About You?

Aside from needed technical skills, what do you think is the most important quality for a graphic designer to possess? Does this career interest you? Why or why not?

Chapter 7

Resumes: Your Personal Advertisement

7.1 Where to Begin

7.2 Content and Structure

7.3 Resume Formats

CAREERS IN MARKETING

Staples

Staples, known for its "Easy Button" marketing campaign, sells a wide range of office products and supplies, including office furniture, technology, and business services. It operates super-stores with retail store, online, and business contract formats.

A copywriter at Staples focuses on business-to-business communications that support the brand image, generate sales, and enhance relationships. The copywriter writes clear, concise, and compelling copy for everything from direct mail and promotional pieces to online work such as e-mail and landing pages.

Working collaboratively as part of the creative team, including designers, art directors, sales associates, and delivery drivers, the copywriter must develop a thorough understanding of the contract business. Strong writing skills and exceptional proofreading and editing skills are essential. The position requires a college degree with a background in English, journalism, or marketing, in addition to advertising experience and comprehensive knowledge of marketing, media, and technology.

Think *Critically*

1. Why is it so important for a copywriter to have excellent proofreading and editing skills?

2. How can you apply the skills required of a copywriter to the process of preparing your resume?

©Mircea BEZERGHEANU, 2009/Used under license from Shutterstock.com

PORTFOLIO BUILDER PROJECT
Your Resume

Project Objectives

Chapter 7 is all about building a resume and learning how and when to use different formats. While searching for a job, you need to prepare yourself for the different ways that potential employers learn about workers. This preparation involves creating different resumes for different purposes. In this project, you will:

- Gather the information you need to create a traditional resume.
- Write your own traditional resume.
- Create scannable and online versions of your resume.

Getting Started

Read the Project Process below. Look at the supporting material on the Portfolio Builder CD.

- Skim Chapter 7 before beginning the portfolio project. As you develop the two resumes for this project, you will need to refer to each lesson.
- From the Portfolio Builder CD, print out and examine the sample resumes.
- Explore the web resource links on the CD. Write down any tips that you think will be useful for creating resumes.

Project Process

Part 1   Lesson 7.1   Read Lesson 7.1. Complete the personal inventory worksheet. Focus on the information you will use to write a clear, one-page resume that highlights your skills and experience.

Part 2   Lesson 7.2   Read Lesson 7.2. Plan which resume sections you will include in your traditional resume. Read about resume style and organization, and review the traditional resume samples. Write your own traditional resume.

Part 3   Lesson 7.3   Read Lesson 7.3. Follow the guidelines to create your own scannable and online resumes, based on your traditional resume.

Project Wrap-Up

Your resume is a working document that you will adapt and improve over time. Putting together a resume now will help you choose activities that will move you closer to your goals. Just for fun, create a "future resume" that shows what you would like your actual resume to look like in 10 years. Include the skills, education, and experience you hope to have acquired by then.

©Jackhollingsworth.com, LLC, 2009. Used under license from Shutterstock.com

Where to Begin

Goals
- Create a personal inventory
- Understand how to fill out a job application

Key Terms
- resume
- personal inventory
- job application

Your Personal Inventory

What makes you special? You've heard that "it's an employer's market" and that "times are tough," but you believe you have a lot to offer. How can you communicate this value to potential employers? The most important document you will use during your search for employment is your resume. A **resume** is a brief summary of your education, job history, and skills. Your resume introduces you to an employer by providing a snapshot of your background and accomplishments. More importantly, it serves as an advertisement that may spark a reviewer's interest enough to get you an interview.

Have you ever been tempted to buy a product because you saw an eye-catching advertisement? Marketers recognize that consumers sometimes make purchase decisions based on exposure to brief television or radio commercials or quick glances at magazine ads. Just as you are exposed to countless ads during a week, an employer may sift through hundreds of resumes to find a candidate for one job. The resume that prompts action will be the one that attracts the most positive attention.

marketing matters

Alex was just about to put together his resume—he hoped to find a position as an assistant at a veterinary office—when a friend said he could get Alex a job at a pet supply warehouse loading merchandise onto trucks. The warehouse job pays better than the assistant job, but it does not relate as well to Alex's career goal of becoming a veterinarian. Alex is very busy and feels he doesn't have time to develop a resume. Plus, the higher wages would help him with future college expenses. If Alex spends the time writing a resume and then sends it out to local veterinary offices, he will have to wait for their responses. Why might Alex want to decline the high-paying warehouse job to explore jobs with local veterinarians? If Alex decides to accept the warehouse position, why might he want to develop a resume anyway?

Blend Images/Jupiter Images

©emin kuliyev, LLC, 2009/Used under license from Shutterstock.com

You can begin developing your resume by creating a personal inventory. A **personal inventory** helps you identify your job-related skills by listing details of your education, experience, and other qualifications. It is a personal document—not intended to be given to an employer—that lists the hard data you will need to write your resume, draft cover letters, fill out job applications, and prepare for interviews. The process of applying for a job will go more smoothly if you take the time to develop your personal inventory ahead of time. Having the information at your fingertips will prevent you from forgetting key items.

What to Include

The following sections will help you understand what to include in your personal inventory.

Education Include the name of the schools you've attended, degrees earned, and graduation dates.

Work Experience Include your previous work experience, including company names and addresses, job titles, and dates of employment.

Extracurricular Activities Include activities in which you participate. These activities may be school-related, such as the drama club or track team. They also may be outside of school, such as volunteer work or community service. These activities, along with your education and work experience, can demonstrate your potential as an employee.

Identify five long-term goals that you could fulfill through your work. Perhaps you'd like to travel, help other people, or work with the environment. How can you achieve the goals you've listed through your target career?

Personal Qualities Include your best qualities—for example, a positive attitude, the ability to get along with others, responsibility, punctuality, and flexibility—and examples of how these qualities have been helpful in the workplace.

Hobbies Include your hobbies—for example, woodworking or traveling.

Career Goals Include your future career goals—for example, creating unique floral designs or managing a business.

Personal Inventory Tips

When listing your qualifications, be as detailed and precise as possible.

- List both the month and the year that you started and ended a job. For example, May 2008 through September 2008.

- Avoid abbreviations, and spell out the complete names of schools and other organizations.

  Correct: *South Florida After School Buddies Program*
  Incorrect: *S. FL After School Buddies Prog.*

- List specific job titles and responsibilities.

- Qualify and quantify your accomplishments. For example, instead of mentioning that you increased sales, tell how you did so and provide an exact figure: *Through suggestive selling, increased gelato sales by 75%.*

- Detail your fluency in a foreign language. For example, instead of noting that you are fluent in Russian, note if you are a native speaker, how many years you have studied Russian, if you can read and write the language, and if you have ever acted as an interpreter.

- Identify your computer skills. Note any experience you may have repairing hardware, and identify by name any software you have mastered or programming languages you know.

- Use appropriate terminology to identify any special skills or knowledge you may have.

  Effective: *Member of design team, trained volunteers, and assisted with the final grouting of the Northside Community mosaic*

  Less effective: *Helped with community mosaic*

Check Point

List three additional categories that could be included in a personal inventory.

Job Applications

A **job application** is a form provided by an employer that asks you to list your qualifications, work history, and work-related personal information (see the sample on page 180). Because application forms are uniform, reviewers find them easy to use when comparing applicants for certain positions. You can use the information on your personal inventory to complete an application. Some employers require only a job application, while others may require a resume as well.

Many employers accept online job applications and resumes. Visit the company web site to find out if you can apply online. For more information about online job applications and resumes, see the Skills for Occupational Success feature on page 203 of this chapter.

Follow these tips for filling out an application.

- Ask if you can take the application home with you, where you will have more time to complete it. Always have your personal inventory with you, though, in case you can't take the application home.

- Request an extra copy or make your own copy to use for practice. The final application should be error free and easy to read.

- Read the application from beginning to end before you start to fill it in.

- Answer questions with measurable statements. For example, instead of mentioning that you wrote for the school paper, list the number of articles you submitted during the time that you worked on the paper.

- Respond to every question. Write NA (not applicable) next to questions that do not apply to you to show the employer that you didn't miss a particular question.

- If possible, scan the form into your computer, fill in the blanks electronically, and print it. Otherwise, hand print the answers neatly, using black or blue ink.

- When applying online, be sure to carefully read and follow the directions provided, and include all information requested.

- Before you submit the application, be sure to proofread it carefully.

Truth in Advertising

Interviewers focus on accuracy. Do the dates on your application match the dates listed on your resume? Are you able to explain how you achieved the accomplishments you listed? Can the human resources department verify the dates of the internships that you list? Whether inconsistencies occur because of exaggeration or simple sloppiness, employers disregard candidates who provide inaccurate information. Update your personal inventory when necessary to ensure the information you provide on your resumes and applications is accurate.

APPLICATION FOR EMPLOYMENT

Please print or type.   An Equal Opportunity Employer

Name	Address	City/State/Zip
Maria Vasquez	123 Spring Meadow Ct.	Cedar Park, TX 78613

Telephone Number	Social Security Number	
(512) 555-0025	123-45-6789	

U.S. Citizen? Yes No	Position Applying for?	Desired Salary
Yes	Marketing Coordinator	Open

WORK EXPERIENCE

Current/Most Recent Employer	Address
Community College of Austin Cypress Creek Campus	1555 Cypress Creek Rd. Cedar Park, TX 78613

Job Title	Dates of Employment from 07 / 2009 to / Present
Admissions Assistant	

Supervisor	Salary	Reason for Leaving?
Jamison Dahn	$9.50/hour	Seeking full-time career position

Previous Employer	Address

Job Title	Dates of Employment from / to /

Supervisor	Salary	Reason for Leaving?

Previous Employer	Address

Job Title	Dates of Employment from / to /

Supervisor	Salary	Reason for Leaving?

EDUCATION

High School	City and State	Attended from 8 / 20-- to 6 / 20--
Cedar Park High School	Cedar Park, TX	

GPA	Degree	Activities, Honors
3.3	Diploma	Junior Achievement club member

College	City and State	Attended from 9 /20-- to 6 / 20--
Austin Community College, Northridge Campus	Austin, TX	

GPA	Degree	Activities, Honors
3.75	A.S., Marketing	Honors graduate

SPECIAL SKILLS, LICENSES, TRAINING, OR MILITARY EXPERIENCE

Course work in marketing communication, sales, and strategy.

REFERENCES *(Do not include the names of relatives or former employers)*

Name	Address	Telephone Number
1. James Lerner (instructor)	Austin Community College Austin, TX 78752	(512) 555-1100
2. Rosa Sanchez (guidance counselor)	Cedar Park High School Cedar Park, TX 78613	(512) 555-3854
3. Tom Garcia (teacher)	Cedar Park High School Cedar Park, TX 78613	(512) 555-3854

CERTIFICATION

I certify that all information on this application is true. I understand that termination may result if any information is found to be untrue. I understand that employment is subject to passing drug tests conducted at the direction of the Company.

(sign) *Maria Vasquez*	July 6, 20–
Signature	Date

Form 956 Rev.8/08

Sample Application Form

Check ▶ Point

If you make a mistake on a hard copy application, is it better to turn it in as is or ask for another? How can you avoid this situation?

7.1 Assessment

THINK CRITICALLY

1. How can the information in your personal inventory be converted to marketable skills on a resume? Choose one category, and explain why you would include this information on your resume.

2. When advertisers create an ad, they aim it toward a particular audience. Who is the audience for a resume? Explain how the size of a company might affect how it processes resumes.

3. What are the advantages and disadvantages of resumes, as compared to job applications?

MAKE ACADEMIC CONNECTIONS

4. **SOCIAL STUDIES** Questions about age, race, gender, and religion don't appear on most job applications. Use the Internet or your local library to research discrimination. Develop an oral presentation about why employers are careful not to discriminate on the basis of any of these factors. Discuss instances in which an employer may wish to hire someone because they are a certain age, race, gender, or religion.

5. **LITERATURE** Choose a well-known author to research. Learn about his or her education, personal interests, group memberships, major works published, and other jobs. Create a personal inventory for this author based on what you learn. Include any life experiences that may have contributed to this author's knowledge about his or her subjects.

Content and Structure

Goals
- Recognize common resume sections
- Learn ways to organize a resume

Key Terms
- job objective
- reverse chronological order
- functional resume
- chronological resume

Resume Basics

Just as every person looking for a job is different, so is every resume. One size does not fit all, and there is no right or wrong way to write a resume. For example, someone who has been in one career for 10 years may have a fairly long, detailed resume. But a high school student entering the job market for the first time will want to stick to one page. A graphic designer applying to a small advertising agency might submit a resume with a layout that emphasizes creativity, while an office worker submitting a resume to a large corporation will want a plainly formatted resume that can be read by a computer.

Despite these differences, resumes do have certain elements, or sections, that every employer looks for. These sections include contact information, an objective, and special sections that list the applicant's qualifications. Each section should have a heading to make it easy for a resume reviewer to find desired information. Experiment with organizing your resume so that it highlights your special skills and reflects your personality, but remember to include standard resume sections so employers can locate key information at a glance.

marketing matters

Jasmine Gregory feels like she has a split personality. She has a part-time job helping children handle live animals in the hands-on exhibit of the natural history museum. Her other passion is art: This year she won the Best Sculpture prize in her high school's art contest. During the upcoming summer, Jasmine hopes to work either in a full-time position at the natural history museum or as an apprentice with a local sculptor. She is beginning to wonder how she can write a resume to cover both of her interests. What advice would you give Jasmine? Is there an alternative to creating and sending out a single version of her resume? Explain.

g_studio/iStockphoto.com

Common Resume Sections

The following resume sections are considered standard. Some, such as *Contact Information* and *Objective*, should be included in every resume. Others, such as *Bilingual Skills* and *Honors and Awards*, are optional.

Contact Information Employers need to know who you are and how they can reach you. At the top of your resume, list your legal name, address, telephone number, e-mail address, and any additional information (for example, your fax number). Be sure to spell out your street name, city, and state and include your ZIP code.

Job Objective Every resume should have a **job objective**, which identifies the job you are applying for. You can state the objective as a job title, as an occupation, or by the qualifications you want the job to require. If you have multiple career targets, you'll want to have a few versions of your resume, each with a different objective.

Never write a vague objective—it gives the impression that you don't know what you want. A clear, appropriate job objective will focus your resume. If you develop your objective first, you can tailor the rest of the resume to fit your objective. Consider these sample objectives.

- **Strong** To obtain a position as a public relations assistant with a non-profit organization
- **Strong** To obtain a position as an office associate where my organizational skills will contribute to the efficiency of the company
- **Vague** A job where I can use my people skills

Education Supply education information on your resume in reverse chronological order. **Reverse chronological order** lists the most current information first and the least current information last. Begin with your most recent school or training program, and work backward, listing the full names of schools and any diplomas, certificates, or honors you received. Include school activities and courses related to the job. Include your class rank or GPA if they are impressive (GPA of 3.0 or higher).

Related Coursework List any relevant courses you have completed. This section is useful if you have little work experience or do not have a degree in your field of interest.

Related Experience Use this category to list experience related to your field that is not part of a paid job, such as extracurricular activities, volunteer work, and unpaid apprenticeships and internships.

Work Experience This section is the most important section of a chronological resume. List your work experience in reverse chronological order. Include the full name and location of each company you worked for, the dates of your employment, and a brief, results-oriented description of your duties. Your descriptions should emphasize your major responsibilities

com-mu-ni-cate

Contact a human resources or office manager in your community. Conduct an interview to determine what he or she looks for in a resume. How much time is spent looking at each resume? What is the worst resume he or she has ever come across? Write a report to share with the class.

Working Abroad

In this global environment, you will quite possibly be asked to conduct business abroad. You may travel to attend a trade show or meeting. Or you may embark on an exciting international assignment. No matter your destination or the length of your stay, your success in conducting business will depend on understanding the host country's culture and adapting to it.

The best way to learn about how to combine a new culture with your career is through employer-provided cross-cultural training. If your company does not provide pre-departure training, ask someone who's worked in the country or region for detailed information. You should research such topics as work priorities and values, dress, decision protocol, and scheduling and punctuality. Communication is the tool you will use most often—and the tool that will give you the greatest opportunity to make or break your experience. Therefore, make sure you ask about communication styles, such as directness, modesty, and use of non-verbal communication (including body space).

Research has shown that the most successful employees in international assignments: (1) are excited to learn about the new culture, (2) have a healthy sense of adventure, (3) possess the flexibility and willingness to adapt to new situations, and (4) enter the country with knowledge about the culture. These attributes are more important than technical knowledge or any other factor. Employees with these qualities have described their experiences as "the chance of a lifetime" and "a wonderful opportunity for personal growth."

and any measurable accomplishments. To strengthen your work experience section, follow these tips.

- Use present tense verbs to describe what you do in your current job; use past tense verbs to describe your responsibilities in previous jobs.

  Present: *Schedule plant deliveries to tri-county area*
  Past: *Developed inventory system for perennial bulbs*

- Use measurements, when appropriate, to describe responsibilities and accomplishments (for example, *Increased August–October bulb sales by 50%*).

- Use strong, active verbs and descriptive nouns (for example, *Conducted survey of customer's landscaping needs and recommended implementation of landscaping consultation service*).

Workplace Skills List your abilities and skills that relate to the job you are seeking. Pack this section with job-related terms that describe skills that are consistent with your objective. Be sure to include specific expertise,

A resume receives only five to ten seconds of consideration before an employer decides to review it more thoroughly or reject it.

technical knowledge, computer skills, and specialized certifications. You can highlight certain skills by breaking this section up into separate labeled sections, such as *Computer Skills* or *Childcare Experience*.

Bilingual Skills Include whether you are a native speaker, how many years you have studied the language, and your fluency level.

Honors and Awards Employers want to see evidence of high work standards and achievement. List any awards that show you are highly productive (for example, *Dean's List, August 20-- Sales Associate of the Month*, and *Helen Baskin scholarship recipient*).

Summary of Qualifications In many situations, your resume will most likely be "read" by a computer first. And when a computer reads your resume, it is looking for keywords—special words related to specific jobs and skills that are used to search computer databases. Effective keywords are:

- **Nouns** When a computer searches your resume for keywords, it will not be looking for verbs! You may still use some action verbs, but you will get more database matches if you rephrase your experience. For example, an online library services trainer will want to say "online services trainer for county library system" instead of "trained county library staff to use online services."

- **Career related** Be sure to include words that are specific to your career objective and job title. Include position titles, certifications, computer programs, programming languages, and other specific skills.

The easiest way to pack your resume with career-related keywords is to include as many keywords as you can in the summary of qualifications section.

References Make a list of references, or people who can provide positive information about you. Include each person's job title, address, and telephone number on the list. Put your contact information at the top of the list, followed by the title *References*, and then list each reference. Do not include the reference list on the resume itself. Be sure to ask permission of all those you list as references. You also might want to update them on the type of work you are looking for, so they can speak intelligently about what you would bring to the position. Employers expect all applicants to have references but differ regarding when and where they want to see an applicant's reference lists.

Workshop

Think about a position that someone close to you has held for several years. List four precise action verbs to describe some of that person's tasks and accomplishments.

Check Point

Why do you think it's standard practice to list education and work experience in reverse chronological order?

careerbuilder®

Seven Things to Know Before Writing Your First Résumé

Kate Lorenz, CareerBuilder.com Editor
Copyright 2008 CareerBuilder, LLC.—Reprinted with permission.

There are many rites of passage in every young person's life. Getting your driver's license, graduation day and turning 21 are just a few. But another rite of passage can be even more important to your future—writing your first résumé.

While it's not as exciting as learning to drive, creating your first résumé is a vital step in launching your career. The process may seem daunting. You have to put all of your best qualities on paper, make yourself look more attractive than the next person and completely sell yourself, all on one sheet of paper. "You have only a few seconds to snag the employer's attention," writes Seattle-based career coach Robin Ryan in *Winning Résumés*, (John Wiley & Sons, Inc., 2003). "You must sell the employer within 15 seconds of looking at your résumé, or you'll lose the job." Here are seven tips to help you catch an employer's attention.

1. Start with the basics.
It sounds obvious, but your résumé must include your name, address, phone number and e-mail address. Be mindful of the address you include. College students, in particular, tend to move often, so include a permanent address, such as your parent's address. Take care with your e-mail address too. "Make your user ID related to your name, not any nickname attributions," Ryan says. If you want to appear professional to an employer, a user ID like "sexylegs2000" will not work. If your personal e-mail address is not appropriate, set up a new account just for job searches.

2. Include an objective and summary of skills.
These sections come right after your personal information and, for a first-time job seeker, should be concise.

For example:

Objective: Editing Position

Summary of Skills: Excellent writer proficient in copy editing and familiar with AP style. Extremely organized, with ample experience meeting deadlines and working in high-pressure situations.

Your "summary of skills" should highlight experiences and qualifications that the employer is seeking. Remember, Ryan says, "a résumé is not about what you want. It's about what you offer an employer."

continued on page 187

3. Choose the right résumé style.

There are three basic types of résumés: chronological, functional and combination. Chronological résumés focus on work experience, and list professional experience in order from most to least recent. Functional résumés concentrate more on skills. A combination style works well for first-time job seekers. You can point out professional experience, but also draw more attention to your skills, since your work experience is probably limited. Ryan suggests that first-time résumé writers divide their résumé into these categories: work experience, academic experience and community service/extracurricular experience.

4. Brainstorm your experience and skills.

While you may be struggling to think of pertinent work experience, Ryan says that you have more than you realize. For example, if you have worked in a retail operation, your skills and qualifications include customer service skills, dependability, accountability, the ability to work as a part of a team and experience in managing money. Were you a full-time summer babysitter? This means you coordinated schedules, handled finances, and were extremely responsible. Many skills learned in part-time positions are quite relevant to the corporate world. Don't underestimate the skills you have gained.

5. Your academic and volunteer experience is relevant.

Don't think that your schooling means nothing to an employer. Your computer skills will be particularly attractive and should be highlighted. You can also demonstrate your aptitude and strengths by project-specific examples of class work you have done. For example, if you were a journalism major in college, tell the employer about major articles you wrote and the legwork you did to complete those projects. Also consider your volunteer and extracurricular experience. If you held an officer position in a club or fraternity/sorority, were an athlete, volunteered or took a leadership role in any other extracurricular organization, you have valuable experience to list.

6. Know the cardinal rules of résumé writing.

First, use strong action verbs and leave out the word "I." Words like created, developed, organized, motivated, and produced all say much more than "did." Next, remember that your résumé should be one page only—no exceptions. And, finally, never send a résumé without proper proofreading.

7. Never, ever lie.

So you were just two courses short of your college degree and think the company won't figure out that you didn't actually get it? Think again. If you lie on your résumé, you will be caught. Don't misrepresent your past—it will come back to haunt you.

Fine-Tuning Your Resume

You want your resume to attract attention. But does that mean you should print it on bright orange paper? Probably not. Employers prefer white or off-white paper and standard typefaces, so you can skip the flashy colors and let your words do the work.

Follow the tips below to create a polished resume that attracts positive attention.

- **Use correct spelling and grammar**   Your resume speaks for you—and it should be perfect.

- **Keep it neat**   Check your resume for spills and smudges before you send it, and never use correction fluid. Make sure your envelope stationery matches your resume stationery, and neatly write or type the address on the envelope.

- **Make it clear**   Use clear, concise, and professional language.

- **Keep it brief**   Use just one page for your resume. You should extend your resume beyond one page only when you have years of experience.

marketing math connection

Radio advertising costs are determined by the rate card provided by the radio stations. The rate card below refers to different quarters during the year. Suppose a business wants to purchase four 60-second spot advertisements per day for four weeks during the spring quarter. The business wants to run these spots between 10 A.M. and 3 P.M., Monday through Friday. How much will these advertisements cost the business?

Time Slot	Spring	Summer	Fall	Winter
6 A.M.–10 A.M.	$170	$180	$190	$200
10 A.M.–3 P.M.	$70	$80	$80	$90
3 P.M.–7 P.M.	$110	$120	$130	$140
7 P.M.–12 A.M.	$30	$30	$30	$30
12 A.M.–6 A.M.	$90	$100	$110	$120

SOLUTION

Cost per day = Spots per day × Cost per spot
= 4 × $70
= $280

Total cost = Cost per day × Number of days per week × Number of weeks
= $280 × 5 × 4
= $5,600

Resume Types: Functional and Chronological

Job seekers with plenty of work experience in their areas of interest should have little difficulty listing the past and current jobs that have led them to the next steps in their careers. But what if you are pointed in a certain career direction by your abilities and interests and lack actual work experience? Just as you include only the resume sections that reinforce your objective, you can also emphasize certain sections through strategic formatting and placement. Two main resume types present different ways to structure your information.

Functional Resumes A **functional resume** focuses on personal characteristics, skills, abilities, and work experiences. It highlights your strengths. For example, if you have strong skills and abilities but not much work experience, you can emphasize your skills by listing *Skills and Abilities* above *Work Experience*.

Use a functional resume:

- For your first job.
- When your career goals change.
- When your skills are more impressive than your work history.
- When you've made frequent job changes.

Chronological Resumes A **chronological resume** arranges work experience in reverse chronological order. Use it to show steady, relevant work experience or years of education related to your career. Employers tend to prefer this format.

Use a chronological resume:

- When your past jobs are in the same field.
- When your job history shows real growth or advancement.
- When your prior job titles are impressive.
- When your previous employer's name might impress a potential employer.

The models on the next two pages show different ways to organize the same resume information.

Check > Point

Why do you think an employer might prefer to see a chronological resume?

JEFFREY YI

1451 Jamestown Road
Pittsburgh, Pennsylvania 15220
(412) 555-9876
jeffreyyi@email.com

OBJECTIVE

To obtain a full-time position as a counselor at a summer day camp

SKILLS AND ABILITIES

Responsible Childcare Worker

- Coordinated and monitored youth activities to ensure maximum safety for children
- Completed childcare safety course at Lebanon Community Health Center
- Completed lifeguard training course and obtained certification

Creative Childcare Worker

- Skilled at introducing new activities and encouraging all children to participate

Leader

- Spearheaded camp clean-ups, organized new games, earned two Counselor-of-the-Week awards

Teamworker

- Cooperated with peers and camp directors to achieve camp goals

EDUCATION

Keystone High School, Pittsburgh, PA
- Completed Child Development I and academic coursework, August 2010 through present

EXPERIENCE

Camp Aim, Bethel Park, PA
- Assistant Counselor, June through August 2011 and June through August 2012

Lebanon Recreation Center, Pittsburgh, PA
- Weekend lifeguard, June through August 2010

ACTIVITIES

- Volunteer, Habitat for Humanity
- Member, Blue Devils Swim Team

Functional Resume

JEFFREY YI
1451 Jamestown Road
Pittsburgh, Pennsylvania 15220
(412) 555-9876
jeffreyyi@email.com

OBJECTIVE
To obtain a full-time position as a counselor at a summer day camp

WORK EXPERIENCE
Camp Aim, Bethel Park, PA
- Assistant Counselor, June through August 2011 and June through August 2012
- Responsible for 4th-grade boys (2011) and 2nd-grade boys (2012)
- Organized boat building workshop for boat race
- Led camp clean-up at the end of each session
- Earned two Counselor-of-the-Week awards

Lebanon Recreation Center, Pittsburgh, PA
- Weekend lifeguard, June through August, 2010
- Ensured the safety of swimmers using the facilities

EDUCATION
Keystone High School, Pittsburgh, PA
- Completed Child Development I and academic coursework, August 2010 through present

SKILLS AND ABILITIES
Responsible Childcare Worker
- Coordinate and monitor youth activities to ensure maximum safety for children
- Completed childcare safety course at Lebanon Community Health Center
- Completed lifeguard training course and obtained certification

Creative Childcare Worker
- Skilled at inventing new activities and encouraging all children to participate

Teamworker
- Cooperate with peers and head counselors to achieve camp goals

ACTIVITIES
- Volunteer, Habitat for Humanity
- Member, Blue Devils Swim Team

Chronological Resume

THINK CRITICALLY

1. If you were Jeffrey Yi, the author of the resumes shown in this lesson, which resume would you submit: the functional or the chronological resume? Why?

2. Why do you think some employers prefer to receive references along with your resume while others prefer to receive references after they contact or interview you? When do you think references should be submitted?

3. Match each item listed with the resume section where you would place it.

   a. Work Experience
   b. Honors and Awards
   c. Skills and Abilities
   d. Objective

   1. To obtain a position as a sales associate at an adventure travel service
   2. Named employee of the week eight times during a two-year period
   3. Teamworker: Cooperated with department to increase international travel sales
   4. Responsible for orientation of new hires

MAKE ACADEMIC CONNECTIONS

4. **PROBLEM SOLVING** Mira Lampi just sent out resumes to six prospective employers she has targeted for a job. She is away at school during the day, no one else is at home to take messages, and her family doesn't own an answering machine. Mira is worried that she will miss important calls from employers. What should she do?

Resume Formats

Goals
- Prepare a scannable resume
- Prepare an online resume

Key Terms
- scannable resume
- online resume

Keeping Up with Technology

You have spent valuable time identifying and acquiring the work skills that will make you marketable in the current job market. You have developed multiple paper resume versions that highlight your skills and target employment positions matching your objective. Your resume is attractively formatted and error free. So why isn't the telephone ringing off the hook with employers clamoring for interviews? Did you overlook something?

Just as the job market continually changes, so do the ways employers select the resumes that lead to interviews. The two main resume formats you need to be aware of are scannable resumes and online resumes. A **scannable resume** is a resume that is mailed or faxed to a company, which then scans it into a computer database. An **online resume** is a document that you send by e-mail, as an e-mail attachment, or submit directly through a specified web site. Many companies now prefer to receive scannable or online resumes instead of traditional paper resumes. This lesson will show you how to format your resume to keep up with current technology.

marketing matters

Justin Matthews has heard about job openings for photocopy clerks at three different companies in his community. One of the openings was listed in the local paper, and his network contacts told him about the other two. He wants to send resumes to the companies, but he isn't sure whether to send traditional resumes, online resumes, or scannable resumes. Should Justin send more than one type of resume to each company? Explain. Can you think of a time when you received multiple types of marketing information for the same product?

szefei/iStockphoto.com

The technology used for resume databases utilizes a search-matching function—a set of rules that allows a search result to be displayed based on the input given by the user (for example, an employer). Search technology for career sites usually is based on keyword searches (searches for specific words or phrases). Click on **www.cengage.com/school/marketing/yourself** and follow the links to this activity. Visit one of the job search sites and perform a keyword search on a position category of interest to you. Find at least two positions. What keywords are mentioned under job description or position requirements?

Scannable Resumes

Scannable resumes have more in common with traditional resumes than you might think. Like traditional resumes, scannable resumes are paper-based. The difference lies in the formatting, as the example on the next page shows. The scanners now used by many organizations to read resumes do not understand some common formatting elements used in paper resumes, such as columns, bullets, and italics. By creating a scannable version, you can ensure that no "misunderstandings" occur. If you're not sure which resume to send, send your scannable resume.

Follow these instructions to create a scanner-friendly resume:

- Use hyphens instead of parentheses around telephone and fax number area codes, for example, 610-555-0178 instead of (610) 555-0178. Many scanning programs cannot read parentheses.

- Use one simple font, such as Arial or Times Roman, 10 to 14 points.

- Use *basic* formatting, such as boldface type. Do not use italics or fancy typefaces.

- Print your resume on white, high-quality paper—lighter colors scan more effectively.

- When faxing, turn on the "fine print" feature of your fax machine if one is available. It will help the scanner read your resume. Some computers have a fax feature as well, so you may be able to scan your resume into the computer and then fax it directly to the employer.

- When mailing, do not fold or staple your scannable resume.

Workshop

Technology usually evolves to become more user friendly. Think of several examples of technologies that became easier to use as they advanced.

Check ▸ Point

Does a scannable resume replace a traditional resume? Explain.

Tasha L. Diaz
406 Whitford Lane
Independence, MO 62843
315-555-1112
cdiaz@email.com

OBJECTIVE
Librarian aid position in a public library utilizing research and organizational skills to promote patron satisfaction

SUMMARY OF SKILLS
Researcher adept at using online search engines, directories, and other online tools
Certified user of Innovative Interfaces for checking and returning patron materials
Computer programs: Word, Excel, Access, PowerPoint, Acrobat, and LexisNexis

EXPERIENCE
Independence Community Library, Independence, MO

Children's Library Aide, April 20-- to present
- Teach children how to use age-appropriate online search engines and directories
- Coordinate prizes for the children's summer reading programs
- Show children how to use Innovative Interfaces, the county's online catalog system
- Notify patrons when their interlibrary loan materials are received

The Book Nook, Kansas City, MO
Sales Associate, January 20-- to April 20--
- Unboxed and shelved new book shipments
- Rang customer purchases and closed out cash register at end of day
- Recommended and implemented used book sale table

EDUCATION
Graceland University, Independence, MO
- Expected graduation date: June 2010
- Related Courses: Library Science, Research Methods, Strategic Management

Independence Senior High School, Independence, MO
- Diploma received: June 20--

HONORS AND AWARDS
Dean's List, Fall 20--, Spring 20--

Scannable Resume

Did You Know?

According to a study by the Society for Human Resource Management, social networking and other online sources—including Internet job postings, Internet advertisements, online job web sites, and blogs—were found to be effective recruiting methods.

Online Resumes

Online resumes, also known as electronic resumes, do not require paper. They are either e-mailed as a computer file or uploaded to a job board or company web site. When uploading your resume, be sure to follow all instructions carefully. You may be able to upload your resume as a Word document, but some sites might require a specific format or software version. When employers ask you to e-mail your resume, clarify what they mean:

- **Do they want a formal resume?** Perhaps they want to print it, but do not want to wait to receive your paper resume by mail. If so, e-mail or upload your traditional resume with formatted elements, such as columns, centering, boldface, and italics.

- **Do they want to enter your resume into their database?** E-mail or upload your online resume.

Formatting Your Online Resume

The main rule for formatting your online resume is to avoid any formatting elements that cannot be found on your keyboard. In addition, do not use tabs. Although tabs appear on your keyboard, they confuse database search tools. Instead, use the space bar or the Enter key to make all spacing. See the example on the next page.

If you have access to a version of Word or another word-processing software that allows you to save your resume as a PDF file (check the "Save As" options for your software), this will allow you to maintain your resume's format. If not, follow these basic instructions for formatting your online resume. Of course, if the employer requests a specific format, you will want to follow the employer's recommendations.

- Avoid using bullets, italics, and boldface.
- Left-justify the text—do not use center, full, or right justification.
- Do not use lines or columns.
- Use only 10- to 12-point Courier, Times Roman, Arial, or Helvetica.

When to Use an Online Resume

You can use your plain text electronic resume:

- When an employer or contact asks you to e-mail a resume
- When you want to post your resume to a career site database
- When you want to e-mail your resume to a company web site
- When a job posting includes an e-mail address

Check ▶ Point

Online resumes are also referred to as plain text resumes. Why do you think this is so?

Tasha L. Diaz
406 Whitford Lane
Independence, MO 62843
315-555-1112
tdiaz@email.com

OBJECTIVE
Librarian aid position in a public library utilizing research
and organizational skills to promote patron satisfaction

SUMMARY OF SKILLS
Researcher adept at using online search engines, directories, and
other online tools
Certified user of Innovative Interfaces for checking and returning
patron materials
Computer programs: Word, Excel, Access, PowerPoint, Acrobat, and
LexisNexis

EXPERIENCE
Independence Community Library, Independence, MO
Children's Library Assistant, April 20-- to present
- Teach children how to use age-appropriate online search engines
and directories
- Coordinator of prizes for the children's summer reading
programs.
- Show children how to use Innovative Interfaces, the county's
online catalog system
- Notify patrons when interlibrary loan materials are received

The Book Nook, Kansas City, MO
Sales Associate, January 20-- to April 20--
- Unboxed and shelved new book shipments
- Rang purchases and closed out cash register at end of day
- Recommended and implemented used book sale table

EDUCATION
Graceland University, Independence, MO
- Expected graduation date: June 20--
- Related Courses: Library Science, Research Methods, Strategic Management

Independence Senior High School, Independence, MO
- Diploma received: June 20--

HONORS AND AWARDS
Dean's List: Fall 20--, Spring 20--

Online Resume

THINK CRITICALLY

1. Some companies will not accept online resumes sent as e-mail attachments because they are concerned about virus contamination. How can you avoid having your online resume rejected?

2. Resume scanning equipment has its limitations. In what ways do you think people can spot qualified applicants better than computers?

3. If you were an employer, which resume format would you prefer from job applicants: a traditional paper resume, a scannable resume, or an online resume? Explain.

MAKE ACADEMIC CONNECTIONS

4. **MATCHING GAME** Pair off with a partner and practice identifying keywords that might be found in an employment database. Think of a career you are familiar with, such as basketball coach, teacher, or restaurant manager. Write a skills summary section packed with descriptive keywords that describe the job you selected. Do not show your partner. In the meantime, without showing you, your partner should list 10 keywords that he or she would enter into a database to search for applicants for the job you selected. How many of your keywords match? Select another career and reverse roles. With your partner, create an oral presentation to report your results to the class.

5. **GRAPHIC DESIGN** Search several web sites that have suggestions about resume formats. Download and print some of the sample resumes and compare their components. Create a poster that emphasizes the components that are suggested by all the sites.

INTERNET

VOCABULARY BUILDER

Choose the term that best fits the definition. Write the letter of the answer in the space provided. Some terms may not be used.

_____ 1. A resume that is scanned into a computer and kept in a database

_____ 2. In order by time, with the most current information first and the least current information last

_____ 3. A resume section that identifies the job you are applying for

_____ 4. A resume that you send by e-mail or as an e-mail attachment

_____ 5. A form provided by an employer that asks you to list your qualifications, work history, and work-related personal information

_____ 6. A brief summary of your education, job history, and skills

_____ 7. A type of resume that focuses on personal characteristics, skills, abilities, and work experience

_____ 8. A document that helps you identify your job-related skills by detailing your education, experience, and other qualifications

_____ 9. A type of resume that arranges work experience in reverse chronological order

a. chronological resume

b. functional resume

c. job application

d. job objective

e. online resume

f. personal inventory

g. resume

h. reverse chronological order

i. scannable resume

REVIEW CONCEPTS

www.cengage.com/school/marketing/yourself

10. List and describe three categories of information that can be included in a personal inventory.

11. How should you respond to questions on an application that do not apply to you?

12. Which two resume sections should be included in every resume? Explain.

13. List three situations where you would use a functional resume.

14. List three situations where you would use a chronological resume.

15. How is a scannable resume similar to a traditional resume? How is it different?

16. How do you send a scannable resume?

17. Where are online and scannable resumes frequently stored so they can be searched?

18. What types of keywords should you use in your resume?

APPLY WHAT YOU LEARNED

19. During the past three summers, Ibrahim Sharif has worked on the loading dock for Laser Tech. This summer, the company will be hiring interns to work in the office and run errands for the engineers. Resumes are required and Ibrahim is interested, especially because engineering is in his field of interest. Should he submit a functional resume or a chronological resume? Explain.

20. Describe four situations where you would use an online resume.

21. Why do you think many large businesses and organizations prefer to recruit employees online?

22. Sonya Cherniak is well prepared for her job search. She has a traditional resume with formatted elements, a scannable resume, and an online resume. On a job board, she read about an opening for a home health-care aid. The listing gives both a post office box and an e-mail address, but it does not specify which resume format is required or how to send it. Because the listing does not provide a telephone number, Sonya has no way of finding out which resume to send. What advice would you give her?

MAKE ACADEMIC CONNECTIONS

23. **TECHNOLOGY** Go to **www.cengage.com/school/ marketing/yourself** and follow the links for this exercise. Look up 10 jobs, and take notes about the resume requirements for each. Which resume format is specified, if any? How and where are applicants supposed to send resumes? Is a contact person's name given?

24. **COMMUNICATION** Predict the future of job hunting and recruitment. Can you think of ways that technology might advance even further to change the way people go about looking for jobs? Will it change the methods employers use to hire employees? How could resume formats and the interviewing process change in the future?

25. **ART/DESIGN** Create a diagram that illustrates the differences in formatting among the three resume formats featured in this chapter: the traditional resume, the scannable resume, and the online resume. Include directions for sending each one.

26. **ECONOMICS** Not every job requires a resume. Think of five jobs that require a resume and five jobs that do not. Think about whether education and income have a connection to the types of jobs that require resumes. Are there any high-paying jobs that do not require resumes?

27. **LANGUAGE ARTS** Locate a dictionary that explains word origins, and look up the word *resume*. What are its various meanings? From what language did *resume* originate, and what does it mean in this original language? Does the original meaning have anything to do with its present meaning?

28. **SOCIAL STUDIES** Work occupations have changed significantly in the United States over the last 100 years. Farming used to be the most common occupation. During the middle part of the 20th century, factory jobs were plentiful. During the last several years, service jobs have become most common. Create three resumes, one for a farmer in 1905, one for a factory worker in 1948, and one for a service worker in 1993. Research the types of things these people would have done, the skills they would have needed, and their education. Use fictional names and addresses.

Presentations Management Team

Participants in this event will use current desktop technologies and software to prepare and deliver an effective multimedia presentation. A team will consist of two to four members. The team shall design a computer-generated multimedia presentation on the assigned topic. A new topic is selected by BPA every year. A word-processed copy, including cited works, must be submitted at the time of the presentation. The team must make effective use of current multimedia technology in the presentation (examples: sound, movement, digital video, etc.).

The United States has focused much attention on improving education to become more competitive internationally. Much emphasis has been placed on math, science, and English. You understand the value of Career and Technology Education and active involvement in professional student organizations like Business Professionals of America. Your team must prepare a presentation for your state government representatives to explain the importance of student involvement in Business Professionals of America.

Participating teams will have from seven to ten minutes for oral presentations. Judges have an additional five minutes to ask questions about the presentation.

Online Job Applications and Resumes

Because job search information now is available with the click of a mouse, you may no longer need to read classified ads or go door-to-door to apply for a job. If you have access to the Internet, you can complete many steps in the job search process, including submitting your resume and job applications. In fact, many companies prefer that candidates apply online.

Company Web Sites

Many companies have web sites that not only provide information about the company, but they also provide information about job openings as well as a means to apply for these openings. The first step is to visit the company's web site. To find the company's employment opportunities check the navigation bar for a link to Human Resources (HR) or Employment, and select the link. If there is not a direct link, try an "About Us" or "Company Background" tab, from which you may find an HR or Employment link. Another option is to view the site map to find the link to HR or Employment. A link to the site map generally can be found in the upper right or at the bottom of the home page.

Once you have located an employment-related link, you may have the option to do an online job search, similar to what is found at job search sites, with categories such as keyword, department, or location. After pulling up positions of interest, you may be able to apply directly to the company through a provided link.

Job Search Sites

General job search and career information sites also provide opportunities to apply for positions online. In fact, when you find a position of interest through a job search site such as Career Builder or Monster.com, selecting it may connect you directly to the company's site for application purposes. If it does not connect you directly to the company, it will still provide instruction regarding how to apply for the position.

Applying Online

After locating the position information, you may have the option of applying for the position online. Typically, the online application process is very specific, and you will be required to complete information about yourself by selecting responses to questions and typing responses into provided fields. Online applications often ask for contact information, education and employment history including dates, as well as any other information the company deems important to the hiring process at this stage. Some sites might ask that you upload your resume as a text file or Word file. Others might request that you type the information from your resume into the application site itself.

Be sure to read and follow all instructions carefully, and proofread your information before submitting the application. Your application might not be considered if you do not follow instructions properly. Another consideration is automated resume screening. Many sites screen resumes for keywords that match the job description. Only those applicants meeting prescreening criteria are forwarded on to HR or hiring managers at the company, so be sure that you address the job description requirements when you apply, and, most importantly, be honest and ethical.

Develop Your Skill

Understanding a company's recruiting process can be very beneficial when you are searching for a job. Select a company in which you are interested. To determine if the company accepts virtual job applications and resumes, first visit the company's web site. Next, visit an online job search site and search on the company's name. If you don't have access to a computer and the Internet from home, you may have access either at your school or at a local public library. What did you learn about this company's virtual recruiting process? If you were to apply to this company, what steps would you need to take?

Chapter 8

Pricing Your Product

8.1 Money and Value

8.2 Salary Research

8.3 Salary Negotiations

CAREERS IN MARKETING

The TJX Companies

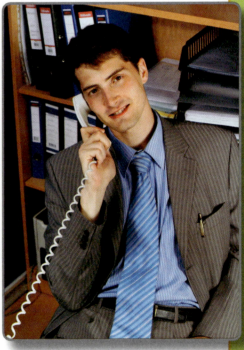

The TJX Companies, which includes retail brands T.J. Maxx, Marshalls, HomeGoods, and A.J. Wright in the United States, is the world's largest off-price retailer. It also has retail stores in Canada and Europe. TJX focuses on diversity in its customers and associates as well as in its merchandise mix.

Media Planners at TJX are responsible for producing and executing media plans for retail grand openings and advertising campaigns, as well as planning, buying, and negotiating media placement. Media Planners need to stay current regarding market trends and new developments in media. The Media Planner also resolves discrepancies with internal and external customers and recommends new media strategies.

The position typically requires a bachelor's degree, advertising experience, excellent communication skills, and in-depth knowledge of broadcast, print, and online media.

Think *Critically*

1. How does a media planner help maintain TJX's image?
2. Why do you think an organization such as TJX is concerned with media planning?

©Kuz'min Pavel, 2009/ Used under license from Shutterstock.com

PORTFOLIO BUILDER PROJECT
Demonstrating Your Value to an Employer

Project Objectives

What should you say when an employer asks what you think you are worth? Whether you are negotiating an hourly wage for a part-time job or an annual salary for a position in your field of interest, you should be able to speak knowledgeably about compensation and prove that you are worth what you believe you should be paid. In this project, you will:

- Research salaries for positions in your field of interest.
- Determine your salary and benefits requirements.
- Prepare a statement that summarizes what you are worth and why.

Getting Started

Read the Project Process below. Look at the supporting material on the Portfolio Builder CD.

- Examine the salary calculator table. You can use it to calculate your salary.

- Use the web resources to begin researching salary ranges.
- Study the sample employment value statement.

Project Process

Part 1 Lesson 8.1 Various factors influence the salaries and benefits employers are willing to offer, including the supply of applicants, the level of education and experience required, and the local cost of living. Use the web resources and your network contacts to research and list salary ranges for jobs you are interested in.

Part 2 Lesson 8.2 Reread your resume and personal inventory. Do your experience and education put you in the low, high, or middle salary range for your field of interest? Wherever you fall, think about how you can justify asking for the upper end of the range within this category.

Part 3 Lesson 8.3 To gain confidence in speaking about what you are worth, write a statement that summarizes the value you will provide an employer. Describe the compensation package you desire and why you believe you deserve it.

Project Wrap-Up

Write a paragraph about what your salary requirements say about you to employers. What would low requirements say? Unrealistically high requirements?

PhotoObjects.net/ Jupiter Images

Money and Value

Goals
- Explain the use of money in exchange
- Discuss how economic concepts affect salary

Key Terms
- commodity
- price
- salary
- supply
- demand

The Value of Exchange

As you learned in Chapter 1, all marketing involves some kind of exchange, where two parties see value in what the other has to offer. Monetary transactions and barter transactions are two types of exchange. Modern day exchanges are commonly thought of in terms of simple monetary transactions, such as exchanging a dollar for a chilled bottle of water. But a job is an exchange as well. You go to work, and, in exchange for your time and your skills, an employer pays you a salary.

Money as a Commodity

Have you ever gone to the local convenience store and paid for a loaf of bread with a bag of shells? Have you ever given the record store a piece of iron ore in exchange for a new CD? As ridiculous as these questions may seem, at one time shells and iron ore held exchange value in barter transactions, just as money does in monetary transactions today. Anything that holds exchange value is known as a **commodity**.

Preferred Commodities Although almost anything could be a commodity, certain items were chosen as preferred items for barter transactions. These preferred commodities were chosen for many different reasons—including ease of storage, ease of transport, and durability. They

marketing matters

Chao Hsu wants to sell his VCR and use the money toward the purchase of a DVD player. Five years ago, he paid $160 for his VCR. Because it is in excellent condition, he wants to sell it for $80, half the original price. Is $80 a reasonable asking price? What factors should Chao consider when pricing the used VCR? Where would you recommend that Chao advertise his VCR?

hidesy/iStockphoto.com

were widely desired and, thus, easy to exchange for other items. Following are some examples of preferred commodities.

- Cacao beans were used in Mexico by the Aztecs.
- Wampum, a string or belt made of small, polished shell beads, was used in North America.
- Metal objects known as manillas were used in Africa.
- Sugar was used in the West Indies.
- Whales' teeth were used in Fiji.

Coins How did coins come to replace such commodities as the preferred medium of exchange? The transition was a gradual one that began with the use of weighed amounts of precious metals as a preferred commodity. As technology advanced, coins were created. These were round pieces of precious metal, each guaranteed to be identical in weight and composition. Because they were identical, these coins did not need to be weighed—they could be counted instead.

Photodisc/Getty Images

The European colonization of the Americas stimulated an increase in the use of coins for exchange. Gold and silver flowed into Spain, Portugal, and England from the Americas, creating new trade and new markets. This flow of wealth soon affected bartering for goods, and even common people began using coins as their preferred commodity.

Paper Money The next important transition was to paper money. The use of paper money developed separately in different countries to meet advancing needs for more flexible commodities. For example, the American colonies had a constant shortage of official coins. As a result, colonists in Virginia began using tobacco as a commodity. But, as you might imagine, tobacco leaves are difficult to regulate, so certificates attesting to the quantity and quality of tobacco deposited in public warehouses came to be used as money and were made legal tender in 1727.

Today's paper money, unlike the original precious-metal coins, does not have any value of its own. It only *represents* value. Its acceptance is dependent on its being backed by some commodity, usually a precious metal such as gold or silver. Money has no value until it is exchangeable for goods and services.

Money and Price

The **price** of a good or service is the amount of money that must be exchanged for it. Using money creates a standard by which the prices of products can be compared. The unit of value, money, is consistent—the common denominator of exchange. Knowing that price is expressed in monetary terms allows you to compare seemingly incomparable items and make purchase decisions based on perceived value. You can compare the prices of two very different products when making exchange decisions. The price of each product is expressed in money.

RapidEye/iStockphoto.com

Compare, for example, a pair of shoes and a wristwatch. The shoes are priced at $59.95, while the wristwatch (a very different product that may seem incomparable) is priced at $79.99. Assume you have only $85 to spend. You really like the watch: It's made by a trendy designer, and it looks great on your wrist. You also like the shoes, and you need a new pair for gym class. But you can only afford to purchase one of the products. How do you decide which to buy? The shoes hold more perceived value based on the need that they satisfy (gym class). You are willing to exchange your hard-earned money for the shoes. You would have liked to purchase both items, but you were forced to make a value determination.

Check ❯ Point

Why is paper money accepted as a commodity?

Value in Salary

Your **salary** is the compensation you receive for your services. Salary, stated in terms of money, helps employers make *exchange decisions*. When you val-

ued the shoes over the wristwatch, you made an exchange decision and paid money for them. When an employer values the labor of a potential employee over the price, or salary, that will be paid for that labor, the employer makes an exchange decision and the employee is hired and paid. When you value the salary you will receive over the time and effort you put into a job, you make an exchange decision and go to work in exchange for your paycheck. The value of these exchange decisions is stated in terms of your salary, or price.

Why, then, is a retail sales associate paid less than a retail pharmacist? Why does a computer programmer earn more than a data entry special-ist? Why is a marketing manager's salary higher than a receptionist's salary? Employers value some positions more or less than other positions, just as you value some products more or less than other products.

© Photodisc/Getty Images

Did You Know?

In 1963, Congress passed the Equal Pay Act, which protects men and women who perform substantially equal work in the same establish-ment from sex-based wage discrimination. This law is enforced by the U.S. Equal Employment Opportunity Commission (EEOC).

The Economics of Salary

Chapter 2 briefly discussed the economic concepts of supply and demand. **Supply** refers to how much of a product is offered to the market. **Demand** refers to how much of a product consumers are willing to purchase. If a prod-uct is in short supply and high demand, consumers are often willing to pay more for it. If a large quantity of a product is available, its value to consumers will be lower. When several alternative products are available, often due to competition, consumers tend to consider price more carefully.

If Ekaterina attends a computer expo with many participating compa-nies selling computers, she has many options and will probably seek out a competitively priced computer that she believes to be a good value. If only a few companies are selling computers, Ekaterina has fewer alternatives and, therefore, may be willing to pay a higher price for a computer.

In a market economy, perceived value, and subsequent price, is often based on the market. The laws of supply and demand affect salaries. Some jobs, such as anesthesiologists, pay more because the skills required are scarce in the labor force, meaning fewer people possess these skills. Such skills are in short supply. Other jobs pay more because certain skills, such as computer programming, are in high demand, which means that many employers are in need of employees with those skills. When a particular

diversity in the workplace

Comparable worth is the concept that, when jobs require comparable skills, efforts, responsibilities, and experience, male and female employees should be paid equally. Consider this resolution by the National Education Association to protect the rights of educational employees and advance their interests and welfare.

The National Education Association believes that all workers should be paid on the basis of the requirements, skills, and worth of their jobs and that factors such as the gender or race of the individual performing the job should never play a role in determining salary.

The Association supports all efforts to attain accurate and unbiased forms of job evaluation and to raise the pay of those jobs that are presently undervalued. The "market value" means of establishing pay cannot be the final determinant of pay scales since it too frequently reflects the race and sex bias in our society.

The Association encourages efforts by education employees and others of the work force to gain salary levels appropriate to the skill, value, responsibility, and requirements of their jobs.

Source: National Education Association 2005–2006 Higher Education Resolutions: F-2. Pay Equity/Comparable Worth

position earns a high salary, it usually means that position is valued over one that earns a lower salary. When there is competition for a position (many people possess the needed skills), its salary may be lower because numerous alternative candidates are available.

Making Career Decisions

How you communicate and demonstrate your value through your skills, accomplishments, and benefits affects how much money an employer is willing to exchange for your services. Remember, satisfying exchanges are often based on benefits, because you believe that what you have given up is worth what you are given in return. In addition, the performance of the product purchased must meet expectations.

Considering market forces can help you make informed career decisions. A high salary for a particular occupation might signal an increased demand for workers with necessary qualifications in that occupation. Of course, salary should not be your only consideration when setting your career objectives. You will spend many years of your life working, and if not today, at some point in your career, you will want to work for more than just a paycheck. Your values, goals, skills, interests, and personality will help lead you to a career that enhances your life.

How do the economic concepts of supply and demand affect salaries for different positions?

8.1 Assessment

THINK CRITICALLY

1. How does an employment situation function as an exchange?

2. Provide an example of how money is used as a medium of exchange.

3. What is the common denominator of exchange? How does it relate to price?

4. How does salary relate to exchange decisions?

MAKE ACADEMIC CONNECTIONS

5. **SOCIAL STUDIES** In his book *The History of Money*, Jack Weatherford states, "Money did not make people smarter, it made them think in new ways, in numbers and their equivalents." Write a two-page response paper discussing some of the ways money could have changed people's thinking.

6. **HISTORY** Research the use of bartering during the Great Depression. How common was the practice? What sorts of items were bartered? Did this return to bartering have any lasting effects on purchasing? Compile your results into a PowerPoint presentation, which you will display to the class.

7. **CULTURAL STUDIES** Do all cultures use money as a commodity? Use the Internet or the resources at your library to answer this question. Provide examples, if they exist, of cultures that do not use money for transactions. What do they use instead? If you find that all cultures do use money as a commodity, choose a culture you're unfamiliar with and learn about its use of money. Prepare an oral presentation of your results.

INTERNET

@

Salary Research

Goals

- Explain how to determine realistic salary ranges
- Identify methods of researching salary information

Key Terms

- salary range
- cost of living

Setting Your Price

Have you ever traveled an extra five miles to a store offering a sale price on a product you wanted to buy? Have you ever bought a different brand than usual because it was offered at a better price? Marketers conduct research to determine how much consumers are willing to pay for a product. As you enter the job market, you will need to conduct similar research to determine the salary ranges that employers are willing to pay for particular positions.

Price is an important factor to consider when searching for employment. If you aim too high, you may price yourself out of the job. If you aim too low, you may get the job but be disappointed when you eventually learn that your salary is lower than it could have been. Or, you may not get a job offer because an employer believes that, because you aren't knowledgeable about appropriate salary ranges, you also aren't knowledgeable about the position, the industry, the organization, or the work involved.

Realistic Requirements

Every person has his or her own definition of success, but for most people, success in a job search means obtaining employment that meets their *realistic requirements*. Realistic requirements are those requirements that you can,

marketing matters

Domenic D'Antonio is looking for an entry-level job as a sales associate. He has a second interview next week, and he's been told to be prepared to discuss a salary and benefits package. To figure out his ideal salary range, Domenic has added up all his expenses, including mortgage payments, car payments, cable, phone, Internet connection, electricity, and groceries. Based on these expenses, he has determined that he needs to earn a salary of at least $50,000 per year. Do you think Domenic should ask for this salary at his interview next week? What else should he research before the interview?

© Daisy Daisy, 2009/ Used under license from Shutterstock.com

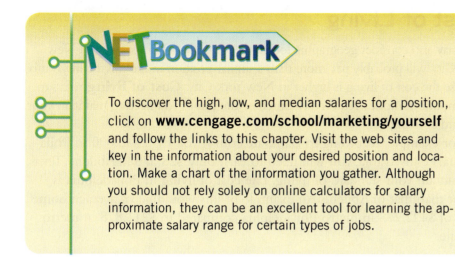

NETBookmark

To discover the high, low, and median salaries for a position, click on **www.cengage.com/school/marketing/yourself** and follow the links to this chapter. Visit the web sites and key in the information about your desired position and location. Make a chart of the information you gather. Although you should not rely solely on online calculators for salary information, they can be an excellent tool for learning the approximate salary range for certain types of jobs.

with some effort, attain in relation to employment. To be employable, it is important to have realistic salary requirements.

Gina recently graduated from college with an associate's degree in graphic design. She is looking for an entry-level design position at an advertising agency or graphics firm. She wants to make at least $55,000 per year. After doing some research, however, Gina learns that the *average* salary for graphic designers in 2009 was $51,000. Most *entry-level* positions pay even less. If she had neglected her research and asked for $55,000 for an entry-level position, Gina would have seriously hurt her chances of being hired.

How much are you worth in the job market? You have identified your skills, accomplishments, and benefits and considered packaging. You have researched positions and industries. Now you can put a price on your product—you—by determining your appropriate salary range.

Determining a Salary Range

Many employers have a salary range in mind for their open positions. A **salary range** has identified maximum and minimum salaries. Supply and demand can affect the salary ranges designated as appropriate for particular positions. The level of education, experience, skills, and responsibilities required of the position also contribute to the salary range.

If, for example, you are interested in a market research position that requires high-demand skills, such as the ability to analyze statistics, the salary range for the position will probably be higher than for a market research position that involves conducting phone surveys. The industry itself can also affect salary ranges. A market research position in a fast-growing high-tech industry may have a higher salary range than a similar position in the nonprofit sector.

Knowing the salary range for positions you are interested in means you understand your worth in the employment marketplace. This requires research. As you conduct research, remember that you are looking for salary information for entry-level positions, for someone with your background, education, and experience.

Cost of Living

You may also consider geographic location. A graphic design position in New York City will probably pay more than a similar position in Dubois, Pennsylvania, because the cost of living is higher in New York City. **Cost of living** refers to the amount of money required to purchase the things you need to maintain your standard of living.

For example, according to Bankrate.com if you earn $40,000 in Philadelphia, Pennsylvania, you will need to earn only $28,578 in Abilene, Texas, to maintain your standard of living. The cost of living in Philadelphia is higher than that of Abilene. An example of this would be an average home price of $422,778 in metro Philadelphia compared to $211,878 in metro Abilene.

Check Point

What are realistic requirements?

Sources of Salary Information

Where can you find salary information? Once you have identified positions and industries, you can research salaries using job listings and employers, associations, career/placement offices, network contacts, and the Internet.

Job Listings and Employers

Some organizations provide salary information, such as a starting salary range, when advertising an opening. If a salary is not mentioned, you may be able to get information from the human resources department, but organizations are not always willing to share salary information, and if they do share, they may tell you the low end of the range. Before you begin searching for a job, contact employers you have researched and ask about salary as part of an informational interview.

Career/Placement Offices

These offices, located in most colleges, can help you research salaries through career publications they may subscribe to, such as the *Occupational Outlook Handbook*, or surveys they conduct with alumni and area businesses.

Associations

You researched professional and industry associations related to positions of interest in Chapter 5. Associations often conduct employment surveys that may include salary information, or they may have access to other salary surveys. Visit the association's web site or contact its headquarters office to check on availability of salary information.

Network Contacts

As you build your network of contacts as described in Chapter 5, you might ask those who work in areas similar to your positions and industries of interest about starting salary ranges. Because they are employed in related areas, they may be good sources of inside information. Keep in mind that many people consider salary to be personal, and may not be willing to share the details of their specific salary. When asking about salary information, be sure to ask for salary ranges for specific types of positions, or salary ranges in specific industries or fields. This may help to make your network contacts more comfortable discussing salaries with you, as they can address the issue with generalities, and they will not feel that you are trying to obtain personal information about them.

© Photodisc/Getty Images

The Internet

The Internet provides a wealth of salary information that is relatively easy to find. Go to **www.cengage.com/school/marketing/yourself** to access a variety of web sites that contain salary information.

State government web sites also may provide salary information. The Bureau of Labor Statistics (BLS) is one such government source of salary information. This site provides links to national, regional, state, and metropolitan area wage data. It also includes a link to the National Compensation Survey. You can also find salary information by industry and occupation. Go to **www.cengage.com/school/marketing/yourself** to visit the BLS wage information site.

Salary data for government jobs can be found through the U.S. Office of Personnel Management (OPM). This site includes salary information by occupation and locality.

Some state sites may also provide salary information. The formula for state sites is generally **www.state.xx.us**, where xx is the two-letter state abbreviation. For example, Texas' web site is **www.state.tx.us**. Use the search feature to research salary information.

Check Point

How can professional and industry associations help you find salary information?

8.2 Assessment

THINK CRITICALLY

1. What factors can contribute to the salary range employers are willing to offer for their open positions?

2. How can cost of living affect salary requirements?

3. List and describe three sources of salary information.

MAKE ACADEMIC CONNECTIONS

4. **INTERNATIONAL BUSINESS** Find professional associations related to your career interests but in other countries. Write a brief report comparing and contrasting those association sites with U.S. sites. Can you get a glimpse of professional life in these other countries?

5. **CAREER RESEARCH** Many happily employed people are perpetual "passive job seekers," meaning that they are employed and don't need a new job, but they keep track of available jobs in their field or location, new credentials and skills that are becoming essential in their field, and their worth in the job market. What advantages and disadvantages can you think of for this behavior? Interview five of your network contacts. Do any of them perform this type of career research? Why or why not? Write a brief description of each of the contacts you chose and describe their thoughts on perpetual job searching.

6. **BUSINESS DECISIONS** Many large corporations choose to build new factories in rural areas (auto manufacturers, for example). Research this trend and make a poster explaining the factors behind such business decisions. Be sure to include such information as rural versus urban cost of living and salary information and non-economic reasons for such decisions.

Salary Negotiations

Goals
- Understand compensation packages
- Discuss common salary negotiation tactics

Key Terms
- compensation package
- benefits
- flexible benefits plan

Discussing Salary and Benefits

A recent college graduate, Sasha is searching for an entry-level sales position. He wants to make a good salary so he can afford to repay his college loans and rent an apartment. He has researched salary ranges in his area for sales positions and has determined that a base salary between $28,000 and $33,000 is average. Because he is looking for an outside sales position, meaning he will have to drive to clients' offices for meetings and sales calls, he also wants a car allowance.

Salary

Sasha has been asked in for an interview with Cabot Industries. He knows that he should not bring up salary during a first interview. It is better to let the employer bring up the topic. Sasha is selling his skills, accomplishments, and benefits to the organization, and he doesn't want the employer to think he is only interested in working for the company for the money. He wants to sell his value in terms of what he can bring to the organization.

If the employer asks about his salary requirements, Sasha can begin by commenting that he expects a salary that is comparable to the going rate for someone with his abilities in this position and industry. He might even ask about the salary range that the organization generally pays for the position. Some salary ranges are set through the human resources department, not by the hiring authority. Sasha may simply be told what

marketing matters

Delia has been offered a position as a sales associate at a local retail clothing store with a starting salary of $8.00 per hour. Through research, she has determined that her starting salary should be between $8.50 and $10.00 per hour. How should she address this difference with her potential employer? Should she accept the position and then ask for more money?

Photodisc/Getty Images

Workshop

In groups, list some benefits that an employer may offer as part of a compensation package. Rank them in order of importance to you, and compare your list with those of your classmates.

© Getty Images/photodisc

the position pays, with little room for negotiation. In this situation, he should ask about the frequency of salary reviews. If Sasha is pushed to state a figure, he should provide a range based on the results of his research.

Compensation Packages

When you are considering a position, take into account the entire compensation package offered. A **compensation package** includes salary and any other benefits. **Benefits** are financial, professional, or personal incentives offered as part of a position's compensation. Many organizations offer a **flexible benefits plan**, allowing employees to choose from a variety of benefit options. When employees select benefits, typically they share in the cost by paying a portion of the premiums. The costs often are deducted from an employee's paycheck as pre-tax dollars, so the employee does not pay employment taxes on the portion that he or she pays. The smart job seeker examines the benefits—and the costs—before making a career decision.

Salary   Your salary will often include more than just your hourly wages or annual salary. It may also include:

- **Commission** A percentage of sales
- **Overtime** Dollars per hour for extra hours worked
- **Bonus** Special earnings based upon performance
- **Stock options** Opportunities to invest in the company's stock at a lower price than the current price per share
- **Profit sharing** A share of the profits earned by the company

Insurance   Many organizations offer employees medical, dental, and vision insurance through private insurance carriers. Few organizations pay the full cost of the insurance premiums. Most require employees to contribute. Some organizations also offer life insurance benefits.

Education and Training   Some employers help employees pay for education and training through benefits such as tuition reimbursement or funding to attend seminars and conferences.

Retirement   Depending on the size of the organization you want to work for and the industry it's in, your retirement plan possibilities will vary.

- **Pension** An accumulation of money that an employee can access upon retirement

marketing math connection

There are two methods of pricing merchandise when the markup percentage and cost are known: the retail method and the cost method. Both are designed to ensure that the business charges enough for its merchandise to cover operating expenses and to make a satisfactory net profit. Knowledge of both is important in determining the proper price at which merchandise should be sold.

The cost a retailer pays for a sweater is $60.00, and the initial markup percentage desired is 30 percent. Use the following formula to calculate the retail price of the sweater.

Retail price = Cost ÷ (100% − Markup %)

SOLUTION

Retail price = Cost ÷ (100% − Markup %)
  = $60.00 ÷ (100% − 30%)
  = $60.00 ÷ 0.70
  = $85.71

- **401(k)** An individual investment plan in which contributions to stock or mutual funds are deducted directly from an employee's paycheck
- **403(b)** Similar to a 401(k), an investment plan available to employees of government agencies

Vacation Days Paid vacation days are generally offered as an employee benefit. The number of days and the formula for calculating them varies from organization to organization. Some organizations offer paid vacation days at the onset of employment, while others have a waiting period.

Sick Leave and Family Leave Sick leave is an allotment of days for which an employee can be paid while being absent due to illness. Family leave is a certain length of time that employees may be absent to care for infants or sick or elderly relatives without jeopardizing their employment.

Other Benefits Other benefits offered by employers may include flexible scheduling, telecommuting, compensatory ("comp") time, child care, and health club memberships.

Check Point

What is a compensation package?

careerbuilder®

How to Get Paid What You're Worth

Kate Lorenz, CareerBuilder.com
Copyright 2007 CareerBuilder, LLC.—Reprinted with permission.

It's a catch-22 when it comes to salary talks with a potential employer. Ask for too much and you might be dropped from consideration; ask for too little and you could be earning less than what your employer is willing to pay.

The way to escape this seesaw is to do your research and find out exactly what the position you're vying for earns in the industry you're seeking. This way, when it comes to talking cash, you have facts to back yourself up, not just the need to feed your shopping addiction.

How do you find out whether your salary is at market value for your profession, position and location? You can turn to your friends, but they may embellish their salaries, so reliability is suspect. Your dad's input as to what people make may be outdated. Finding good sources is not easy, but here are some tips for assembling information that might lead you to the answer.

Determine your needs

First, figure out what you'll need to make each month to make ends meet. Draw up a budget for your necessities including rent, credit card bills, school loans, cell phone, car insurance and food. You'll probably also want to factor in extra money for going out with friends, clothes and savings. That's what your minimum take home pay should be ideally each month.

Salary sites

Check out a web site that specializes in salary information, like CBsalary.com. You can search by job title and metro area. Ad hoc searches on search engines can sometimes direct you to fruitful results. A search engine query for "salary information" and "salary guides" can lead down various paths and you might get a little lost. Even better is to narrow the search by profession, say, to "accounting salaries" or "accounting salary guides."

Occupational Outlook Handbook

The Bureau of Labor Statistics (BLS) provides comprehensive occupation information for specific jobs. Pick your industry and then your job title—median earnings are given for a range of roles per job description. This information is based on national figures, though, and might not reflect median earnings in your geographic location.

Trade publications and professional associations

Association sites for a particular profession might be one of the most reliable sources of salary information. Some sites do not have salary surveys listed among their menus, but a call or e-mail to the site administrator might reveal how that information can be obtained. Trade publications often run their own salary surveys, so search their Web sites. For example, Ad Age features salary information that is fairly detailed. One pitfall about trade and association web sites: you often need to be a subscriber to access information.

Negotiating Your Salary

You should be fully prepared to negotiate your salary. Conduct research, and have an appropriate salary range in mind based on the open position, the industry, and the geographic location.

Image Source Black/Jupiter Images

Help the employer see the benefits you could bring to the organization. Be honest, straightforward, and courteous with the interviewer. Look at the big picture, including the benefits, such as the number of vacation days and a 401(k) plan. Conduct relevant research that provides an objective measure of your salary requirements. Never mention your reason for needing a certain salary. That is not how business decisions are made, and you will appear unprofessional. You also risk losing ground in the negotiations. Instead, speak in terms of how hiring you will benefit the organization.

Sasha spoke with a representative at Cabot Industries about salary. He presented his research and objectively explained the basis for his figures. He focused the discussion on his potential contributions to Cabot based on his skills and accomplishments and the benefits he could bring to the company. He provided a salary range based on his research, and, after some negotiation, received a job offer.

Negotiation Tactics

The topic of compensation (salary and benefits) is inevitable if you are being seriously considered for a job. To put yourself in the strongest bargaining position, try to postpone discussion of salary until you receive a job offer. If the topic of salary comes up too soon, the interviewer's focus could shift too far away from your qualifications, costing you the job. As any salesperson knows, first concentrate on what the "buyer" will gain (your qualifications) before focusing on the price (your compensation).

The following tips will help you achieve a win-win solution that both you and your future employer are satisfied with.

- Do not accept the job offer without discussing compensation.
- Whenever possible, let the interviewer raise the topic of compensation.

- Aim for a salary that equals your qualifications. The higher you start, the higher the final offer is likely to be. Don't specify a minimum requirement. If you do, the employer will likely select it.

- If the interviewer asks what salary you want, ask what figure or range the company is planning to pay. If the number is higher than you expected, you have helped yourself by not stating a lower figure first. If it's lower, you now have a place to begin negotiations.

- When the interviewer presses you for your salary requirement, respond by stating the national average for a person with your experience, education, and training. Then discuss what range you expect based on the local costs of living. Be sure to research the facts first!

- If the interviewer brings up the subject of salary too early in the interview (before you have adequately covered your qualifications), delay discussion of the topic by asking to first discuss the position further.

- Do not discuss your expenses or any other sources of income.

- While discussing salary, always return to your assets. Review all you have to offer the company.

- Once you state your salary range, do not back down, particularly if you think it is equal to your qualifications. The employer will respect your confidence about the quality and worth of your work.

- Always discuss the benefits along with the salary.

- Ask how the organization determines compensation increases and the frequency of salary reviews. If increases are good, they can offset a somewhat lower starting salary.

- If the salary offer is made in a letter and the salary is too low, arrange an appointment to discuss it in person, not by letter or telephone.

- If the salary isn't acceptable, state the salary you would accept, and close by reaffirming your interest in the company and the job. If the interviewer needs more time to consider your request, wait one week and then call back. If the interviewer refuses your request, express regret that you were unable to work out a compromise, and restate your interest in the position and the organization. Send a follow-up thank-you letter within two days; it could swing the decision in your favor.

Check Point

What is a compensation package?

THINK CRITICALLY

1. How would you react if an employer's salary offer, which is set through the human resources department and is non-negotiable, did not meet your requirements?

2. List and describe five components of a salary other than hourly wages or annual salary.

3. Explain the difference between a 401(k) and a 403(b) plan.

4. Why should you try to postpone the discussion of salary until you receive a job offer?

MAKE ACADEMIC CONNECTIONS

5. **SURVEY** Do most organizations pay the full cost of insurance premiums? Or do most require employees to contribute? Survey your network contacts to find out. If you need more information, contact the human resources departments of some local companies and ask about their insurance benefits. Create a graph of your results and be prepared to discuss it in class.

6. **COMPANY RESEARCH** Employers are getting more creative in the benefits they offer employees. For example, some give employees a day off on their birthdays and some arrange weekly chair massages. Use company web sites to find more examples of creative benefits. Pay attention to the industries and locations of the companies you research. Do you see any trends? Are companies in certain industries or locations more or less creative in their benefits than those in other industries of locations? Create a PowerPoint presentation to report your results.

VOCABULARY BUILDER

Choose the term that best fits the definition. Write the letter of the answer in the space provided. Some terms may not be used.

_____ 1. The amount of money that must be paid for a good or service

_____ 2. How much of a product is offered to the market

_____ 3. A combination of salary and other benefits

_____ 4. An addition to a base salary that consists of dollars per hour for extra hours worked

_____ 5. An addition to a base salary that consists of opportunities to invest in the company's stock at a lower price than the current price per share

_____ 6. How much of a product consumers are willing to purchase

_____ 7. An addition to a base salary that consists of a percentage of sales

_____ 8. An accumulation of money that an employee can access upon retirement

_____ 9. An addition to a base salary that consists of special earnings based on performance

_____ 10. An individual investment plan in which contributions to stock or mutual funds are deducted directly from an employee's paycheck; available to employees of non-government organizations

a. 401(k)

b. 403(b)

c. benefits

d. bonus

e. commission

f. commodity

g. compensation package

h. cost of living

i. demand

j. flexible benefits plan

k. overtime

l. pension

m. price

n. profit sharing

o. salary

p. salary range

q. stock options

r. supply

REVIEW CONCEPTS

www.cengage.com/school/marketing/yourself

11. How does price communicate value?

12. How was paper money first used in the American colonies?

13. What does it mean to have realistic requirements related to employment?

14. Explain why money has no value until it is exchangeable for goods and services.

15. Describe how coins replaced earlier commodities.

16. Why do some positions pay higher salaries than others?

17. How can considering market forces help you make informed career decisions?

18. Why is researching salaries before determining your ideal salary range so important?

19. What is cost of living?

20. What are benefits?

APPLY WHAT YOU LEARNED

21. List four characteristics of preferred commodities.

22. You have decided to buy a new television. Currently, two TVs are on sale for the same price. Explain how you would decide which TV to buy.

23. What usually happens to salary when there is a lot of competition for a position? Why? List some examples of positions for which competition is high.

24. How can you affect the salary you are offered by an employer?

25. Why are some organizations unwilling to share salary information?

26. Why should you avoid using only one source for your salary research?

MAKE ACADEMIC CONNECTIONS

27. **HISTORY** Research the history of paper money further. You've learned that it came into use in the American colonies as a way to certify tobacco as a commodity. How did it come into use in other parts of the world? Can you find out where paper money was first used? Create a poster to display your results to the class.

28. PROFESSIONAL ASSOCIATIONS Have other associations released resolutions similar to the National Education Association's resolution on pay equity and comparable worth (from the *Diversity in the Workplace* feature in Lesson 8.1)? Use your local library or the Internet to find such statements. How are they similar to the NEA's resolution? How are they different?

29. INTERNET RESEARCH Choose an occupation that you're interested in. Then go to www.cengage.com/school/marketing/yourself to access the web sites for this exercise. Find salary information and other useful information on the web sites that you can use in your job search. Organize your results into a table, using the columns headings shown below. Write a two-page description and analysis of your results. Which site or sites would you use again to research salary information?

Web Site	Salary Information	Other Useful Information

Business Financial Plan

A financial plan is essential to the success of any business. You and your teammates are challenged to establish a complete financial plan for a successful restaurant that wants to open two additional locations in a community with 250,000 people. The financial plan must be economically and financially sound within a realistic time frame.

You will prepare a synopsis of 400 words or less that summarizes the loan needed to open two additional locations for a successful local restaurant. Plans must not exceed 15 pages. The financial plan must include a Synopsis; Company Description (legal form of business, company mission, company governance, company location, long- and short-term goals); Operations and Management (business facilities, management personnel, workforce); Target Market (current target market and future sales potential); Financial Institution (name of financial institution and rationale for choosing the financial institution); Loan Request (purpose, amount, planned expenditures, planned repayment for the loan and projected future stability of the company); and Supporting Documents.

You have seven minutes to present the plan to convince the judge to extend a loan for a successful business expansion. The judge(s) will have three minutes to ask questions about your proposal.

"Diabetes can be really challenging sometimes. It's hard to know what I can and can't eat or do. I signed up for a diabetes management workshop at the local hospital to learn how to manage my diabetes as part of my lifestyle."

Health educators help individuals and communities understand and adopt healthy lifestyles through education. Health educators teach the public how to detect possible health problems in their early stages, how to avoid some illnesses through lifestyle changes, as well as the impact of their behaviors on overall health and well-being. They determine the kinds of needs that exist for an audience and determine how to most effectively meet those needs. They may organize a class, workshop, demonstration, or even a health screening. They also are involved in developing marketing materials for these initiatives, such as brochures, pamphlets, posters, DVDs, and web sites, as well as grant writing, curriculum development, and logistics.

Employment Outlook

Jobs are expected to grow much faster than average.

Job Titles

- Public health educator
- Clinical instructor
- Community health consultant
- Health promotion specialist
- Nurse educator
- Community health education coordinator

Necessary Skills

- A bachelor's degree usually is the minimum requirement, and many positions may require a master's degree.
- The ability to work with many different people with diverse needs and backgrounds and to maintain effective relationships is essential.
- Creativity and effective writing skills are important for the development of new programs and materials.

- Strong public speaking skills are essential for classroom teaching and presentations.

What's It Like to Work in Health Education?

Colin is a health education specialist at the local hospital. To prepare for this job Colin worked for several years as an RN, and then he went back to school. He studied education and communication and earned a bachelor's degree. He puts his education and experience to good use assessing the health education needs of the local community and planning initiatives to address those needs. He has been on the phone all morning finalizing the schedule for the senior expo and confirming the speakers and participants so he can get the information to the marketing department.

Colin is meeting with the lead science teacher at the high school during lunch, hoping to plan an anti-drug program that will be co-sponsored by the police department. He wants to make sure the program will cover not just the legal ramifications, but also the effects of drugs on the health and development of teens. After lunch, he plans to research support groups for the families of patients with life-threatening illnesses, as he hopes to begin a support group at the hospital. Before he ends the work day, he needs to review the curriculum for the diabetes education program that starts next week with the doctor and nurse who will be helping teach the program.

What About You?

What health-related issues do you think are important to the students at your school, and what kinds of programs would you develop to address them if you worked in health education? How would you generate student interest?

Chapter 9

Product Promotion: Correspondence and Other Tools

9.1 Business Correspondence

9.2 Structure and Etiquette

9.3 Employment Correspondence

CAREERS IN MARKETING

AT&T

AT&T provides wireless service, local and long-distance telephone service, directory publishing, advertising services, and high-speed Internet access to millions of customers worldwide. A leader in smartphones, Wi-Fi and mobile broadband, AT&T focuses on communication innovation and continues to explore new opportunities.

©iofoto, 2009/ Used under license from Shutterstock.com

The eCommerce Market Development Manager at AT&T is responsible for managing business-to-consumer eCommerce initiatives. In addition to working with the catalog, marketing, and product teams, the eCommerce Market Development Manager works with supply chain partners to coordinate merchandise for promotions.

The position requires strong communication and analytic skills, eCommerce experience, an understanding of web technology, and a college degree, preferably in business and marketing. The position also requires the ability to prioritize tasks while working in a fast-paced, dynamic environment.

Think *Critically*

1. Why is the ability to prioritize tasks important for this position?
2. Why does AT&T innovate and explore new opportunities?

PORTFOLIO BUILDER PROJECT
Writing Effective Letters

Project Objectives

Cover letters, letters of inquiry, and thank-you letters may seem secondary to your resume and interview skills, but they can make all the difference. In this project you will:

- Understand what goes into an effective cover letter.
- Learn how to write an engaging letter of inquiry.
- Write an appropriate thank-you letter.

Getting Started

Read the Project Process below. Look at the supporting material on the Portfolio Builder CD.

- Read the sample cover letter, paying attention to the focus of each paragraph.
- Note the differences between the sample cover letter and the sample letter of inquiry (also called an unsolicited cover letter).
- Study the sample thank-you letter.

Project Process

Part 1   LESSON 9.1
Read the section in this chapter about cover letters. Use the Internet or newspaper classifieds to find an advertised position in your field of interest. Research the employer by browsing its web site or visiting a library. Draft a cover letter that responds to the advertisement.

Part 2   LESSON 9.2   Read the section in this chapter about letters of inquiry. Research an employer that you would like to work for but that does not have an advertised position in your area of interest. Write a letter of inquiry. Note that a letter of inquiry, unlike a cover letter, focuses its opening paragraph on the employer's needs and concerns. As with a regular cover letter, though, the purpose of this letter is to convince the employer to read your resume and offer you an interview.

Part 3   LESSON 9.3   Read the section in this chapter on thank-you letters. Thank-you letters show that you are professional and courteous. They also re-mind interviewers of your name so they will be more likely to remember you. Write a thank-you note for this situation: You followed up your interview with a telephone call, but you do not know whether you will be offered the position.

Project Wrap-Up

Write a thank-you letter for a situation in which you learn that you did not get a position. Why is it important to write a thank-you letter in this situation?

©Galushko Sergey, 2009/Used under license from Shutterstock.com

Business Correspondence

©mangostock, 2009/Used under license from Shutterstock.com

Goals

- Discover the importance of writing for your audience
- Learn to focus on the purpose of your document
- Understand the basic elements of persuasive business correspondence

Key Terms

- audience
- business correspondence
- purpose
- informative correspondence
- request correspondence
- goodwill correspondence
- persuasive correspondence

Finding Your Audience

What do successful comedians, politicians, talk-show hosts, advertisers, and writers have in common? They all understand the importance of the **audience** —the people who view, read, or listen to their material. Successful professionals in every industry know that different people respond to material in different ways.

Imagine you're a speech writer for the President of the United States. You know the President's new budget will cut funds for the military and increase funds for public schools. This week, the President will speak at a public school convention, at a military banquet, and on national television. Would you write the same speech for all three events? A savvy speech writer would consider the different audiences and compose three versions.

You've probably noticed that the same stories, news items, and films are entertaining or interesting to some people and boring or unpleasant to others. Identifying, understanding, and relating to your audience are critical when developing **business correspondence** —letters, e-mail messages, phone conversations, and other forms of workplace communication.

Who Is My Audience?

Before you develop business correspondence of any kind, always determine who your audience is. Think about who you are trying to reach and who

marketing matters

Freda Gray is responsible for setting up the brochure displays for her travel agency. Spring Break at the local college is just around the corner, and Freda plans to make a special display of travel destinations to warm climates. What kind of images should she use in these brochures? How would the images differ if the brochures were geared toward senior citizens?

diversity in the workplace

Think about how you view different groups of people. Do you have a certain perception about police officers? When you think of librarians, what comes to mind?

Although your perceptions may be true for one person, or even many people, in a particular group, they are not accurate for the entire group, and they lead to false assumptions. You should try to abandon your preconceived notions and see each person as unique.

One of the most important things to learn is that we all carry prejudices. Think of how you feel about different cultural groups. Like faulty perceptions, there are damaging generalizations that are never true for every member of a particular group. It's important to acknowledge your prejudices and work to eliminate them. Give each person a fair chance to prove himself or herself as an individual.

will receive your message. Will your message be received by everyone you try to reach? Might it be received by some people you weren't trying to reach?

Imagine you're writing a letter to existing customers about a new version of your company's software that is faster than the version they currently use. Look at the job titles of your readers. A computer engineer or network administrator will probably be more interested in the technical details of the software, while a CEO will probably be more interested in the general benefits to the company, such as increased productivity or decreased costs.

Knowing your audience will help you focus on the information that matters most to those people. Finding your audience involves three steps.

1. Identifying what kinds of people make up your audience

2. Understanding the interests and outlooks of those people

3. Relating to those people by focusing on their interests and outlooks

Identifying To identify your audience, consider their ages, socioeconomic backgrounds, ethnic backgrounds, knowledge of your subject, and any other factors that may influence how they receive the information.

Understanding To understand your audience, think about how the factors you've identified will affect the way you present the information. Put yourself in their shoes. What interests them? Why do they need this information? What may they have difficulty in understanding?

Relating To relate to your audience, adjust your content and style to their needs and interests. For example, an audience with a solid understanding of your subject may be insulted if you tell them too much about what they already know. Be sure not to offend anyone by communicating exclusively to one group: Don't address your audience as "ladies" unless you are *positive* there are no men present!

Workshop

Imagine you are a graphic designer giving two presentations next week about your work experience—one to a potential client and one to a group of fourth-graders learning about different careers. In groups, make a list of differences between the two presentations.

Check > Point

Why do audiences warm up to certain presenters, performers, or teachers?

Establishing Your Purpose

Once you've found your audience, it's time to think about your purpose for communicating. Your **purpose** is your reason for communicating. If you establish your purpose before beginning, you'll find that business correspondence—from quick phone calls to potential employers to letters of apology to clients—is much easier to prepare and easier to understand.

What Is My Purpose?

Several common purposes are described below. Most business correspondence combines more than one of these purposes.

Informative correspondence describes or explains something. Examples include describing ordering policies to customers or teaching new employees how to operate office equipment.

Request correspondence makes a request or asks the audience to clarify something. Examples include inquiring about services offered or asking your supervisor for an opportunity to give a presentation.

Goodwill correspondence expresses support, thanks, or care. Examples include thank-you letters or memos that recognize achievements.

Persuasive correspondence attempts to convince the audience to believe or take action toward something. Examples include describing the benefits of a product or explaining why a new procedure should be adopted.

Crowther & Carter/GettyImages

Persuading Your Audience

Think of a time when you wanted something from a parent or caregiver. Perhaps it was a new pet, a pair of running shoes, or a privilege, such as staying out late or going to a concert. While nobody gets everything they want, you probably fared much better when you justified your opinions with facts and demonstrated the benefits of getting what you wanted.

Photodisc/Getty Images

As a professional in the business world, you will want many things—sales, new clients, promotions, and opportunities to carry out your ideas, just to name a few. While you won't get everything you want, you'll fare much better when you learn how to communicate persuasively.

Essentials of Persuasion

Although the purpose of your business correspondence might not be directly persuasive, everything you communicate is persuasive on some level. Your business correspondence influences how people perceive you and will be one of your most valuable tools for marketing yourself. The following strategies are all essential elements of persuasion.

Meet the Needs of Your Audience Identify and focus on your audience's wants or needs. Why does your audience need this product? What information do they need most?

Relay the Benefits and Features Talk about the features and benefits of what you're offering. As you learned in Chapter 3, *features* are part of a product or proposal's design, such as the type of material used or a project schedule. *Benefits* are descriptions of how those features will help the audience, such as saving them money or increasing productivity.

marketing math connection

Advertising rates are based on an ad's reach through a particular medium. Reach refers to how many people see or hear an ad. The number of people reached by an ad is usually a measurable number. It may be the number of subscribers, readers, listeners, households in a geographic area, or cars passing a certain location. Internet sites may define reach as the number of hits, registrations, or searches beyond the home page. The cost per person of an ad is found by dividing the ad's cost by the number of people reached.

A furniture store spent $3,640 on a newspaper ad featuring a sale on leather sofas. In the next two days, 130 people who looked at the sofas said they saw the ad. What was the cost of the ad for each shopper who was attracted by the ad?

SOLUTION

Cost per shopper reached = Total cost of ad ÷ Shoppers reached

$$= \$3,640 \div 130$$

$$= \$28$$

Validate Your Opinions Your opinions will carry more weight when you back them up with research, facts, expert opinions, case studies, and real-life experiences.

Establish Your Qualifications Before an audience will accept what you have to say, they must feel that you are a reliable and trustworthy resource. Show why you are qualified to present the information. Talk about past successes that relate to your topic.

Express Your Position Clearly Like all business communications, persuasive correspondence should be logical and well structured. Make clear points with smooth transitions between major topics.

Check Point

Why is persuasive business correspondence an important way to market yourself?

THINK CRITICALLY

1. List the three steps involved in identifying your audience.

2. Why should you be careful when using humor in business correspondence?

3. Match each passage to its primary purpose:

   a. Informative; b. Request; c. Goodwill; d. Persuasive

   1. I think you will be pleasantly surprised by our new merchandise! As a preferred customer, you may use your 10% discount.

   2. This letter shall confirm your acceptance of the verbal order communicated to you on November 16, 2010.

   3. We are writing to ask for permission to reprint an excerpt from the commencement speech given at Pierce Community College on May 30, 2010.

   4. Congratulations on achieving the November sales goal!

4. Explain how to consider your audience when developing persuasive business correspondence.

MAKE ACADEMIC CONNECTIONS

5. **BUSINESS PRACTICES** When businesses want to sell their products to an extremely large audience, they often mail form letters—letters that have the same text—to thousands of people on their mailing lists. Your family has probably received hundreds of form letters in the mail. In your opinion, how effective are form letters? Write two paragraphs to defend your position.

6. **HISTORY** The Civil War made the 1860s a turbulent time in American history. One of the most eloquent writers of all time, President Abraham Lincoln wrote several letters to citizens, military personnel, and politicians about what the country was facing. Search the Internet or the library for these letters. Choose one letter, and evaluate it based on what you've learned in this lesson. How does Abraham Lincoln relate to his audience, convey his purpose, and persuade his audience?

INTERNET

@

Structure and Etiquette

Goals
- Create effective business correspondence
- Revise and check your work
- Discover the fundamentals of phone correspondence

Key Terms
- structure
- etiquette
- letterhead
- salutation

Business Letters, Memos, and E-Mail

Business letters are used for external communications—communications from your company to a client or customer or from you to a potential employer, for example. Memos are used for internal communications—communications within a group or organization, such as notices about policies, procedures, and events. E-mail is used for a variety of internal *and* external business communications.

Letters, memos, and e-mail messages reflect your ability to think, express ideas, sell, and distribute information. They also reflect your ability to act professionally and follow accepted standards. To ensure your business letters, memos, and e-mail messages place you in the best light, they must employ appropriate **structure** (organization and format) and **etiquette** (rules of social behavior).

Business Letters

To paint a good picture of yourself and your company, your business letters should conform to the following rules of etiquette.

- Be polite. Use an accommodating, courteous tone. Express appreciation and a willingness to help.

marketing matters

José is looking for a child care provider to look after his toddler while he is at work. He calls four day care centers and asks them to send information about their services. Happy Kids sends him a hand-written message on a post-it note, clipped to one of their newspaper advertisements. José immediately eliminates them. What did Happy Kids do wrong? If you worked at a day care center, what would you send to impress José?

Cultura/GettyImages

- Be professional. Though you don't want to sound arrogant or cold, use a formal tone that reflects the manners and behavior appropriate to your profession.

Letterhead Business letters are typically written on **letterhead**—special stationery with the company's name, logo, and contact information. Make your own letterhead if you are sending a personal business letter, such as a letter to a potential employer. *Never use company letterhead for your personal business.*

Other essential components of a business letter are placed in the following order, from top to bottom. Each part should be separated by one blank line.

Date Include the month, date, and year.

Reader's Address Include the reader's name, title, company, and complete address.

Salutation A **salutation** is a formal introductory greeting. Your salutation should begin "Dear Mr. _____:" or Dear Ms. _____:". If you don't know the recipient's name, a title such as "Dear Sales Manager:" would be appropriate. If you know the person well, you can end the salutation with a comma instead of a colon.

Body The body includes the entire message, or content, of your letter. Always break main ideas into separate paragraphs. A paragraph can be one sentence long if that sentence is something that should stand out, such as an important selling point or a statement expressing goodwill.

Closing Close your letter with "Sincerely," "Best regards," or another appropriate expression. Leave two to four blank lines between your closing and your typed name to allow space for your signature.

Sender's Signature Sign your name below your closing.

Sender's Name and Position Type your name and your position (if appropriate). If you have a business e-mail address and/or phone extension that isn't included in the company letterhead, include that information.

See the sample letter on page 239.

Memos

Though internal company communications, such as memos, are less formal in tone than business letters, you must still be polite and professional!

Main Headings The first lines of a memo are the main headings. They are:

- TO:
- FROM:
- SUBJECT:
- DATE:

Salutation Not all memos include salutations, but you can use one if you like. If you are writing to a supervisor who prefers being addressed formally, use a formal salutation. If you have a casual relationship with a

---

Workshop

The copier in your office has been jamming for weeks! You've just discovered what has been causing the trouble. In small groups, write an office memo to all employees in your company explaining how to prevent the paper jams.

supervisor or coworker, using their first name only is fine. In many cases, you will be addressing a group of people, such as a department (for example, "Dear Sales Team:").

Body Keep the body short. Include only the ideas that make your point most effectively.

Sender's Name or Initials Include your full name or your initials. A closing is not necessary, but you can include one if you like.

Attachments If you are enclosing or attaching a document relevant to the memo, alert the audience by adding an "Attachment:" line.

Notice of Other Readers Identify the names of people who are receiving a copy of the memo by adding a "c:" or "cc:" line. List only people who are not included in the "TO:" line.

See the sample memo on page 240.

E-Mail

E-mail has become an extremely popular means for conveying information in the workplace. Workplace e-mail ranges from casual reminders to coworkers to formal letters to customers. Though your most casual forms of business correspondence may be e-mail messages, your workplace e-mail should be as formal as the situation requires.

Include a Subject Line It is common courtesy to alert your readers to the topic of your message. Filling in the subject line also helps recipients organize their e-mail messages.

Use Short Paragraphs Long paragraphs are difficult to read on screen. Split main ideas into brief paragraphs. When transferring a large amount of information, attach a longer document to your e-mail message.

Be Professional Though business e-mails may be less formal in structure and more casual in tone, it is important to convey your message professionally. Use proper capitalization and punctuation. NEVER USE ALL CAPITAL LETTERS—it is the e-mail equivalent of shouting. Avoid potentially confusing language, such as humor, sarcasm, slang, and jargon. And, as you learned in Lesson 5.3, don't use emoticons in business correspondence.

Respond Promptly A quick response lets your reader know that he or she is important to you.

See the sample e-mail message on page 240.

Check Point

How would an e-mail to a potential client differ from an e-mail to a client you've talked with nearly every day for over a year?

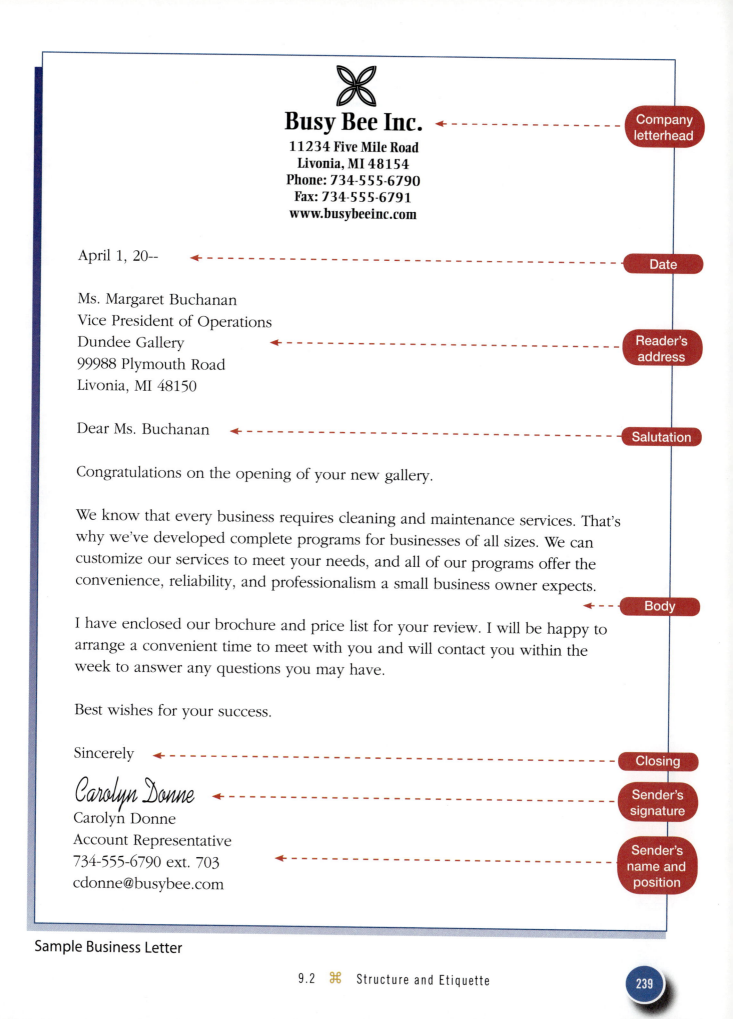

Busy Bee Inc.
11234 Five Mile Road
Livonia, MI 48154
Phone: 734-555-6790
Fax: 734-555-6791
www.busybeeinc.com

Company letterhead

April 1, 20--

Date

Ms. Margaret Buchanan
Vice President of Operations
Dundee Gallery
99988 Plymouth Road
Livonia, MI 48150

Reader's address

Dear Ms. Buchanan

Salutation

Congratulations on the opening of your new gallery.

We know that every business requires cleaning and maintenance services. That's why we've developed complete programs for businesses of all sizes. We can customize our services to meet your needs, and all of our programs offer the convenience, reliability, and professionalism a small business owner expects.

Body

I have enclosed our brochure and price list for your review. I will be happy to arrange a convenient time to meet with you and will contact you within the week to answer any questions you may have.

Best wishes for your success.

Sincerely

Closing

Carolyn Donne

Sender's signature

Carolyn Donne
Account Representative
734-555-6790 ext. 703
cdonne@busybee.com

Sender's name and position

Sample Business Letter

Interoffice Memo

TO:	Christopher Reid, Sales Team Manager
FROM:	Josefina Vaughn, CEO
SUBJECT:	"Selling Technology" Seminar
DATE:	June 18, 20--

Christopher:

A seminar on "Selling Technology" is being held at the Mabrick Hotel on August 15. It is being conducted by Tech Industries, and should be extremely informative.

I strongly recommend that every member of the sales force attend this seminar. The department will, of course, pay the entrance fees. Please encourage everyone to attend and provide me with the names of attendees no later than July 15. Thank you.

JV

Attachment: Selling Technology seminar brochure

cc: Jack Michaels, Heath Walker

Main headings

Salutation (optional)

Body

Sender's name or initials

Attachment

Notice of other readers

Sample Memo

FROM:	Anne Fleming
TO:	Susan Morganza
SUBJECT:	Training schedule

Good morning Susan,

I've attached training schedules for everyone in your department. Please tell everyone to bring along some snacks--the training will overlap lunchtime by an hour or so. Thanks!

Anne

Sample Casual E-Mail

Accuracy and Revisions

All letters, memos, and e-mail messages should be factual, grammatically correct, and free of spelling errors and typos. No written business correspondence is finished until it has received a thorough review for textual errors and accuracy. Be sensitive to the writer's feelings when suggesting revisions, and be willing to accept revisions from others. Even the best writers rely on feedback from editors.

Checking Your Facts

Checking your facts and figures is a big part of the revision process. Don't send business correspondence that is incorrect or misleading. Pay special attention to numbers, factual statements, and specific details. Being "pretty sure" is not good enough—do your research.

Making Revisions

Revising written documents involves adding, deleting, and rearranging information. It also involves checking for spelling and grammar errors. When making revisions, you need to check the structure, content, and language of the document.

- **Check the structure** Are all of the necessary parts present? Are they in the correct order? Are the main ideas easy to find? Would the document be easier to read if it used a different font type or font size?

- **Check the content** Is the information accurate? Are the facts correct? Is the information complete—do you need to add information to address the reader's questions? Is any of the information unnecessary?

Photodisc/Getty Images

- **Check the language** Are there grammar, punctuation, or spelling errors? Is the tone professional? Is the writing style appropriate for the audience? Are any sentences or paragraphs unclear?

Check Point

Your supervisor gives you a five-page business report and asks you to revise it. You notice that the organization is hard to follow and the headings have too many different font styles. What kind of revision will this be?

Telephone Correspondence

Every day, businesses rely on the phone to stay in touch with customers, business contacts, and coworkers. The phone is also an important tool for making contacts when you're looking for work.

Business Telephone Etiquette

You've probably been using the phone since you could talk. However, it's important to understand that phone correspondence in the workplace requires more than basic phone manners. Poor business phone etiquette could "disconnect" you from a potential sale or a potential job.

Answering Calls Always answer the phone by the third ring—it make your caller feel valued. Identify yourself when you pick up the phone, for example, "Hello, Red Marble Marketing. This is Alonzo." Be pleasant when you answer. Don't sound hurried or annoyed. Learn your company's phone system, so that you can effectively transfer calls and place callers on hold. When taking a message for someone else, be thorough.

Making Calls Before you make a call, think about your purpose for calling. To establish a friendly relationship with the person you're calling, start with a greeting and a brief opening remark, for example, "Hello Mr. Gold. Do you have a few moments to discuss our proposal?" While you shouldn't rush yourself or the person you're calling, be sure not to waste your listener's time. When you've finished, quickly summarize the conversation, confirm any commitments you've made, and close with a pleasant good-bye.

Speaking and Listening Speak slowly, keep your voice at a conversational volume, and use the caller's name occasionally. Be efficient, sound confident, and be an attentive listener. Take notes as you listen—record the purpose of the call, the caller's name, the date, and the time.

Using Voice Mail or an Answering Machine Program your voice mail to answer by the third ring as well. Create an answering machine or voice mail greeting that is brief and clear, and avoid messages that are clever or cute. Check your messages a few times each day (several times each day when you're away from the office). Return calls promptly—a missed call is often a missed opportunity.

Leaving Messages When leaving a message with a business contact, speak more slowly than normal, so that the other person does not need to listen to your message more than once. Pronounce your name clearly, and spell it slowly if necessary. Be brief—give your company name, title, your reason for calling, and the best times to call back. If the message must be long, repeat your name and phone number at the end.

Check▶Point

Why should you check your messages regularly?

THINK CRITICALLY

1. How are business letters and memos used in the workplace? Give examples.

2. Why should you include a subject line in your e-mail messages?

3. List the three main things to look for when revising documents. Give an example of each revision type.

4. How should you adjust your speech when leaving a message? Why?

MAKE ACADEMIC CONNECTIONS

5. **TECHNOLOGY** A teleconference is a meeting held among people in different places by means of a speaker phone. Businesses use teleconferences to cut down on expenses and lost productivity that comes with business travel. However, teleconferences present some structural hurdles and unique standards of etiquette. For example, how would you ensure that everyone doesn't speak at once? How would you ensure that the meeting is comprehensible to those who are not in the room? Make a short list of teleconference etiquette, explaining why each etiquette rule is necessary. Think about special considerations, such as planning and equipment, in addition to general etiquette.

6. **BUSINESS PRACTICES** When you use your company e-mail, you are using your employer's time and equipment. That's one reason that your company e-mail should only be used for work-related communication. Another reason is a common business practice—e-mail monitoring. Employers are entitled by law to read what you send from your company e-mail address and many will not notify you that they are doing so. Monitoring employee e-mail allows employers to track and prevent illegal activity. It also tells employers who is spending work time on personal business. However, many employees feel that e-mail monitoring is an invasion of their constitutional rights. What do you think? Use the Internet to research the practice of monitoring e-mail, and write a one-page report arguing for or against this business practice.

Employment Correspondence

Goals
- Create effective traditional and e-mail cover letters
- Create effective inquiry letters
- Understand the importance of thanking employment contacts and potential employers

Key Terms
- cover letter
- networking
- inquiry letter
- networking letters
- cold cover letters

Crafting Your Cover Letters

Throughout the course of your working life, you may draft, write, and revise hundreds or thousands of business letters. While much of that correspondence will be instrumental in selling yourself and the people you represent, the most important letter of all is your cover letter. A **cover letter** introduces your resume and is used when submitting a formal application for a job opening.

Why is a cover letter the most important letter? Combined with a winning resume, it is your gateway to the job of your dreams. When recruiters and hiring managers place advertisements for job openings, they may receive tens, hundreds, or even thousands of applications! For that reason, cover letters should not be taken lightly. They should grab the employer's attention and explain why you are the person who best meets the employer's needs.

Traditional Cover Letters

Before the Internet and e-mail, only one type of cover letter was used in a job search—a formal, one-page letter, printed on "good" paper. Today's job searches use e-mail cover letters more frequently, but the formal, traditional cover letter is still a major player in employment correspondence. The success of your job search will largely depend upon your ability to write traditional cover letters that sell.

marketing matters

Donna Wang is looking for a job. She doesn't feel secure about her writing skills, so she decides to hire a writing service to develop one cover letter that she can use for all of her job applications—all she has to do is change the contact information, the place of business, and the position title. What do you think about Donna's strategy? How do you think employers will respond to her cover letters?

Blend Images/Getty Images

When an employer specifically asks for a cover letter, you'll want to send a traditional cover letter printed on matching resume paper. Traditional cover letters should demonstrate knowledge about the hiring organization and explain how you meet the employer's needs.

Like all business correspondence, your cover letter should be concise, clear, professional, polite, and free of errors. Pay special attention to the spelling of the company's name, the addressee's name, and the addressee's title. Check for smudges, unattractive format, or other elements that will detract from the content. Don't forget to sign the letter—it shows that you are attentive to details. If you are sending your cover letter and resume through e-mail or a web site, a signature isn't necessary.

Traditional Cover Letter Structure

The overall structure of a cover letter is exactly like that of a business letter. The body of the letter, however, has a unique structure. The best formula for writing the body of a traditional cover letter uses three main paragraphs. See the example on page 249.

Paragraph 1: The Opening Briefly state the name of the position and where and when you found the listing. Include a concise statement about how your skills match the required qualifications. Then, focus on what you know about the company's accomplishments.

Paragraph 2: The Sales Pitch Most important to a prospective employer is whether you meet the company's needs. Be careful not to simply reiterate the experience section of your resume. Describe specifics about how your experience uniquely qualifies you for the position. You may want to list your relevant experiences in a bulleted form for the second paragraph.

©Eduard Titov, 2009/Used under license from Shutterstock.com

Paragraph 3: The Closing Begin with a statement confirming that you are the best candidate for the job. Then, express interest in an interview and indicate that you will follow up with a phone call. Don't use the word "interview" directly. Instead, express an interest in meeting to discuss how your experience meets the requirements of the position. Never directly ask for a job in a cover letter.

Workshop

Most jobs require communication skills. Even professionals in high-tech careers must be able to express ideas and distribute information. Write down everything from your experience that could be considered a communication skill. Then, formulate a one- or two-sentence summary that you could use in a cover letter.

NETBookmark

Many web sites have resources for writers. Go to **www.cengage.com/school/marketing/yourself** and click on the Net Bookmark for this chapter. After visiting several of the web resources for writers, write a cover letter to an employer with which you would like to work.

E-Mail Cover Letters

More and more job seekers and hiring managers are using e-mail to communicate during the recruitment process. In addition to the occasional quick e-mail about interview schedules or directions to a place of business, you'll use e-mail to create shorter versions of your traditional cover letter. Why? Because some hiring managers and human resources professionals don't have time to read stacks of long cover letters, and they prefer a simpler, shorter version. Always send an e-mail cover letter when:

- You are applying for a job online, directly through a company web site or Internet job board.
- A newspaper advertisement gives an e-mail address or web site for applications.

E-Mail Cover Letter Structure

In addition to being much shorter than traditional cover letters, e-mail cover letters are always sent as e-mail text, generally as an accompaniment to an attached or pasted resume. An e-mail cover letter should identify the specifics of the job opening and briefly state that your qualifications meet the employer's needs. The best formula for writing an e-mail cover letter uses one short opening paragraph and a one-sentence closing statement. See the example on page 248.

Opening Paragraph Briefly state the name of the position, job number (if given), and where and when you found the listing. Include a concise statement that expresses your qualifications.

Closing Sentence Express interest in a meeting or an opportunity to discuss the position.

Check Point

How does the structure of a cover letter differ from that of a business letter?

careerbuilder®

Cover Letter Do's and Don'ts

By Kate Lorenz, CareerBuilder.com
Copyright 2007 CareerBuilder, LLC.—Reprinted with permission.

Most people are familiar with the importance of a well-constructed resume, and put a fair amount of time into creating one. But just as important is the cover letter that accompanies and introduces your resume.

In an extremely competitive job market, neglecting your cover letter is a big mistake. Why? A cover letter is your first opportunity to tell a prospective employer about yourself, and to do so in your own words. Like a written interview, a cover letter gives you the opportunity to point out applicable experience and qualities that make you right for the job. And just like any other important job searching tool, there are definite dos and don'ts to follow to make sure your cover letter is an asset, not a hindrance.

Do personalize your letter.
Nobody likes to receive impersonal mail. Cover letters that begin with phrases like "To Whom it May Concern," sound like random junk or bulk mail, rather than an important correspondence. You expect the company to take the time to read through your material, so you too need to take some time to research the correct addressee. Call the company, look on its Web site or talk to others to find the correct contact.

Don't send a generic cover letter to many different companies.
Hiring managers can spot a mass mailing a mile away. What gets their attention are letters that address the company—and its needs—specifically. Research the company prior to writing the letter. Check out recent news and read through the company's Web site, and then incorporate what you learned into your letter. Doing so will demonstrate to employers that you are informed, motivated and willing to go the extra mile.

Do address the specific position advertised.
Companies that post openings are making your life easier by telling you the qualities they are seeking. Show the company that you paid attention. If a company advertises that it is looking for sales experience, make sure you address your sales experience. One way to do this is by making a table for yourself before writing your letter. List the company's stated needs in one column, and your corresponding experience and qualifications in another column. You can then use that information to write a letter that tells them exactly what they want to know.

Don't make the reader work too hard to see that you are right for the position.
Include specific examples about your past successes and experience. If you are looking for a marketing position, give the reader detailed information about a marketing campaign you successfully executed. Don't just tell the reader that you are motivated. Give an example that shows your motivation. You need to lay all of your pertinent information out in a way that lets the

continued on page 248

person making the hiring decision easily see how your experience and qualities fit the company's needs.

Do get to the point.

Hiring managers receive letters and resumes from dozens and even hundreds of applicants, and often just don't have the time to read lengthy, wordy letters. Be direct. In the first paragraph, include the title of the position you are interested in and then move on to your specific qualifications immediately.

Don't end your letter passively.

Nobody gets a job by sitting at home waiting for the phone to ring. Similarly, not many people get a call once a resume or cover letter is sent. Since you are the one looking for work, you need to take the initiative and follow up. Instead of ending the letter with "I look forward to hearing from you," close with "I will call you next week to discuss a time for us to meet." Once you've included this call to action, however, make sure you follow your own promise.

Do write and edit your letter with great care.

Nothing says "I don't really want this job" like a cover letter with typos, incorrect information, or spelling errors. Make sure the company's name is spelled correctly. Check to see if the contact is a male or female. And, while it sounds almost too obvious to mention, be sure to sign your letter. Careless—and easily correctable—mistakes tell the company that you did not take this simple task seriously.

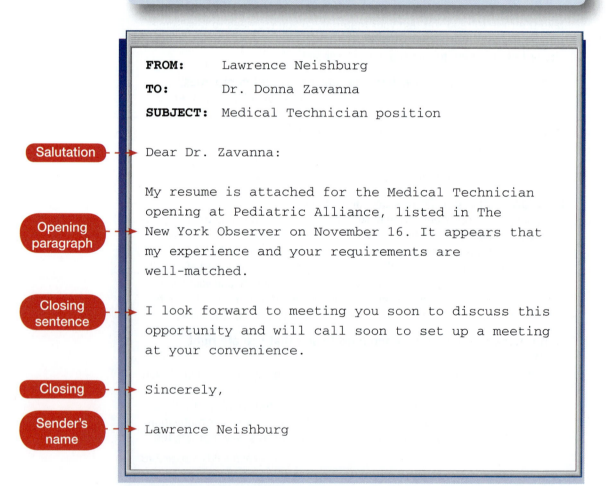

FROM: Lawrence Neishburg

TO: Dr. Donna Zavanna

SUBJECT: Medical Technician position

Salutation → Dear Dr. Zavanna:

Opening paragraph → My resume is attached for the Medical Technician opening at Pediatric Alliance, listed in The New York Observer on November 16. It appears that my experience and your requirements are well-matched.

Closing sentence → I look forward to meeting you soon to discuss this opportunity and will call soon to set up a meeting at your convenience.

Closing → Sincerely,

Sender's name → Lawrence Neishburg

Sample E-Mail Cover Letter

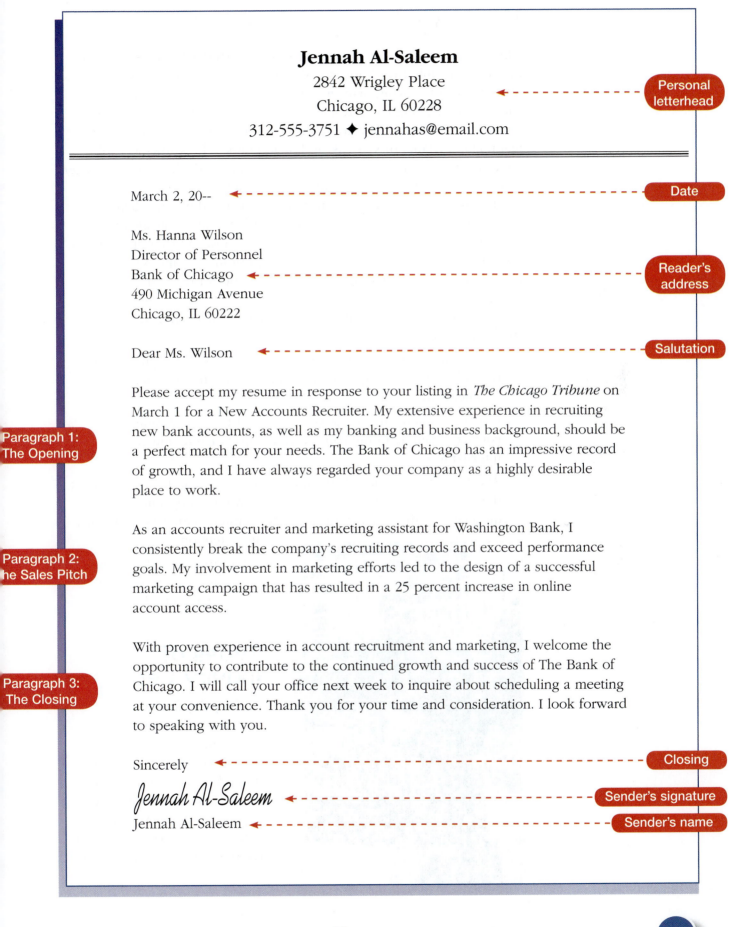

Jennah Al-Saleem

2842 Wrigley Place

Chicago, IL 60228

312-555-3751 ✦ jennahas@email.com

Personal letterhead

March 2, 20--

Date

Ms. Hanna Wilson
Director of Personnel
Bank of Chicago
490 Michigan Avenue
Chicago, IL 60222

Reader's address

Dear Ms. Wilson

Salutation

Please accept my resume in response to your listing in *The Chicago Tribune* on March 1 for a New Accounts Recruiter. My extensive experience in recruiting new bank accounts, as well as my banking and business background, should be a perfect match for your needs. The Bank of Chicago has an impressive record of growth, and I have always regarded your company as a highly desirable place to work.

Paragraph 1: The Opening

As an accounts recruiter and marketing assistant for Washington Bank, I consistently break the company's recruiting records and exceed performance goals. My involvement in marketing efforts led to the design of a successful marketing campaign that has resulted in a 25 percent increase in online account access.

Paragraph 2: The Sales Pitch

With proven experience in account recruitment and marketing, I welcome the opportunity to contribute to the continued growth and success of The Bank of Chicago. I will call your office next week to inquire about scheduling a meeting at your convenience. Thank you for your time and consideration. I look forward to speaking with you.

Paragraph 3: The Closing

Sincerely

Closing

Jennah Al-Saleem

Sender's signature

Jennah Al-Saleem

Sender's name

Writing Inquiry Letters

The most successful job seekers are skilled at **networking**—reaching out to the people they know to ask for job leads, job referrals, and introductions to hiring managers. Friends, family, previous supervisors and coworkers, neighbors, teachers, and members of your clubs and associations are all part of your employment network. Though you may feel uncomfortable or silly asking Uncle Frank if he knows any job contacts in your career field, he may go fishing with the hiring manager of your preferred company—you never know!

Thousands of positions are created and filled without ever being advertised. When you use your network of friends and acquaintances to create new business contacts, you can uncover those hidden opportunities. You can also increase your odds of standing out in an employer's mind, instead of competing with hundreds of applicants for the same advertised listing.

When asking friends, family members, and acquaintances for employment contacts:

- Give them a synopsis of your work experience and explain what type of work you're seeking. You might want to give them a copy of your resume, as well.

- Get as much information as you can about the new business contact—spelling of full name, title, company name, and contact information.

- Ask if you can mention their name when contacting this person or ask them to suggest your name for a position. Mentioning a mutual acquaintance is the best way to earn a new business contact's trust, time, and attention.

Photodisc/GettyImages

- Graciously thank everyone you ask, even those who don't have a lead.

Types of Inquiry Letters

An **inquiry letter** is used to inquire about employment openings, career advice, job leads, or any other information related to your job search. Unlike traditional and e-mail cover letters, however, inquiry letters are not written in direct response to job advertisements.

Their purpose is to generate new job opportunities. There are two main types of inquiry letters.

- **Networking letters** are written to the contacts you've generated from networking. Do not directly inquire about employment in a networking letter. The purpose of networking letters is to request help with job contacts or career strategies.

- **Cold cover letters** are used when your job-search network does not generate contacts in your preferred companies. Though they are not written in response to an advertised opening (hence the term "cold"), they *do* directly inquire about employment.

Inquiry Letter Structure and Etiquette

Both types of inquiry letters—networking letters and cold cover letters—use standard business letter format and etiquette. Like traditional and e-mail cover letters, both should include an attached resume and focus on why you are qualified for the type of work you are seeking. An inquiry letter sent electronically will be shorter than one that is mailed, but it should maintain a professional tone and appearance. Refer to page 238 for guidelines for writing e-mail messages.

Networking Letters Unless you are close friends with the person you are writing to, the first sentence of a networking letter should establish your connection with the reader. (*I attended the "Women in Retail" luncheon last Wednesday and introduced myself to you following your presentation.*)

The remainder of the first paragraph should communicate that you are looking for employment and should state the purpose of your inquiry.

Did You Know?

You might want to express your interest in freelance or full-time work in a cold cover letter. Freelancing gives the employer an opportunity to try you out and gives you an opportunity to show what you can do.

(I am in the process of a job change and am writing to professionals whose opinions I value. If you know of any retail operations that could benefit from the experience of a top-notch retail buyer, I would be grateful for the leads. I have attached my resume for your review.)

The second paragraph should be a brief version of your "sales pitch" paragraph in your cover letter. Offer a short synopsis that focuses on the key selling points of your work experience.

The third paragraph should convey goodwill and express thanks for the reader's time. Be extremely gracious—you are asking your reader to do you a favor. (*I understand the demands of our profession and appreciate your time and consideration. Good luck in all of your endeavors.*)

Cold Cover Letters If you've exhausted your networking options, and no position in your field is available at the company of your dreams, a **cold cover** letter might be your best shot at getting in the door. The body of a cold cover letter is exactly like a traditional cover letter, with the exception of the first paragraph. In the first paragraph, you'll ask about unadvertised opportunities that may be available instead of responding to a specific advertised position (see the example below). The second and third paragraphs will still perform the same functions as a traditional cover letter.

> I first heard of ExtraTech while working as the call center manager at DialUs, Inc. Jill Scott, a colleague who handled your consumer survey, mentioned how much she enjoyed working with you and the staff at ExtraTech. Since then, I've heard nothing but good things about the work you do. I am currently looking for new opportunities in consumer surveys and telephone research, and am certain my experience will benefit your ventures. I have attached my resume for your consideration.

Sample First Paragraph of Cold Cover Letter

Before you write a cold cover letter, do your research. Find out as much as much as you can about the company, and convey that knowledge in the first paragraph. Don't inquire about a specific job title when asking about opportunities. Mentioning a career field or a range of positions you qualify for will increase your chances of finding an opening.

Check▸Point

Describe two ways that cold cover letters differ from networking letters.

Thanking Potential Employers and Job Contacts

Sixty to seventy percent of job seekers find work through networking.

In the business world, time is money. That's why it's so important to thank every person who plays a part in your job search, whether it's a potential employer who interviewed you or a network contact who provided career advice. If you prefer, you may handwrite thank-you letters on professional-looking stationery or cards, instead of typing it on your personal letterhead.

After the Networking Meeting

Maintain strong relationships with your networking contacts by expressing thanks for their time and expertise. A networking letter can be slightly more casual in tone than a post-interview thank-you letter, and should be shorter as well. Try to mention details that will help your contact remember your meeting. See the sample below.

> Thank you for taking time from your busy schedule yesterday to answer my questions about careers in web design. I am now revising my resume to include your helpful suggestions. I will send you a copy next week.
>
> I will keep in contact and follow through on your suggestion to see Julian Valencia about opportunities at CreaTech Designs. Thank you again for your time and thoughtfulness.

Sample Body of Networking Thank-You Letter

After the Interview

A brief, well-written thank-you note may swing the balance in your favor when the employer makes the final decision. Send the interviewer a thank-you letter immediately following your interview—put it in the mail no later than one day after your meeting. A post-interview thank-you should reaffirm your interest in the position, restate your qualifications for the position, and express appreciation for the interviewer's time and courtesy. See the example on the next page.

Check > Point

Think of one way in which thank-you correspondence differs from other business correspondence.

July 19, 20-- ← **Date**

Ms. Theresa Stanzino
Director of Marketing
Miller Media Group ← **Interviewer's name, title, and company name**
3952 Kanawha Blvd.
Charleston, WV 25302

Dear Ms. Stanzino ← **Salutation**

Thank you so much for taking the time to discuss the account representative position at Miller Media Group on July 18th. I enjoyed meeting you and the members of your staff. They were very welcoming, especially when they added my name to the sales board followed by a "0" in new sales! ← **Expression of thanks and details from meeting**

The interview convinced me of how compatible my experience is with the goals of Miller Media. As I mentioned during our conversation, my successful history of developing effective marketing materials for new businesses, such as Karaway Sports and Paul & Sons Supply is a perfect match for the requirements of your position. ← **Reaffirmation of interest in and qualifications for position**

I am looking forward to joining your excellent team, and will be contacting you soon to inquire about the status of the position. ← **Restatement of interest and promise to follow up**

Best regards ← **Closing**

Mary Kay Medine ← **Sender's signature**

(304) 555-2744
mkmedine@email.com ← **Sender's contact information**

THINK CRITICALLY

1. Which paragraph of a traditional cover letter will be of most interest to potential employers? Support your answer.

2. Why do some employers prefer e-mail cover letters?

3. Describe the content of a networking letter's second paragraph.

4. Describe how a post-interview thank-you letter can be an effective tool for marketing yourself. Give at least two examples.

MAKE ACADEMIC CONNECTIONS

5. **MATH** Using your comprehensive list of networking contacts, imagine that each person on your list gives you two new business contacts. Those new contacts then each give you one new business contact. How many contacts do you now have? How many did you have when you started? Show the formula you used for finding your new total.

6. **ART/DESIGN** Use the Internet or the library to find pointers for writing effective post-interview thank-you letters. Combine what you find with the pointers from this lesson to create a poster entitled "Effective Thank-You Letters." Share the poster with your school placement or career office.

VOCABULARY BUILDER

Choose the term that best fits the definition. Write the letter of the answer in the space provided. Some terms may not be used.

_____ 1. A letter used to inquire about employment openings, career advice, job leads, or any other information related to your job search

_____ 2. A letter written to the contacts you've generated that requests help with job contacts or career strategies

_____ 3. A letter used when your job-search network does not generate contacts in your preferred company; the letter directly inquires about unadvertised employment

_____ 4. Reaching out to the people you know to ask for job leads, job referrals, and introductions to hiring managers

_____ 5. Letters, e-mail messages, phone conversations, and other forms of workplace communication

_____ 6. Correspondence that describes or explains something

_____ 7. The people who view, read, and listen to your material

_____ 8. Rules of social behavior

_____ 9. A formal introductory greeting in a letter

_____ 10. Correspondence that expresses support, thanks, or care

_____ 11. Correspondence that asks the reader to clarify something

_____ 12. Special stationery with the company or individual's name and contact information

a. audience

b. business correspondence

c. cold cover letter

d. cover letter

e. etiquette

f. goodwill correspondence

g. informative correspondence

h. inquiry letter

i. letterhead

j. networking

k. networking letter

l. persuasive correspondence

m. purpose

n. request correspondence

o. salutation

p. structure

13. What do successful comedians, politicians, talk-show hosts, advertisers, and writers have in common?

14. List some strategies for validating your opinions.

15. What types of business correspondence are used for internal communications?

16. What are the two basic rules of business correspondence etiquette?

17. Why should you use short paragraphs in your business e-mail messages?

18. When checking your facts, what should you look for?

19. Describe proper phone etiquette when answering calls.

20. Why is a cover letter your most important business letter?

21. What are the two basic parts of an e-mail cover letter?

22. What should you attach to every inquiry letter?

23. When should you send a post-interview thank-you letter?

APPLY WHAT YOU LEARNED

24. Most audiences relate better to benefits than to features. Why do you think this is true? How does this relate to employment correspondence?

25. You are writing a business letter to Janet Johnson, a close friend and colleague. How will you address her in your salutation?

26. You've just asked your coworker, Mohammed, to revise a rough draft of your business report. He hands it back with marks for grammar, spelling, and punctuation only. What did Mohammed miss?

27. How has the Internet changed the way job seekers apply for advertised positions?

28. Why do most job seekers find work through networking instead of through advertised job openings?

MAKE ACADEMIC CONNECTIONS

29. INTERNATIONAL COMMUNICATION Use the Internet to research tips for overcoming communication barriers between people from different countries. Create a short chart that gives pointers on how to understand and relate to audiences with diverse languages and cultures.

30. COMMUNICATE Call five businesses and politely ask them for information about their services. After each call, answer the following questions: Did someone answer within three rings? Did the person politely identify himself or herself? Was your question managed effectively? Did the person reflect positively on the company? Find the two most common etiquette problems, and write up the results of your findings in a business e-mail.

Enterpreneurship

Many Americans dream of owning and managing a business. Teams of two or three members must demonstrate the knowledge and skills needed to establish and manage a business. Participants will learn and apply business decision-making skills and demonstrate the speaking ability and poise through oral presentation.

Case Study Gifts to Impress is a family-owned marketing specialty company that has been in operation for 30 years. The Gifts to Impress owners are originally from China and use this connection to obtain great financial deals on marketing gifts that can be engraved. Gifts to Impress has never followed a strategic marketing plan. Their success has resulted from the word-of-mouth advertising provided by satisfied customers. Three things customers like about Gifts to Impress are the high-quality gifts, reasonable prices, and excellent service. The owners of Gifts to Impress have been swamped taking care of orders and developing relationships with new clients. They have asked your marketing team to develop a national campaign to advertise Gifts to Impress.

You have 20 minutes to determine a national marketing strategy for Gifts to Impress. No reference materials, visual aids, or electronic devices may be used during the preparation or performance. You have seven minutes to present your plan to the judge(s).

Professionalism with Electronic Communications

Have you "friended" anyone or read a "tweet" recently?

Electronic communication has not only added new terms to everyday conversation, but it also has made 24/7 contact a reality. Electronic communication takes many forms, including e-mail, instant messaging, texting, blogging, and posting through social networks. These are all tools that support or facilitate communication.

Accessibility

An important consideration as you utilize various means of electronic communication is accessibility. Who will have access to the communication? Blogs, web sites, and social networking sites often are accessible globally, and employers often use the Web when conducting background checks. If, for example, your Facebook profile is not private, potential employers and others have the ability to access your profile. They may be able to read your posts, read the posts of your friends, and view your photos and notes. Schools and other organizations often have policies regarding electronic communication. If you are using your school's or organization's e-mail system, that organization may have access to incoming and outgoing messages. There also may be concerns about security and privacy.

Permanence

While electronic communication is a dynamic form of communication, it also has an element of permanence. When you delete a message, it may disappear from your computer screen immediately, but it can remain on your hard drive. It also can be printed. Once you click on "send," your message has entered the public sphere and others will have a record of your communication. Posts to social networking sites usually can be deleted after posting, but if the comment has been printed, it becomes permanent.

Degree of Formality

While electronic communication may lend itself to a less formal communication style, if you are using these tools for employment purposes, keep in mind that employers likely will expect professionalism. Do not use abbreviations, slang, or other informal elements of communication. Because electronic communication may not fully communicate the tones and subtleties of the interaction, practice restraint and use sarcasm and jokes cautiously, if at all.

Develop Your Skill

Prepare an e-mail message to a co-worker who has not effectively participated in a workgroup. Assume that the coworker has missed numerous team meetings and failed to submit reports on time, which has led to the workgroup's missing an important company deadline. After preparing the e-mail message, review it to check for sarcasm or other elements of communication that may be easily misinterpreted.

Chapter 10

Product Promotion: Selling Yourself in Interviews

10.1 Interview Basics

10.2 During and After the Interview

10.3 Listening and Nonverbal Skills

CAREERS IN MARKETING

Giant Eagle

Giant Eagle is an award-winning regional supermarket serving parts of Pennsylvania, Ohio, West Virginia, and Maryland. A privately held company founded in 1931, Giant Eagle values sustainability, inclusion, and innovation.

The Category Manager is responsible for the merchandising of fresh products and services for retail sales including product selection, presentation, pricing, and promotion. He or she is expected to understand the competitive environment and maintain strong positioning against competitors.

The Category Manager needs to have a college degree along with experience in buying and merchandising. He or she also must have knowledge of store operations, familiarity with marketing and finance concepts, and excellent communication and time management skills.

Digital Vision/Getty Images

Think *Critically*

1. The Category Manager must research sales/profit information and understand merchandising/product development. Explain how these are related.

2. List ways the Category Manager can research competitors. What information would he or she need?

PORTFOLIO BUILDER PROJECT
Answering Tough Interview Questions

Project Objectives

One of the best ways to prepare for an interview is to anticipate the questions that will be asked and plan answers to those questions. For this project, you will:

- Learn to recognize and respond to common interview questions.
- Practice answering challenging interview questions.
- Identify illegal questions and get tips for responding to them.

Getting Started

Read the Project Process below. Look at the supporting material on the Portfolio Builder CD.

- Read through the lists of questions and begin thinking about your answers.
- Go to the web resource links. Take notes on any interviewing tips you find.

Project Process

Part 1   Lesson 10.1 The purpose of most interview questions is to obtain factual information. However, some questions are open-ended and require careful thought (for example, "Why do you want this job?"). Read the list of common questions, and write a response to each question. Answer honestly, but positively.

Part 2   Lesson 10.2 Read over the list of challenging questions, and write a response to each question. Give examples of how you overcame obstacles in previous jobs or assignments. Give examples that show measurable accomplishments. Be sure to frame each answer positively. Next, read the questions out loud into a tape recorder. Replay the tape, and practice answering each question without the aid of your notes.

Part 3   Lesson 10.3 Most employers will not ask illegal questions about your religion, race, ethnicity, national origin, age, marital status, membership in certain organizations, or physical condition. Unfortunately, though, some will. Read the list of illegal questions, and write a response to each question. With a partner, role-play responses.

Project Wrap-Up

Don't forget to ask your own questions. Figure out in advance what you want to know about the employer and the position, and jot down appropriate questions. The interviewer will see that you have done your research and can take initiative when appropriate.

jhorrocks/iStockphoto.com

Interview Basics

Goals
- Describe relationship selling and traditional selling
- Explain the interview process

Key Terms
- traditional selling
- relationship selling
- rational motives
- emotional motives
- punctuality
- closed-ended questions
- open-ended questions

Building Relationships

If you don't make a "sale" during an interview, you don't get a job. Regardless of how well you—the product—can satisfy a need, if you can't sell yourself in an interview by convincing a potential employer of your benefits, you will not get a job offer.

You have built your self-knowledge, have learned how to package yourself, have defined your target market and how to reach it, and have prepared effective promotional pieces. Yet, even with all your preparation, you may still feel overwhelmed by the thought of interviewing, or selling yourself in an employment situation.

Traditional Selling

When you think of salespeople, what comes to mind? Many people immediately conjure up a negative image of a stereotypical used-car salesperson. Such salespeople—usually aggressive, loud, and manipulative—engage in **traditional selling**—setting appointments, overcoming objections, and closing sales by using memorized techniques (sometimes known as *canned sales presentations*) that don't really consider the client.

In Chapter 1, you learned about the Sales Era, during which organizations and their salespeople, sold what they produced, not what met customer needs. The traditional sales process flourished during the Sales Era.

© Adam Borkowski, 2009/ Used under license from Shutterstock.com

marketing matters

Darryl has just been recruited as a salesperson by Sunlight Windows. In this position, he will call homeowners to schedule appointments to sell replacement windows. The sales manager, Jeff Espana, gives Darryl a sales technique manual, telephone scripts he can read to set appointments, and some videos to watch that show salespeople closing sales with customers. If Darryl wants to build relationships with customers to sell his products, are scripts and videos going to be effective? Explain your response.

Relationship Selling

Relationship selling is a buyer-oriented sales philosophy, as opposed to the seller-oriented philosophy of traditional selling. It is based on trust, needs satisfaction, and mutual goals. Relationship selling has a long-term focus that positions the buyer and the seller as partners, not adversaries.

Trust Buying decisions are made more carefully in slow economic times. Hiring decisions are also made more carefully. Organizations want to hire someone they can trust to satisfy their needs. When you perceive that someone is not being honest with you, you hesitate to do business with that person. When people project honesty and helpfulness, though, you will probably happily do business with them again.

Following are some tips for building trust:

- Project positive self-esteem and self-confidence when meeting and speaking with others. Let them get to know you and become comfortable with you.

- Demonstrate integrity by keeping your word. If you tell an employer you are going to call, be sure to call. If an employer asks you to complete a sample project, complete it on time.

- Don't just talk—listen. Listening shows potential employers you are genuinely interested in the organization, the position, and what they have to say.

Needs Satisfaction As a seller, when your product can meet the needs of a prospective buyer, you increase your chances of making the sale. The same holds true for interviewing. When an employer feels comfortable that your product—you—can meet the needs of the organization and successfully fulfill the requirements of the position, you increase your chances of being hired.

Demonstrate your knowledge of the position, industry, and organization with the information you gathered in Chapter 5, and clearly identify the employer's needs. If, after the interview, you don't feel you can meet those needs, be honest. The employer will respect you and perhaps even refer you to another organization whose needs you *can* meet.

To build a truly win-win situation, you should be comfortable with the organization and the employer should be comfortable with the decision to hire you. Remember, the interviewer is a buyer making a purchasing decision.

Mutual Goals Mutual goals are objectives shared by buyers and sellers. Achieving these goals increases satisfaction, and these goals are more likely to be achieved when the buyer and the seller work together. The desire to achieve mutual goals provides an incentive to maintain a productive, beneficial relationship.

Buying Motives

Marketers believe that consumers make purchasing decisions based on two types of reasons: rational motives and emotional motives. **Rational motives** are conscious, logical reasons. For instance, you may buy a specific book

The phrase "sell like hotcakes" comes from the early 1800s, when hotcakes were a popular food at carnivals and fairs. Hotcake vendors couldn't keep up with the demand for their product.

marketing math connection

Overtime pay is an extra amount of money paid for working more than the usual work hours in a day or a week. Overtime pay is often figured at one and a half (1.5) times the regular-time rate and is called *time-and-a-half pay.*

To find time-and-a-half pay, first multiply the regular pay rate by 1.5 to get the time-and-a-half rate. Then multiply the time-and-a-half rate by the number of time-and-a-half hours.

Last week, Vincenzo Vaughn worked six hours at time-and-a-half pay. His regular pay rate is $9.60 per hour. What was Vincenzo's total overtime pay for the week?

SOLUTION

Time-and-a-half rate = Regular pay rate × 1.5

= $9.60 × 1.5

= $14.40

Overtime pay = Time-and-a-half hours × Time-and-a-half rate

= 6 × $14.40

= $86.40

because you are required to read it for your English assignment. **Emotional motives** relate more to feelings. For example, you may stop to buy freshly squeezed lemonade after class not because you are thirsty (a rational motive) but because it reminds you of your childhood.

Employers also make decisions based on rational and emotional motives. Your skills may provide rational motives for hiring. Providing emotional motives for hiring is more difficult. For example, Leia, a public relations manager is considering both Juan and Tina for an entry-level position. They both have similar skills, and Leia is having a hard time deciding based on rational motives alone. She decides to hire Juan because she thinks he will get along better with the other employees in her department, which will reflect well on her performance as a manager. Leia has made her decision based on emotional motives.

Check Point

How does the relationship selling philosophy differ from the traditional selling philosophy?

The Interview Process

What will your interview be like? Your knowledge of the organization may give you some idea of what to expect, but every interview will be different. Interviews vary in format and length. Your initial interview may be conducted over the phone or in person with a human resources representative. Or it may be with the president or owner, a situation that is more likely to occur in a small business setting. It may occur over lunch in the company cafeteria or at a local restaurant. Or you could have a panel interview, where you are interviewed by a number of people from the organization.

You may meet with one person for 15 minutes, or you may spend all day meeting with various people and touring the organization. You may be required to take tests, such as aptitude tests, computer knowledge tests, personality tests, or even honesty tests. Regardless of the format and length of your interview, though, if you take the time to prepare, you will increase your chances of success.

Preparation

Just as a salesperson would be ill advised to be unprepared for a meeting with a client, an interview candidate should not simply show up for an interview without research and preparation. Almost everyone feels nervous before an interview. But you can use your nervous energy to stay motivated as you prepare. The more prepared you are for the interview, the more comfortable you will feel, allowing your knowledge and self-confidence to shine through.

Research Interviewers often ask questions that test your knowledge of the position, the organization, and the industry. Review the information in Chapter 5 about researching companies to prepare yourself to answer such questions.

Practice As you would with any other oral presentation, you should practice for your interview. Provide a friend or family member with a list of questions you are likely to be asked, as well as some information about the company, and ask them to interview you. Take this mock interview seriously, and, beginning with your entrance into the "interviewer's office," make the experience as real as possible. If you have access to a camcorder, set it up or ask another friend to record the interview. It might seem uncomfortable, but you will have the opportunity to view your "performance" and get feedback from others—all of which can help make your real interviews more successful.

The Interview

Keep in mind the interviewer's responsibility to the organization—he or she wants to find the right person for the position. Your challenge is to convince the interviewer that you are that right person. You want to sell "product you" to the interviewer by pointing out the benefits you could offer to the organization.

Every moment of an interview is important, from your arrival to your departure. Sometimes, seemingly insignificant details can influence whether or not you are offered the job.

Workshop

In small groups, brainstorm questions that you may be asked in an interview. Share these questions with your classmates, and discuss appropriate responses.

Your Appearance In Chapter 4, you learned about the importance of first impressions and how your appearance can affect the impression you convey. Dress conservatively, and appear neat and well groomed. Wear your hair neatly, and minimize jewelry and cologne. "Wear" a positive attitude, and carry yourself with confidence.

Arriving at the Interview **Punctuality**, or arriving at the scheduled time, is a necessity. If you are late to an interview, regardless of how good your excuse is, the interviewer's first impression of you will be tainted by your tardiness. Plan to arrive about 15 minutes early, which will provide some leeway for traffic delays or confusing directions.

Always arrive alone for an interview. Don't bring family members or friends into the building with you. The interviewer wants to interview someone who is capable of working independently.

Greeting the Interviewer When you arrive for an interview, a receptionist or assistant may greet you. Be extremely polite, explain the purpose of your visit, and mention the name of the person you are there to see. When you are introduced to the interviewer, extend your hand in greeting and introduce yourself. Be polite, and wait to be seated until you are asked. Bring extra copies of your resume and your references, and bring your portfolio with items that document your accomplishments, such as sample projects, awards, grades, and letters of recommendation.

Asking Questions Plan to be an active participant in the interview process. Though the interviewer should lead the discussion, your preparation will allow you to ask relevant, important questions that can help set the tone or direct the content of the interview. Try not to ask too many **closed-ended questions**—questions that require only "yes" or "no" answers (such as "Will my performance be reviewed after six months?"). Instead, ask **open-ended questions**—questions that require more detailed answers than "yes" or "no" (such as "Can you tell me about the performance review process?"). Open-ended questions will provide you with much more detailed, and probably more helpful, information than closed-ended questions will.

Be friendly but professional. Answer the interviewer's questions honestly and completely, but don't volunteer any negative information. Remember to let the interviewer bring up the topic of salary and benefits first.

Concluding the Interview At the end of the interview, thank the interviewer and restate your interest in the position, if you are indeed still interested. Ask what the next step in the process will be. Gather any items you brought, ask the interviewer for his or her business card, and shake hands before you leave. If a receptionist greeted you when you arrived, acknowledge him or her as you leave.

Check▶Point

Explain the importance of punctuality in an interview situation.

Chapter 10   ⌘   Product Promotion: Selling Yourself in Interviews

careerbuilder®

The Interview: Body Language Do's and Don'ts

By CareerBuilder.com
Copyright 2007 CareerBuilder, LLC.—Reprinted with permission.

Your heart feels ready to leap out of your chest. Beads of sweat build on your forehead. Your mind is racing.

It's not a full-blown interrogation—although it may feel like it—it's just a job interview. While it's no secret that job interviews can be nerve-racking, a lot of job candidates spend a significant amount of time worrying about what they will say during their interview, only to blow it all with their body language. The old adage, "It's not what you say, it's how you say it," still holds meaning, even if you're not talking. You need to effectively communicate your professionalism both verbally and nonverbally.

Because watching your nonverbal cues, delivering concise answers and expressing your enthusiasm at once can be difficult when you're nervous, here's a guide to walk you through it:

Have them at "hello"

Before you walk into the interview, it's assumed that you will have done the following: prepared yourself by reading up on the company and recent company news; practiced what you'll say to some of the more common interview questions; and followed the "what to wear on your interview" advice. So you're ready, right?

Some hiring managers claim they can spot a possible candidate for a job within 30 seconds or less, and while a lot of that has to do with the way you look, it's also in your body language. Don't walk in pulling up your pantyhose or readjusting your tie; pull yourself together before you stand up to greet the hiring manager or enter their office. Avoid a "dead fish" handshake and confidently—but not too firmly—grasp your interviewer's hand and make eye contact while saying hello.

Shake your hand, watch yourself

If you are rocking back in your chair, shaking your foot, drumming your fingers or scratching your... anything, you're going to look like your going to look the type of future employee who wouldn't be able to stay focused, if even for a few minutes. It's a not a game of charades, it's a job interview. Here's what to do (and not do):

Don't:

- Rub the back of your head or neck. Even if you really do just have a cramp in your neck, these gestures make you look disinterested.
- Rub or touch your nose. This suggests that you're not being completely honest, and it's gross.

continued on page 268

- Sit with your armed folded across your chest. You'll appear unfriendly and disengaged.
- Cross your legs and idly shake one over the other. It's distracting and shows how uncomfortable you are.
- Lean your body towards the door. You'll appear ready to make a mad dash for the door.
- Slouch back in your seat. This will make you appear disinterested and unprepared.
- Stare back blankly. This is a look people naturally adapt when they are trying to distance themselves.

Do:
- Sit up straight, and lean slightly forward in your chair. In addition to projecting interest and engagement in the interaction, aligning your body's position to that of the interviewer's shows admiration and agreement.
- Show your enthusiasm by keeping an interested expression. Nod and make positive gestures in moderation to avoid looking like a bobblehead.
- Establish a comfortable amount of personal space between you and the interviewer. Invading personal space (anything more than 20 inches) could make the interviewer feel uncomfortable and take the focus away from your conversation.
- Limit your application of colognes and perfumes. Invading aromas can arouse allergies. Being the candidate that gave the interviewer a headache isn't going to do anything in your favor.
- If you have more than one person interviewing you at once, make sure you briefly address both people with your gaze (without looking like a tennis spectator) and return your attention to the person who has asked you a question.
- Interruptions can happen. If they do, refrain from staring at your interviewer while they address their immediate business and motion your willingness to leave if they need privacy.
- Stand up and smile even if you are on a phone interview. Standing increases your level of alertness and allows you to become more engaged in the conversation.

Say Goodbye Gracefully

After a few well-thought-out questions and answers with your interviewer, it's almost over, but don't lose your cool just yet. Make sure your goodbye handshake is just as confident now as it was going in. Keep that going while you walk through the office building, into the elevator and onto the street. Once safely in your car, a cab or some other measurable safe distance from the scene of your interview, it's safe to let go. You may have aced it, but the last thing you want is some elaborate end-zone dance type of routine killing all your hard work at the last moment.

THINK CRITICALLY

1. How does relationship selling differ from traditional selling?

2. How can you demonstrate integrity after an interview?

3. Differentiate between rational and emotional buying motives. For the same product or service, give an example of each motive.

4. Explain the importance of preparing for an interview.

MAKE ACADEMIC CONNECTIONS

5. **PEER REVIEW** Create an interview critique form that includes space to record information about the aspects of an interview you think are important. Interview a classmate and evaluate him or her with your critique form. Then switch roles and have your partner interview and evaluate you. Finally, write a one-page summary of your interview skills. Based on your partner's critique form, what are your strengths and weaknesses? How can you improve your interviewing technique?

6. **INTERVIEW** Interview a person who works in sales. Ask questions that allow you to determine if he or she uses a traditional selling technique, a relationship selling technique, or a combination. Create an oral presentation to report your results.

7. **RESEARCH** Click on **www.cengage.com/school/marketing/ yourself** and follow the links in Chapter 10 to this activity. Visit three or four of the career web sites and summarize at least four strategies for effective interviewing. Look for new ideas that may be useful to you. Write a summary of your findings. If you find new information, research the topic(s) further and discuss them with your classmates.

INTERNET

During and After the Interview

Goals
- Identify common interview questions
- Describe tactics for effective follow-up

Key Terms
- follow-up interviews
- pre-employment testing

Interview Questions

Most interviewers, especially those with a lot of experience, have standard questions they ask candidates. Some of these questions may be difficult to answer—especially because your responses can influence your future (or lack of future) with an organization.

When responding to interview questions, remain focused and positive. If you don't understand the question, ask for clarification. An interview is not an interrogation, so resist the urge to become defensive, especially if you are asked complicated or leading questions. Some interviewers may even try to ruffle your feathers a bit to see how you respond to stress.

Initial Interviews

During an initial interview, interviewers assess the overall impression you make, as well as your record. Below are some common interview questions.

- Tell me about yourself.
- Describe your experience and/or education.
- Which courses did you enjoy most (or least)?
- Why did you choose this field of study?

Photodisc/Getty Images

marketing matters

Junipero Kitura is preparing for an interview for an internship at Computer Analysis Associates, Inc. He reviews some questions he thinks the interviewer might ask him, and then writes down his answers and memorizes them. He brings the written answers to the interview, and keeps them inside a folder. How might preparing written answers to interview questions be helpful to Junipero? Do you think memorizing the answers will help him make a good impression in the interview?

- Why did you attend (name of school)?

- Tell me about your past jobs.

- Tell me about your grades and academic achievements.

- What kinds of activities have you participated in?

- What do you know about this organization?

- Describe your ideal job.

Comstock Images/Getty Images

- What are your greatest strengths and weaknesses?

Follow-Up Interviews

Sometimes employers schedule **follow-up interviews**—additional interviews of candidates they are very interested in. During such interviews, the position itself, as well as the organization, may be discussed in more detail. The same person may interview you, or another person, such as the department manager or supervisor, may handle the follow-up interview. You can use a follow-up interview to determine if the position is a suitable match for your career goals. Below are some common follow-up interview questions.

- Why do you want to work here?

- Why do you want to leave your current position?

- Where do you see yourself five years from now?

- How can you benefit this organization?

- How can you effectively meet the position requirements?

- Describe a problem you have had to deal with. How did you handle it?

- Do you prefer to work in a position with well-defined responsibilities or one that frequently changes?

- What salary are you expecting?

NETBookmark

Learn more about illegal interview questions by visiting **www.cengage.com/school/marketing/yourself** and following the links to this activity. After viewing the web sites, write three or four of the illegal questions on a piece of paper and respond to them as you might in a job interview.

com-mu-ni-cate

If you don't know when a hiring decision will be made, you might need to make a follow-up phone call to the interviewer. Think about what you would say, and write a script of a possible follow-up phone call. Compare your script with another student's script. Did he or she include any additional or different information?

Illegal Questions

Some questions are inappropriate for an interview—and some are actually illegal. Interviewers should not ask about your marital status or children, religious affiliation, disabilities (except those that would limit your ability to perform the job responsibilities), race or ethnic background, or age (unless related to a work permit).

When faced with an illegal question, you may choose to ignore the legality and answer it anyway. Or, you may ask the interviewer why the question is relevant. In any case, handle the situation with care and tact. If you are strongly offended, you may choose to contact the Equal Employment Opportunity Commission (EEOC) after the interview.

Asking Questions

Make yourself an active participant in the interview by asking your own questions. You will assume some of the control over—as well as some of the responsibility for—the interview's success. Success, as defined by the relationship selling model, means that both you and the interviewer learn enough about each other to feel that your employment with the organization would be mutually beneficial. You believe that the company is right for you, and the interviewer believes that you are right for the company.

You may think of questions during the course of the interview, based on the discussion or the interviewer's comments and questions, but you should also prepare some general questions ahead of time. Preparing a list of your own questions before the interview will help you obtain all the information you need to reach a decision about whether to take a position.

Avoid asking questions that may require personal or confidential information of the interviewer or questions that imply you think you have the job already. Below are some possible questions you might ask.

- Why is this position open?
- What is the projected starting date for the position?
- How is job performance evaluated?
- What is the career path related to this position?
- How would you describe the job responsibilities?
- What would a typical day be like?
- What results will I be expected to produce?
- Do you foresee any changes in the company that will affect this position?
- Is it possible to tour the facility?
- Are ongoing training and other educational opportunities available?

Asking questions demonstrates your interest in the organization and the position. As the interview ends, stress your interest in working for the company—if, in fact, you are still interested—and ask if you can provide the interviewer with any additional information. You will give the interviewer an opportunity to mention any last minute concerns, and you can deal with any unresolved issues or underlying questions about your chances before you leave. You should also ask what the next step in the process is and when you can expect to hear from the interviewer. Mention that you would like to follow up to check on the status of the position, if necessary.

Pre-Employment Testing

In addition to interview questions, you may be asked to complete some **pre-employment testing** addressing issues such as aptitude, proficiency, personality, honesty, and drug use. These tests may be done on-site before or after the interview, or you may be asked to complete the testing at another location. For example, if an organization requires drug testing, you may be asked to submit a urine sample to the company health office when you arrive for the interview. If the organization does not do the testing on-site, you may be directed to a specific testing facility to complete the drug test.

> ## Check > Point
>
> Provide an example of how an initial interview might differ from a follow-up interview in terms of format and questions.

Follow-Up

Following up can greatly improve your chances of getting a job offer. You can keep your identity fresh in the interviewer's mind and remind him or her why you are a strong candidate. Begin by sending a thank-you letter no later than one day after your interview.

Post-Interview Assessment

After an interview, summarize the key points. Answer the following questions to determine which aspects went well and which need to be improved.

- What did you feel comfortable with?
- What made you feel uncomfortable?
- At what points did the interviewer seem most pleased with the interview?
- Did your appearance seem appropriate for the organization?
- Did you ask the questions necessary to learn more about the organization and the position?

In job interviews, two people with the same qualifications can be evaluated differently depending on how they present themselves. One may show self-confidence, and the other may communicate self-doubt. Brainstorm other factors that might cause an interviewer to evaluate similar candidates differently.

YinYang/iStockphoto.co

Answering these questions will help you improve your interview performance and give you insight into areas that you can improve, which, in turn, will help you feel more comfortable during your next interview.

Record-Keeping Forms

Following each interview, you should complete a record-keeping form. Keep your completed forms and all other information related to the interview together in an interview binder. This will make following up with employers easier when writing thank-you letters, preparing for follow-up interviews, or making follow-up calls.

Your record-keeping forms should include space for the following information.

- Date of interview
- Company name
- Contact's full name, title, address, phone number, and e-mail address
- Position interviewed for
- Key responsibilities
- Key interview points (tour of facility, other employees met, projects discussed, and so on)
- Salary range (if mentioned)
- Next step in interview process

Check > Point

Describe the benefits of following up after an interview.

THINK CRITICALLY

1. Explain some steps you can take to respond effectively to interview questions.

2. Identify some illegal interview topics.

3. Why is it important to ask questions during an interview?

4. Why should you complete a record-keeping form for each interview?

5. What types of pre-employment testing might an employer ask you to complete?

MAKE ACADEMIC CONNECTIONS

6. **EMPLOYMENT COMMUNICATION** Draft a letter you could use as a follow-up to your interview. Include the information listed below.

   - Write an appropriate greeting and a reminder of the position you interviewed for.

   - Include any important information you omitted from your interview.

   - Summarize your job qualifications briefly.

   - Express your interest in the job and your appreciation for the interview.

7. **INTERVIEW** Interview someone who regularly conducts interviews for a company. The person may work in the human resources department or as a manager in another department. Ask the person if he or she wants applicants to call after interviews or if he or she prefers to call applicants. Also ask if the person expects to receive thank-you letters from applicants after interviews. How often does he or she receive one? Write a summary of the results of your interview. Then share the information with the class.

Listening and Nonverbal Skills

Goals
- Understand the importance of effective listening
- Describe common forms of nonverbal communication

Key Terms
- communication process
- nonverbal communication
- personal space
- eye contact
- facial expressions
- gestures
- mirroring

Listening to Others

Have you ever played the "telephone game"? A person tells one person a message consisting of a few sentences, and the listener then whispers the message to another person. The process continues until the last person says the message out loud. The object of the game is to see how much the message changes from beginning to end.

Effective Listening

The fun of the telephone game comes from participants who don't listen effectively and, therefore, don't pass on the message correctly. Poor listeners:

- Don't listen attentively. Their focus of attention is on something else while they should be focused on the message.

- Judge the speaker. If the speaker's views differ from their views about a topic, poor listeners may assume they already know what the speaker is going to say and may "tune out" the message.

- Don't listen actively. They are too busy planning what they will say when the other person pauses.

When you do not listen effectively, you miss information. David was listening to Mrs. Hoffman's lecture on *Romeo and Juliet* in literature class. Taking notes helped him pay attention and focus on Mrs. Hoffman, but

jhorrocks/iStockphoto.co

marketing matters

Alina Vinichko works part time at Perez's Party Store. The owner, Mr. Perez, is not very happy with her. He asked Alina to mop the floors, fill a dozen balloons with helium, and restock the crepe paper. Alina responded, but she was busy thinking about her family and their new dog. Now, over an hour later, the work has not been done. What could Mr. Perez do to ensure that Alina is listening effectively? How can Alina be a more effective listener?

when another student couldn't stop coughing, he began thinking about his neighbor, who was ill. When he began focusing on the lecture again, he realized that Mrs. Hoffman had been reviewing important concepts for the upcoming test.

Luca's father was explaining how to set up the field for an upcoming baseball game that Luca was scheduled to umpire. Luca felt that he already knew what to do and that his father could not possibly add anything of importance, so he began thinking about the game and did not fully absorb his father's directions.

To listen effectively, you should:

- Take a deep breath.
- Make up your mind to listen.
- Maintain eye contact with the speaker.
- Ask helpful questions.
- Listen to the speaker's response.
- Mentally paraphrase (repeat in your own words) the message.
- Confirm the response.
- Ask again if necessary.

The Communication Process

The **communication process**, at its most basic level, involves a sender, a receiver, and a message. In an interview, you will change roles—at times acting as the sender by providing information to the interviewer and at other times acting as the receiver by listening to the interviewer.

When you are the sender, be sure to pause, if necessary, to prepare your thoughts. When you are the receiver, be sure to listen effectively. Don't spend your listening time planning your response. You could miss important information. Focus on both words and meaning, and be sure your response makes it apparent that you have been listening.

Don't forget your relationship with the interviewer. To follow the relationship selling model effectively, you must value the interviewer's time. You want to understand his or her needs to determine if you can satisfy them. The interview is based on trust and mutual goals. You want to benefit the organization with your skills and accomplishments, and you want the organization to benefit you by providing an opportunity for you to achieve some measure of success based on your values and goals. A mutually beneficial employment situation is ideal.

Workshop

With a partner, develop a list of skills that are necessary for effective listening. Share your list with another team. How would these skills help you in an interview setting?

Check Point

What does it mean to listen effectively?

Nonverbal Communication

Have you ever heard the expression "Actions speak louder than words"? **Nonverbal communication** refers to communication other than spoken language. It includes distance, eye contact, facial expressions, voice, posture, and gestures. When meeting with an interviewer, both your verbal and your nonverbal messages will affect the interviewer's perception—and, ultimately, opinion—of you as a potential employee.

Nonverbal communication plays an important role in your interaction with others. Nonverbal "cues" can help you determine another's attitude and personal feelings.

Distance

Distance refers to the actual space between your body and another person's body. The distance you place between yourself and another can convey

diversity in the workplace

The first step in communicating effectively with people from different cultures is to think about the values of the cultural groups and determine whether they apply to your coworkers. Marcelle Du Praw, of the National Institute for Dispute Resolution, and Marya Axner, a consultant in leadership development and diversity awareness, have identified the following six ways that cultures differ.

- **Communication style**   The meaning of nonverbal messages can vary from culture to culture. Included are body language, personal space requirements, facial expressions, and more.

- **Attitudes toward conflict**   Whether conflict is viewed positively or negatively is culturally determined.

- **Approaches toward completing tasks**   Some cultures value building relations first and then beginning the task at hand. Others want to get right to the task. Different cultures also have varying concepts of time.

- **Decision-making styles**   Some cultures emphasize delegating responsibility. Other cultures feel individuals should make their own decisions. Emphasis on majority rule or achieving consensus is also culturally determined.

- **Disclosure**   Cultures differ in how comfortable individuals feel disclosing personal information, the reasons behind a conflict, or individuals' roles in a conflict.

- **Approaches to knowing**   Some cultures tend to consider knowledge acquired through analysis as most valid. Other cultures may place a higher value on knowledge acquired through the senses, feelings, and emotions.

a message, such as attraction, interest, status, or respect. The appropriate amount of distance may vary by culture. For instance, in the United States, **personal space**—the distance that feels comfortable for personal interactions—is about two to four feet. Personal space should be respected. A violation of another's personal space can cause communication problems.

Eye Contact

Eye contact, or gazing directly at another person, is extremely important in an interview. When you look down, up in the air, or away during an interview, you may appear to lack confidence or interest in the position. When you maintain eye contact, you show sincerity and confidence.

This show of sincerity and confidence can help you convey your message and create a positive impression. Looking at the interviewer can also help you determine if he or she is paying attention. Just don't stare him or her down.

Facial Expressions

Never underestimate the power of a smile. **Facial expressions**, the sometimes conscious and sometimes unconscious movements of your facial muscles, communicate emotions and attitudes. Your facial expressions will change during the course of the interview, as will the interviewer's. Keep your expression positive, and watch for less-than-positive expressions on the interviewer's face. A frown, a raised eyebrow, and a yawn all communicate reactions to the conversation.

Gestures

Many people use **gestures**—hand movements—when talking. Positive gestures tend to be open, natural, and smooth. Negative gestures tend to be closed and rigid, such as folding your arms tightly across your chest. You can practice **mirroring**, or moving your body to mimic that of the interviewer. Some psychologists believe that mirroring can make the other person feel more comfortable with you. For instance, if the interviewer leans in toward you, you should lean slightly toward him or her.

Check Point

Describe the importance of paying attention to body language when listening to another person.

THINK CRITICALLY

1. Why is it important to listen effectively during an interview?

2. Label the three basic parts of the communication process.

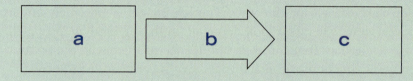

| a | b | c |

3. How can personal space, as a form of nonverbal communication, be respected during an interview?

4. Explain mirroring.

MAKE ACADEMIC CONNECTIONS

5. **ANALYSIS** Do you listen attentively in some situations and inattentively in others? Do you detect a pattern in your listening behavior? Take some time to think about all the listening you've done today. Draw four columns on a sheet of paper. In the first column, write the names of several people to whom you have listened. In the second column, write the subjects of the conversations. In the third column, write "attentive" or "inattentive" to describe your listening behavior. Analyze why you were more attentive some times than others, and write a sentence in the fourth column explaining the reasons for your listening behavior.

6. **OBSERVATION** Go silent and listen to the sounds around you that you usually ignore. Do you hear a computer humming, someone flipping pages at the desk next to you, or cars roaring or accelerating on the street outside? Make a list of the sounds you hear. Then write a one-page report about how the sounds around you can affect your ability to listen without being distracted.

VOCABULARY BUILDER

Choose the term that best fits the definition. Write the letter of the answer in the space provided. Some terms may not be used.

_____ 1. The distance that feels comfortable for personal interactions

_____ 2. Using memorized sales techniques to set appointments, overcome objections, and close sales

_____ 3. A conscious, logical reason

_____ 4. Moving your body to mimic that of another person

_____ 5. Arriving at the scheduled time

_____ 6. A question that requires only a "yes" or "no" answer

_____ 7. An additional interview for a candidate in whom an employer is very interested

_____ 8. Communication other than spoken language

_____ 9. The actual space between your body and another person's body

_____ 10. A reason that relates to feelings

_____ 11. A sometimes conscious and sometimes unconscious movement of facial muscles to communicate an emotion or an attitude

_____ 12. A buyer-oriented sales philosophy, based on trust, needs satisfaction, and mutual goals

_____ 13. Hand movements

_____ 14. A question that requires a more detailed answer than "yes" or "no"

a. closed-ended question

b. communication process

c. distance

d. emotional motive

e. eye contact

f. facial expression

g. follow-up interview

h. gestures

i. mirroring

j. nonverbal communication

k. open-ended question

l. personal space

m. punctuality

n. rational motive

o. relationship selling

p. traditional selling

15. Describe traditional selling.

16. Explain the three concepts important to relationship selling.

17. Provide an example of a rational buying motive and an example of an emotional buying motive.

18. How should you conclude an interview?

19. What is the purpose of a follow-up interview?

20. What is a post-interview assessment?

21. List some of the barriers to effective listening.

22. Describe four common elements of nonverbal communication.

APPLY WHAT YOU LEARNED

23. How can you build trust during an interview?

24. How might you convey to an interviewer that you can meet the organization's needs?

25. Explain how to prepare for an interview.

26. How might a follow-up interview differ from an initial interview?

27. How can you be an active participant in an interview?

28. Why is effective listening an important part of relationship selling?

29. How can you express openness and a positive attitude through nonverbal communication?

30. Why might an employer require pre-employment testing?

MAKE ACADEMIC CONNECTIONS

31. **SELF-EVALUATION** Analyze your body language in the following areas: posture, handshake, facial expression, eye contact, voice qualities, gestures, and distracting nonverbal habits. Do you use any body language that might be construed as aggressive or passive? Make a list of the habits you think are most important to change. Then write a one-page action plan for changing your bad body language habits.

32. **INTERVIEW** Contact at least two organizations in your field similar to your actual job target, and arrange a brief meeting to research common interview questions. Make certain your contacts understand that this is not a request for an interview. During your meetings, ask your contacts to explain the questions they use to evaluate applicants for positions similar to the one you will be targeting. Take notes of the information you find useful, and create an oral presentation to summarize what you've learned.

33. **PRACTICE** Contact an employer in your career field, and ask for help with a course assignment. Ask the employer to give you a practice interview and to complete a copy of the interview critique form you created in Lesson 10.1. After your rehearsal interview, evaluate your performance by completing your own copy of the interview critique form. Compare your form to the interviewer's form, and write a summary of the similarities and differences between the two.

34. **INTERNET RESEARCH** Search the Internet for additional tips on interview follow-ups that could be useful to you. Print relevant articles, and then write your own article summarizing what you've learned.

35. **ROLE-PLAYING** Prepare a draft of a telephone call you could use to follow up on an interview. Write an appropriate telephone greeting for the person who interviewed you. Follow it by a statement of your name and the position you were interviewed for. Include any important information you omitted and any questions you forgot to ask during the interview. Express your interest in the job and your appreciation for the interview. Pair up with another student, and act out your call in front of the class.

Public Relations Project

The Public Relations Project provides the opportunity to demonstrate the skills needed in planning, organizing, implementing, and evaluating a single public relations campaign conducted by the DECA chapter. This project includes the written document and an oral presentation by one to three students. Your team has the challenge of designing a public relations strategy for an important campaign in your community. Examples of projects may include encouraging community beautification, helping people register to vote, and challenging students not to drink.

The written document should be limited to 30 pages consisting of the following parts: summary memorandum, campaign theme or focus, local media and other promotional possibilities, campaign organization and implementation, evaluation and recommendations, bibliography, and appendix. Your paper may include charts and graphs. The written document will be completed in smaller segments that will be combined as the complete project. Your team will have 10 minutes to present your Public Relations Project to the class, judge, or businessperson. The audience will have five additional minutes to ask questions about the project.

"Sarah just started her new job. She had three interviews before the company offered her the position. She had to attend orientation on her first day, and then a two-week training program. She said the starting salary was competitive, and she has great benefits, including medical and dental coverage, a 401K plan, and even life insurance. Sarah is really excited to begin her career!"

Have you ever thought about the people you might deal with as a prospective employee at a company? In many organizations, you will deal with Human Resources Specialists who are involved in recruiting, interviewing, and hiring candidates for available positions. Human Resources Specialists must have a broad knowledge of the organization, including its mission, its structure, and the types of positions that may become available. They also may be involved in setting employment policies, conducting new employee orientations, managing recruitment budgets, handling payroll and employee benefits, training employees, traveling to job fairs, and ensuring compliance with employment regulations.

Employment Outlook

An above-average rate of employment growth is expected.

Job Titles

- Human Resources Specialist
- Employment Manager
- Benefits Coordinator
- Employer Relations Representative
- Director of Human Resources
- Placement Specialist
- Job Analyst

Needed Skills

- A bachelor's degree usually is required, and a graduate degree such as an MBA is often recommended, especially for career advancement opportunities. Certification is available through professional organizations.
- The ability to work with many different people, including those of varied cultural backgrounds, experience, and levels of education is essential.

- A background in sales, teaching, supervising, or administration is helpful.
- A pleasant personality, strong communication skills, discretion, and the ability to handle conflict is important.

What's It Like to Work in Human Resources?

Helenka isn't a teacher, or a sales representative, or even a lobbyist, but she feels like she's all of these and more today. She was recently promoted to be Director of Human Resources after serving as a Human Resources Specialist for the last five years. She wraps up her meeting with the orientation and training director after reviewing and approving the curriculum for the new employee development program that will be rolled out next month. She wants to review her notes before she heads out to the luncheon with the Human Resources Association. She has been booked as the guest speaker and wants to be sure she uses examples from her organization. She believes in supporting her employer, and with several people in her department nearing retirement, she is always on the lookout for qualified candidates.

Back at the office after lunch, she meets with a representative from the company's health insurer. There have been rumors of cost increases, and she wants to discuss this before beginning a benefits review. Her day ends late in the evening, as she is going to dinner with several local legislators who want to discuss employee payroll taxes, benefits contributions, and other human resources issues.

What About You?

How would you explain the role of human resources in the job search process?

Chapter 11

Workplace Success

11.1 Starting a New Job

11.2 Employment Satisfaction

11.3 Issues in the Workplace

CAREERS IN MARKETING

Sony

Sony, one of the world's most comprehensive entertainment companies, manufactures audio, video, communications, and information technology products and employs more than 171,000 people worldwide. In the United States, Sony's businesses include Sony Pictures Entertainment, Sony Music Entertainment, Sony Electronics, and Sony Computer Entertainment America.

The Marketing Analyst handles the marketing needs of studios and networks. This position focuses on relationship-building, as the Marketing Analyst is expected to build and maintain strong relationships both internally across Sony business units, and externally with partners.

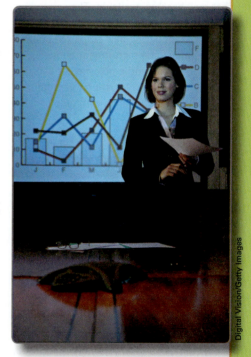
Digital Vision/Getty Images

The Marketing Analyst must possess not only a bachelor's degree in marketing, business, or communication, but also work experience with a studio or network. The person must understand the entertainment business and online marketing. Excellent interpersonal skills, quantitative and analytical skills, mature judgment, and the ability to work with multiple cultures also are important.

Think *Critically*

1. Why is it important for employers to communicate the responsibilities and qualifications required for a position such as this?

2. While this job involves quantitative and analytic skills, how would interpersonal skills help a Marketing Analyst succeed?

PORTFOLIO BUILDER PROJECT
Demonstrating Your Best Work

Project Objectives

Do you lack extensive job experience in your area of interest? You can provide concrete evidence of the work you do in school by featuring it in your career portfolio. In this project, you will:

- Obtain an official transcript.
- Display your best projects and writing samples.
- Document proof of your academic strengths.

Getting Started

Read the Project Process below. Look at the supporting material on the Portfolio Builder CD. Jot down ideas about how to obtain the items you need.

Project Process

Part 1 Lesson 11.1 A transcript lists the courses you take and the grades you receive. Transcripts may also include college entrance exam scores, state graduation or proficiency test scores, and copies of certifications earned.

Part 2 Lesson 11.2 Gather your best research papers, essays, and school projects. Look for completed work that received high marks. Narrow your selections by looking for examples that relate to your field of interest. Focus on samples that highlight your communication skills. Weed out any examples that look sloppy or have smudges. After you have chosen work that reflects your best efforts, display it in your career portfolio.

Part 3 Lesson 11.3 Add evidence of your strength in a particular subject by requesting and including written comments from a teacher. Write a note to this teacher about your work interests, explaining how they relate to the subject. Describe how your skills can be transferred to your career interest. Then ask this teacher to write a one-page letter that you can include in your portfolio. Remember to send a thank-you note.

Project Wrap-Up

Just as your career and interests change, so will your career portfolio. List the items you would like to be able to add to your portfolio that reflect academic success. Think about how you can improve academically to obtain these items.

ManuWe/iStockphoto.com

Starting a New Job

Goals
- Describe a new employment situation
- Understand job changes

Key Terms
- orientation
- mentor
- lifetime employment
- resign

A New Beginning

All your hard work has paid off, and you've accepted a new job. You understand the business environment. You have researched the industry, position, and organization. You feel positive and self-confident. You know how to present yourself in the workplace, with a professional appearance and a positive attitude. You developed and followed a marketing plan. You used your self-promotion pieces to secure an interview. You "sold" your skills, accomplishments, and benefits in the interview. You were offered a position, and you negotiated a fair compensation and accepted the job. Now you're ready to hit the ground running. But where do you begin?

Employee Orientation

Some organizations, particularly larger ones, hold orientations for new employees. An **orientation** is an opportunity for new employees to learn about a company and to adjust to a new working environment. The orientation can provide new employees with information about company policies, organizational structure and culture, and expectations for productivity and conduct. New employees often attend with other new employees from various departments, so orientation can provide an opportunity to get to know others. Teambuilding may be encouraged. Materials such as company brochures, employee handbooks, policy manuals, and benefits packets are provided.

marketing matters

Today is Steven's first day on the job. He was hired as the shift supervisor at On-Time Deliveries, and he's a little nervous. He reported to work a few minutes early so he would have time to prepare himself for the day. Steven wants to make a good impression on his manager, as well as build strong working relationships with the people he will supervise. What are some things Steven can do to get off to a positive start in his new position?

jacomstephens/iStockphoto.com

When Ryan began working at Solutions Software, he attended an orientation held by the human resources department with other new employees. He learned about Solutions Software's founder, John Lanashia, as well as the history of the company. He also learned about the company's products, target markets, key competitors, mission, and differentiation strategies. Ryan received organizational charts that outlined reporting relationships and listed the names of key managers. He felt more comfortable with his role as a sales representative after he learned the "inside details" of the company.

A human resources manager then talked about the culture of Solutions Software, including the dress code, diversity awareness, and the company's focus on teamwork and customer support. Flexible work arrangements, ongoing training opportunities, the "promote from within" mindset, vacation guidelines, the performance evaluation system, harassment policies, and company events were explained. The orientation concluded with a tour of the facility.

The First Day

Remember your first day of school? Did you experience "first day jitters"? You may have known some of your classmates, perhaps even some of your teachers, but you were probably still a little anxious. This anxiety may have come from the uncertainty of new classes, new activities, and new experiences.

Did**You**Know**?**

Eleanor Roosevelt said, "The future belongs to those who believe in the beauty of their dreams."

Stockbyte/Getty Images

Workshop

In small groups, make a list of behaviors to avoid in a new position. Include behaviors that create a bad first impression. Share the list with your classmates, and discuss appropriate behaviors.

When you start a new job, you may feel the same sort of uncertainty and anxiety. You probably don't know your boss very well, you may not have met your new coworkers, and you certainly don't have the understanding of the inner workings of the organization that can only come with experience.

Learning the Ropes Tracy was excited to begin her new job as a receptionist for an advertising agency. She felt that this position was her "foot in the door" and could lead to her real goal, working as a copywriter in creative services. The night before the big day, she reviewed her notes about her interviews and visits to the agency and planned her outfit according to company policy.

Tracy arrived 15 minutes early so she would have time to get settled and introduce herself to her coworkers, hoping to make a good first impression. She was friendly and polite, yet reserved, staying out of the morning chitchat. She attended orientation, where she met new employees from other departments, completed paperwork, and learned more about the agency.

When she returned to her desk around noon, she was invited to go to lunch with a few of her coworkers, including Aziz, whom she was replacing because he was being promoted. She readily accepted, knowing that this would be a good opportunity to socialize and show enthusiasm for the organization and her new position.

Tracy also hoped that Aziz would act as a **mentor**, an experienced employee who helps a new employee learn about the ways of the organization. That afternoon, Aziz worked with Tracy, teaching her the phone system, providing helpful information about employees, and explaining the agency's policies for voice mail and forwarding calls. Tracy was exhausted by the end of the day but knew that it had been productive. She reviewed the orientation information that evening and felt less anxious when she returned to work the next day.

Look Before You Leap The first day of a new job can be anxiety ridden, but you can take some steps that will reduce your anxiety and prepare you for a smooth transition.

- **Prepare yourself** Review your interview record-keeping sheet. Be sure you know where and to whom you will report on your first day. Plan your transportation so you arrive early. Set out your clothes the night before, and be sure you have identification, a notebook, and anything else you have been asked to bring.

- **Be on time** Allow more than enough time to get to work and introduce yourself to your new coworkers.

- **Plan to listen** Especially on the first day, resist the urge to demonstrate how much you know. Instead, listen more than you speak.

- **Be friendly and positive** Be open and polite to others, and project a positive attitude. Don't participate in gossip, and don't criticize. Offer assistance, ask for advice, and demonstrate your willingness to learn.

- **Take notes** Remembering every detail required to master a new set of job tasks is impossible. A notebook provides a quick review and a reminder of procedures.
- **Accept responsibility** Be accountable for your actions, and portray your abilities and experience honestly. You should be well on your way toward earning the respect of your new coworkers.

Check > Point

What are the benefits of attending an orientation?

Moving On

While it may seem strange to think about moving on after glimpsing your first day at a new job, labor statistics show that most people hold seven to ten jobs throughout their career. Your first job probably will not be your last. Understanding why people change jobs, how to make the move, and what to say to your employer can help smooth the transition.

In the mid-1900s, **lifetime employment**, or staying with one company for the duration of your career, was typical. Today, most people work for many different companies over the course of their careers.

Why Employees Leave

Employees choose to leave their jobs for many different reasons. Some common reasons include:

- **Loss of interest** Employees feel that their positions do not challenge them, their organizations have lost their appeal, or their work is no longer meaningful.
- **Lack of appreciation** Employees feel that their efforts are not recognized or that they are not rewarded for their contributions.
- **Lack of opportunities** The organization may not follow a "promote from within" structure, leaving employees to feel that there is no room for advancement. Training and development opportunities may also be limited.
- **Low salary** If employees did not research realistic salary ranges, they may have agreed to inadequate pay. If reasonable salary requirements are not met, employees may feel dissatisfied and look elsewhere.
- **Poor skills match** Employees' skills may not adequately match the job responsibilities. Perhaps the information employees presented

during their interviews was unclear, or perhaps the responsibilities have changed. When jobs are too easy, employees may become bored. When jobs are too difficult, they may experience frustration.

Considering a Change

If you experience any of the above situations, you may feel you have reason to leave your job. Before leaving a job, keep in mind that it is probably best to have another job lined up first. It may be easier to find a new job while you are still working, as gaps in employment are sometimes viewed unfavorably. Being employed shows employers that you are employable.

You might also consider the advantages and disadvantages of staying in your current position. If your position is secure, staying may pose little risk because you keep your benefits, such as vacation time, and you will build a reputation for stability. On the other hand, a new job could offer new challenges, more opportunity for advancement, or a better compensation package.

The Internet has made searching for new jobs much easier. Even someone who is satisfied with his or her current situation may choose to browse job listings, looking for that great opportunity. Use the Internet wisely, keeping in mind that you should consider the pros and cons before changing jobs.

Your Resignation

How you **resign**—relinquish or give up—your position within an organization can affect your future employment. To resign gracefully, follow the advice below.

- **Never burn bridges** If you choose to leave an organization, plan to resign professionally. Don't leave in anger or make disparaging remarks. You may find yourself working with your manager or coworkers again in the future.

- **Be practical** Many potential employers ask for references from former employers. Help ensure your employer will provide a fair reference by leaving on pleasant terms; provide at least two weeks' notice of your departure, and cooperate with others to organize your workspace and manage the transition.

- **Be considerate** Show your willingness to complete projects before you leave, offer to help train an employee to take over your position, and remain positive. The impression you make when you leave may be the one an employer remembers when providing a reference.

- **Submit a resignation letter** You should submit a formal letter of resignation when you leave an organization. The letter will serve as notice that you are leaving and provide an effective date for your departure. State the benefits of your employment with the organization, and thank your employer for the opportunities you received.

Why is it best to have another job lined up before leaving your current job?

11.1 Assessment

THINK CRITICALLY

1. How does an orientation help acquaint you with your new company?

2. What is a mentor?

3. How can you decrease anxiety about your first day on the job?

4. What should you include in a resignation letter?

MAKE ACADEMIC CONNECTIONS

5. **BUSINESS PRACTICES** Contact the human resources departments of three companies to determine if they hold orientations for new employees. If they do, ask for a description, including the format, the information covered, and the materials provided. Prepare a PowerPoint presentation reporting your findings.

6. **COMMUNICATION** Christopher is planning to resign from his position as an assistant chef at Southfield Bistro because he has accepted a position as executive chef at Lathrop Village Grille. Write Jesse's resignation letter to Southfield Bistro's owner, Paul Paradis.

Employment Satisfaction

Goals
- Identify the qualities organizations desire in employees
- Understand the importance of customer service

Key Terms
- competent
- initiative
- time wasters
- procrastination
- organization
- external customers
- internal customers
- customer satisfaction

Becoming an Effective Employee

You've made it through the first day of your new job, and now you're thinking about the future. How can you be successful in your new position? How can you add value to the organization? What can you do to be viewed as an effective employee?

All employers value certain behaviors and attributes in their employees. These include putting in a full day's work, taking initiative, being willing to learn, managing your time, being organized, and accepting responsibility.

Competence

Being **competent** means being properly or sufficiently qualified to do a job. It also includes working hard and showing **initiative**—taking on work that needs to be done without specifically being asked. When you begin a new job, especially an entry-level job, you'll be expected to learn quickly and contribute to the organization. You were hired, in part, because you possess the basic skills needed to do the job. You may receive some training, but you will be expected to handle all your assignments and duties effectively, even those you haven't been specifically trained for.

marketing matters

Hunter has just accepted an internship with a local television station. When he arrives on the first day, his supervisor, Josina, explains that he will need to answer the phones, photocopy or print out stories, and help the reporters prepare to go on air. Hunter begins to think he made a mistake in accepting the internship. He wants to gain experience in TV journalism, but instead he'll spend his time on tasks that he thinks are beneath him. How should Hunter view these tasks? What benefits can this internship provide based on his career interests?

©Zsolt Nyulaszi, 2009/Used under license from Shutterstock.com

You may be asked to assist others, complete tasks that seem boring, or handle assignments that no one else wants. You should take the stance that no job is too small. Whether you are washing windows or managing a million dollar sales account, complete the assignment effectively and on time. Though the "small" jobs may seem insignificant to you, they are often very important to the overall functioning and success of the organization.

Be sure to follow instructions, whether they are from a manager or from a reference manual. Double-check your work—turning in incomplete or sloppy work makes a bad impression. Be willing to show initiative. Pay attention to customers, other employees, and work assignments. How can you help? Where can you add value?

To establish effective long-term relationships, you need to provide value. Don't enter a relationship with an employer focused only on how you can benefit. Instead, develop a mutually beneficial relationship.

Learning

Learning refers to the process of gaining knowledge or skills. Have you heard the phrase "lifelong learner"? Learning is a continuous process: No one can learn all there is to know about everything, so you should be aware of all that you don't know and constantly strive to build your knowledge.

When you start a new job, you will need to learn more about the organization, your position, and the company's culture. To learn more about the organization, you can read brochures, policy manuals, annual reports, and so on. Visit the company's web site, and search for press releases that provide

Photodisc/Getty Images

insight into new developments, products and services, or anything else of interest. Observe your coworkers, and ask questions as they arise. How do others behave and interact? How does work get accomplished?

The interviewer may have given you basic information about your new position. You probably have some idea of your responsibilities. Your supervisor may meet with you to discuss your position and his or her expectations in more detail when you begin the job. If not, ask for a clarification of your responsibilities and priorities. As you begin working, you may have additional questions about the position, but you may not need to go to your supervisor for an answer to every question. Instead, ask for assistance from coworkers. Doing this can also help you build relationships with them.

What are some tasks you often procrastinate with? Develop a list of three to five items, and, working in small groups, develop strategies to overcome procrastination.

Time Management

Many employers believe the saying that "Time is money." Managing your time effectively can help you become more organized, meet deadlines, and complete priority projects. To manage your time more effectively, you should be punctual, plan your day, and avoid time wasters.

Being Punctual Sabrina always arrives at work by 7:55 a.m., so she'll have time to put away her things and be at her desk—ready to begin her first project—promptly at 8 a.m. When employees arrive late for work, even by only five minutes, the result is lost productivity. Five minutes per day, five days per week for one month adds up to nearly two hours of lost work time.

Planning Your Day To arrive at work by 7:55 a.m., Sabrina must wake up and begin her day by 6 a.m. She chooses, instead, to manage her time even more effectively by waking up at 5:45 a.m. and using the extra 15 minutes to plan her day and what she wants to accomplish. She writes a list of tasks she plans to accomplish and then ranks them according to priority. Essential tasks are labeled with an "A." Sabrina focuses on completing these first. Supporting tasks are labeled with a "B." She works on these as soon as she has completed the day's "A" tasks. Tasks labeled with a "C" are those she would like to accomplish, if she has time. Sometimes, "C" tasks are carried over to the next day, and sometimes, based on deadlines, they become "B" or "A" tasks.

Avoiding Time Wasters **Time wasters** are activities that limit productivity. They may include interruptions, socializing, or even trips to the document shredder. While you may need to take a break during the day, as it is difficult to be productive at every moment, you should consider ways to limit activities that take time away from your planned tasks. Sabrina realized that she was losing time when a coworker frequently stopped by her desk to talk socially. While she enjoyed talking with Marco, he would sometimes sit down near her desk and talk about topics unrelated to work for 10 to 15 minutes at a time. Sabrina moved unoccupied chairs away from her desk, thinking that he might talk with her briefly if he could not comfortably sit and chat. She also decided to tell him when she was very busy and to suggest that they meet for lunch occasionally to chat socially.

Procrastination, deferring or delaying action, can become habitual. Do you often put off doing things that you need to do? Sometimes people procrastinate because a task seems overwhelming and they don't know where to begin. They may procrastinate because they want to wait until everything is perfect before beginning, or they may be uninterested in a task because they perceive it to be boring or meaningless.

Sabrina realized that she sometimes procrastinated completing the paperwork associated with an assignment because she wanted to wait until she collected all the needed information for her reports. She determined that if she wanted to manage her time more effectively, she needed to get started on paperwork as soon as possible. Rather than waiting for all the information, she began completing as much as she could and made a file for incomplete items. Once she got started, it was easier for her to complete the reports.

Organization

When you complete your homework each night, do you work in a set area where you keep items such as pencils, a dictionary, and a calculator? Or do you set your book down in the most convenient spot and then go looking for the items you need? Do you keep reports, assignments, and projects organized, or are you frequently looking for the information you need?

Organization refers to an orderly structure or system. Getting organized can make completing tasks easier and more efficient. Disorganization wastes time, causes stress, and sometimes leads to procrastination. Have you heard the saying "A place for everything, and everything in its place"? Spend a little time now filing paperwork, keeping a schedule, and organizing your work space, and you can save a lot of time later.

Filing Paperwork Try to handle each piece of paper or e-mail message only once. If you need to take action, do it right away. If you can't do it immediately, put it in an "action" file. If you need to keep it for reference, file it immediately, creating a file if necessary. If you don't need it, throw it away. Do not let clutter consume you. File information as it is received.

Keeping a Schedule You can't remember everything, so write things down. Use a planner or other calendar-based system, and write down appointments, meetings, and tasks. Your written schedule should also include your prioritized "to-do" list.

Organizing Your Work Space Whether you have an office, a station, a cubicle, or a counter, keep it neat. Make sure needed supplies are handy, and put them away as soon as you are finished with them. A surgeon can't make the first incision if she can't find the scalpel.

Responsibility and Accountability

When you accept a job, you assume responsibilities, including getting along with others, timeliness, behaving in a professional manner, and completing job duties. You are responsible for your actions and your performance. Taking responsibility shows maturity and confidence. Don't be afraid of failure. Instead, consider it a learning opportunity.

With personal responsibility comes public accountability. You are accountable to others for your actions. You are accountable to your manager for your job responsibilities. You are accountable to your customers for the service you provide. Rather than placing blame, acknowledge the situation, work to resolve it, and apologize when necessary.

Check Point

Explain the importance of taking initiative on the job, and provide an example.

Customer Relations

Total customer service involves satisfying both external and internal customers. Organizations need external customers to exist. To function effectively in meeting shared goals and objectives, employees should also view each other as "customers."

External customers are customers outside the organization who purchase your products or services. Good customer service is simply good business. Repeat business and referrals from satisfied customers can help build a company's market as well as its reputation. No matter what your position in the organization, you are in the business of serving customers.

Internal customers are employees within the organization. Organizations that promote an environment of teamwork recognize the value of adopting a customer mindset internally. Employees in some departments, such as human resources or accounting, may deal infrequently, if at all, with external customers.

Building Relationships with Customers

Relationships involve reliability, responsiveness, assurance, and empathy. You can demonstrate reliability by following through on your promises and never promising more than you know you can deliver. If the payroll department, an

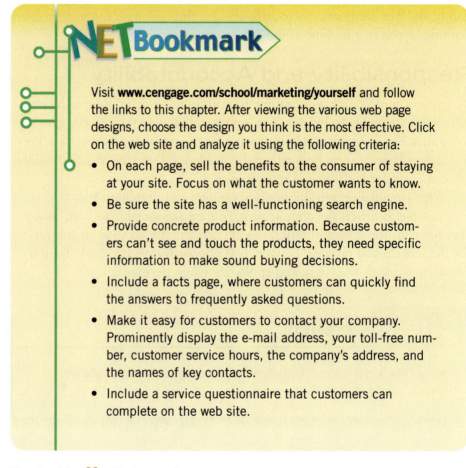

NETBookmark

Visit **www.cengage.com/school/marketing/yourself** and follow the links to this chapter. After viewing the various web page designs, choose the design you think is the most effective. Click on the web site and analyze it using the following criteria:

- On each page, sell the benefits to the consumer of staying at your site. Focus on what the customer wants to know.

- Be sure the site has a well-functioning search engine.

- Provide concrete product information. Because customers can't see and touch the products, they need specific information to make sound buying decisions.

- Include a facts page, where customers can quickly find the answers to frequently asked questions.

- Make it easy for customers to contact your company. Prominently display the e-mail address, your toll-free number, customer service hours, the company's address, and the names of key contacts.

- Include a service questionnaire that customers can complete on the web site.

diversity in the workplace

To embrace the diversity of your customers, you need to demonstrate that you value them. Here are some ways to do that.

- Listen attentively to what your customers say. Keep an open mind; don't judge. Ask questions if you don't understand.

- Strive to understand the causes of communication breakdowns. Take immediate steps to understand what the customer is telling you; for example, ask your manager to join the conversation.

- Speak against stereotypes, prejudice, and harassment. Avoid using language and humor that others may not understand or may find offensive.

- Avoid touching customers or commenting on their physical appearance or attributes.

- Support all of the many varied cultures of your customers. Try saying "hello" in a customer's primary language. If you decorate your workplace for the holidays, be sure to represent all cultures.

internal customer, wants to receive employee time cards as soon as possible, don't promise to provide them by the end of the day if you know that you have other priorities and probably won't meet that deadline.

Being responsive means providing service in a timely manner. Be willing to help customers, even if you are busy, and help them in a reasonable amount of time. Providing assurance means acting so that customers are confident in your abilities and feel secure working with you. Empathy occurs when you consider the feelings of your customers. You think about their interests, give them individual attention, and try to understand their needs.

Satisfying Customers

Customer satisfaction relates to managing the perceptions that customers have of your company's performance in relation to their expectations. When your performance equals or exceeds their expectations, they are satisfied. When your performance does not meet their expectations, they are dissatisfied.

You can affect a customer's expectations. For example, if you exaggerate your abilities to an employer, he or she will expect you to work at a level beyond your capability. If your performance doesn't meet expectations because you don't really have the skills you said you did, your employer will be dissatisfied with you.

Satisfying customers has its benefits. When customers are satisfied, they are more likely to speak positively to others about you and the organization and they are more likely to become loyal customers.

What are the four elements of relationship building?

11.2 Assessment

THINK CRITICALLY

1. Provide an example of each of the four elements of relationship building.

2. Describe three things you can do to improve your organization skills.

3. Why should you avoid stereotyping your customers?

4. How can having satisfied customers benefit an organization?

MAKE ACADEMIC CONNECTIONS

5. **BUSINESS PRACTICES** Customers who receive poor service don't always complain. Sometimes they simply stop frequenting the business. View some case studies on the International Customer Service Association's web site accessible via www.cengage.com/school/marketing/yourself. What are some ways a company can encourage customers to tell them when they receive poor service? Report your findings in a one-page paper.

6. **CONTINUING EDUCATION** Identify appropriate continuing education courses or training workshops you could take to update your skills and knowledge on an ongoing basis once you start working. Include any plans you have to obtain an additional or advanced degree, certificate, or license. Prepare a written or oral report of your findings, including the names of the education or training providers and courses or workshops.

7. **COMMUNICATION** Have you or anyone you know received poor service as a result of discrimination or stereotyping? Describe the situation, then write an explanation of what could have occurred if everyone involved had been sensitive to diversity.

Issues in the Workplace

Goals

- Explain how to deal with conflicts in the workplace
- Understand issues facing employees today

Key Terms

- conflict
- discrimination
- sexual harassment
- substance abuse

Conflict Resolution

Though the organization you work for may want everyone to get along and work together effectively, the reality is that people are different; they have different needs, expectations, and behaviors, and no one gets along perfectly with everyone else all the time. **Conflicts** are struggles or states of opposition. They tend to occur when what one person wants is not compatible with what another person wants.

Good vs. Bad Conflict

Contrary to what you may think, not all conflict is negative. After all, what would a workplace be like if everyone agreed all the time? Workers would say yes to everything, creativity would be stifled, and new ideas would probably not be developed. Conflict is inevitable, and some degree of conflict can provide a balance, generating creativity and innovation. Conflict can even lead to organizational change. When there is too much conflict, though, time and resources are wasted on disagreements, and lack of cooperation can cause chaos and delays.

Managers will generally intervene once a conflict begins to affect productivity. When Christine gets angry and blames Ron for delaying a project, Ron begins to feel uncomfortable. Though they are working

marketing matters

Conway has been working at Hair by Lauren for a few weeks. He notices that Ken and Audrey don't pay much attention to each other, and that when they are forced to work together they either don't speak or make curt remarks to each other. Other employees have told Conway to keep his distance, so rather than asking questions or asking either of them for help, he puts off tasks or leaves his station to find another employee who can help him. How does the conflict between Ken and Audrey affect Conway? How does it affect salon operations?

©Laser222, 2009/Used under license from Shutterstock.com

together on a new project, he starts avoiding Christine, preferring to keep his distance rather than deal with her comments. When a meeting is scheduled with the entire project team, Ron calls in sick. His manager begins to notice the tension between Ron and Christine and recognizes that the team is not functioning effectively because of the strain. Rather than promoting innovation and creativity, the conflict could delay the new project as well.

Resolving Conflict

When a conflict escalates to the point where it affects productivity, try using the following strategies to resolve it.

- **Acknowledge the conflict** The people involved in the conflict should admit that a conflict has arisen, describe the disagreement or dispute, and give others the opportunity to explain their viewpoints.

- **Problem solve** Take an objective, logical look at the issue. Talk in terms of facts, and keep emotions in check. Consider possible alternatives.

- **Compromise** Compromise involves give and take. While compromising can resolve conflicts, most compromises involve emotion and power, which can lead to solutions that may not be in the best interest of the organization.

- **Mediate** The goal of mediation is to use a person who is not involved in the conflict to help find a win-win solution. The mediator may work for the organization or be hired externally. Mediators don't force a solution that is binding, but work with the individuals involved in the conflict to help them resolve the situation in a way that benefits them and the organization.

Avoiding Conflict

The best way to deal with conflict is to avoid it in the first place. Of course, not all conflict can be avoided, but strategies can be used to reduce it. These include:

- An organizational culture that does not tolerate any discrimination.
- Formal grievance procedures.
- Clearly explained responsibilities for each position.
- A focus on teamwork and task completion.
- A management style that promotes tolerance and the open exchange of ideas.
- A focus on training so employees have the knowledge, skills, and support they need to do their jobs.
- A reward system based on cooperation and achievement of overall organizational objectives.

careerbuilder®

Workplace Conflict Resolutions

By Rachel Zupek, CareerBuilder.com writer
Copyright 2008 CareerBuilder, LLC.—Reprinted with permission.

From the guy who thinks his desk is his living room/kitchen/bedroom to the manager who asks for (then steals) your ideas, every worker faces workplace conflict. (And if you don't, let me know where you work—I want an application.)

As offices become more diverse in age, talent and ethnicity, conflict is inevitably prevalent in the workplace. Lori Coruccini, CEO of Predix Link Inc., a work-force development consulting company, says variances usually arise because of the lack of communication and clarity on how to reach common work goals. Employees don't know how to understand each other based on their individual workplace behavior.

"Depending on their behavioral traits, some employees may not appreciate a fast-changing environment because of the need to naturally process through information," Coruccini says. "Others' behaviors may be perceived as being demanding and being 'told' what to do. Every employee has unique behaviors, which, if understood in a team environment, can reduce conflict."

If clashes at work aren't reduced, vital parts of business are affected. For example, conflict causes a distraction, which decreases productivity and is also a de-motivator. Conflict also causes procrastination because your mind isn't focused on the end goal, Coruccini says. If disagreements are taken personally, it causes resentment toward co-workers or the company as a whole.

"When conflict is taken personally, it can shut down communication, cause intimidation, de-motivate, cause health issues if not dealt with, and the lack of interest to complete a mission or common goal," Coruccini warns.

However, some conflict can be healthy if you properly deal with situations to reach a proper resolution. But, this can only be done if you know how other people effectively deal with differences.

"Everyone communicates differently according to their natural behavior; everyone is driven differently based on their behaviors," Coruccini says. "Once there is an understanding of why others respond the way they do, it makes it easier to respect the other person and recognize that statements or comments are not about you and they don't take things personally."

Here are five examples of conflict you might face in the workplace:

- Being told what to do rather than asked. This causes tension, and employees become defensive.
- Employees who have different communication styles. One employee may need specific information while the other may just need the basics. Each will shut down when there is too much (or too little) information.

continued on page 304

- Different behavioral back-up styles. For example, someone may deflect controversy for a while, but when put under too much pressure, he or she may become confrontational. Others may take offense to the back-up style, which causes conflict.
- When there is not a clear vision or mission. This usually means wasted energy and money spent in a workplace.
- Unclear job expectations are sure to cause conflict for the manager and the employee.

Make use of the following tips to resolve conflict at work:

Choose your battles. How important is the dispute really? Does it truly affect you, and is it a chronic problem? If it's a one-time incident or mild transgression, let it pass.

Expect conflict. Friction will occasionally emerge in the course of human relationships—it's natural. Don't fear it—rather, learn to spot the symptoms early and see opportunity in the resolution.

Use neutral language. Avoid judgmental remarks or sweeping generalizations, such as, "You never respond to my e-mails." Use calm, neutral language to describe what is bothering you. For example: "I get very frustrated when you don't return my messages because I never know if you've received important information." Be respectful and sincere, never sarcastic.

Practice preventive maintenance. Avoid retreating to the safety of withdrawal, avoidance or the simplistic view that your co-worker is a bad person. These are defense mechanisms that prevent the resolution of conflict. Instead, focus on the problem, not the person. Never attack or put the other person on the defensive.

Listen actively. Never interrupt the other party. Really listen and try to understand what the other person is saying. Let him know you understand by restating or reframing his statement or position, so he knows you have indeed heard him.

Get leverage on yourself. When disputes between you and a co-worker appear without resolution, get leverage. Ask to be held accountable. This brings your performance evaluation into the equation without taking away your responsibility for resolving the conflict. This is hard to do, but remarkable change can happen when you are held to task.

Check ▶ Point

How can conflict benefit an organization?

Contemporary Workplace Issues

In some ways, the world of work connects an individual's public and private lives. As personal and professional selves become more integrated, issues that affect individuals at home begin to affect them at work as well. For instance, stress in the home due to a family member's illness often translates into increased stress at work. Societal issues, such as the increasing number of mothers who work outside the home, can affect the workplace as well. Organizations must consider policies, such as flexible work arrangements or on-site child care, that may help employees balance the demands of home and work.

Discrimination

Discrimination is the inappropriate treatment of an individual based on a group or class that the individual belongs to. Discrimination may occur on the basis of race, age, ethnicity, gender, or disability. In some cases, laws have been passed in an attempt to eliminate workplace discrimination. The Equal Employment Opportunity Commission (EEOC) was created by the federal government to deal with issues of discrimination and harassment in the workplace.

Affirmative Action The concept of affirmative action calls for minorities and women to be given special consideration in employment, education, and contracting decisions. Affirmative action programs were put in place to encourage the hiring of diverse individuals and to discourage workplace discrimination. Affirmative action was not designed as a quota system, but rather as a way to ensure that all qualified candidates, regardless of race, ethnicity, or gender, were given consideration.

Photodisc/Getty Images

com-mu-ni-cate

Research affirmative action, including its history and its role today. Based on what you learn, decide where you stand on the issue, and write a letter to your U.S. representative explaining your position.

In small groups, consider how diversity benefits the workplace. Share your ideas with your classmates.

Workshop

Special Needs

The Americans with Disabilities Act requires that employers make reasonable accommodations for employees with special needs and discourages discrimination based on disability. If an individual is qualified to perform the essential functions of the job, he or she should be considered.

Sexual Harassment

Most organizations have policies in place prohibiting sexual harassment. **Sexual harassment** includes unwelcome sexual advances or remarks as well as inappropriate language or physical conduct. You may be able to stop harassment by confronting the person involved, and/or notifying your manager. However, if the severity of the situation warrants it and the company does not address the situation, you might consider filing a formal grievance with the EEOC.

Photodisc/Getty Images

Compensation

The Equal Pay Act states that men and women should be paid equally for equal work in the same establishment. The job content, not title, is reviewed to assess if substantially equal skills, effort, responsibility, and working conditions are involved. According to a 2007 U.S. Census Bureau study, women are paid an average of only 77 cents for every dollar a man earns.

Health and Safety Issues

The Occupational Health and Safety Act (OSHA) requires employers to provide a workplace environment free from recognized hazards likely to cause serious physical harm to employees. In addition, employees are required to follow safety and health standards in the workplace. In addition to safety issues, employers also are faced with employee health issues. While health issues affect individuals, they also affect the workplace in the form of lost productivity and absenteeism. Two health issues that often affect workplaces are substance abuse and HIV/AIDS.

Substance Abuse

Substance abuse is the overuse of drugs or alcohol. In some jobs, such as operating equipment or driving, such abuse can present a very dangerous situation. It can also lead to absenteeism, tardiness, diminished productivity, and employee theft. Many employers require pre-employment drug screening, and some have policies allowing for random drug screening of employees.

marketing math connection

Mary Ellen Keeley's employer offers a health insurance plan that covers Mary Ellen, her husband, and their child. The total monthly premium is $285, of which the employer pays 26%. How much does Mary Ellen pay for the health insurance for one year?

SOLUTION

$$
\begin{aligned}
\text{Total annual premium} &= \text{Total monthly premium} \times 12 \\
&= \$285 \times 12 \\
&= \$3{,}420 \\
\text{Employer's share of premium} &= \text{Total annual premium} \times 26\% \\
&= \$3{,}420 \times 0.26 \\
&= \$889.20 \\
\text{Mary Ellen's share of premium} &= \text{Total annual premium} - \text{Employer's} \\
&\qquad \text{share of premium} \\
&= \$3{,}420 - \$889.20 \\
&= \$2{,}530.80
\end{aligned}
$$

Some companies have established employee assistance programs (EAPs) to provide counseling and treatment to employees. Organizations may also provide benefits that cover treatment of substance abuse.

HIV/AIDS Many organizations have developed policies for dealing with employees who test positive for HIV. These policies primarily regulate confidentiality.

Family Issues

Family issues have gained attention as the numbers of women in the workplace, two-income families, and older workers have increased.

Flexible Work Arrangements To keep experienced employees who may have family obligations, such as children or an aging parent, some organizations offer flexible work arrangements. These arrangements can include flexible working hours, job sharing and telecommuting.

Child Care Employees are less productive when they have to solve problems such as finding quality child care and attending to a sick child. Some companies offer on-site day care centers as an employee benefit, while others provide subsidies or flexible spending accounts that parents can use to pay for child care with pre-tax dollars. Some companies provide care centers for sick children so parents don't have to miss work to care for them.

Family Medical Leave Act The Family Medical Leave Act requires employers to allow eligible employees to take an unpaid leave of absence from their positions for up to 12 weeks per year to recover from an illness or to care for a sick child, spouse, or parent or a new child.

What program did the federal government create to help reduce discrimination in the workplace?

11.3 Assessment

THINK CRITICALLY

1. What is a conflict?

2. Identify four strategies to try to resolve a conflict at work.

3. What is the purpose of affirmative action?

4. What can you do if you believe you are experiencing sexual harassment?

MAKE ACADEMIC CONNECTIONS

5. **EMPLOYMENT LAW** For more information on employment discrimination law, visit this textbook's web site at **www.cengage. com/school/marketing/yourself** and follow the links to this activity. Prepare a poster that highlights and summarizes the key employment discrimination laws described on the site.

6. **REAL-LIFE APPLICATION** Think about a recent conflict you experienced with a friend or family member. Using the conflict resolution suggestions in this chapter, write a script that demonstrates how the conflict could be successfully resolved.

7. **CONSTRUCTIVE CRITICISM** Assume you are beginning a team project in which Robert, notorious for his uncooperativeness and ill temper, has to play a major role. Think about how you might approach Robert to advise him to behave cooperatively during the project. How could you begin? What points could you make? How would you try to avoid conflicts before they begin?

INTERNET
@

VOCABULARY BUILDER

Choose the term that best fits the definition. Write the letter of the answer in the space provided. Some terms may not be used.

_____ 1. An experienced employee who helps a new employee learn about the ways of the organization

_____ 2. The ability to take on work that needs to be done without specifically being asked

_____ 3. An opportunity to learn about a company or help new employees adjust to a new working environment

_____ 4. Properly or sufficiently qualified to do a job

_____ 5. Inappropriate treatment of an individual based on the group or class the individual belongs to

_____ 6. Staying with one company for the duration of one's career

_____ 7. Deferring or delaying action

_____ 8. A struggle or state of opposition

_____ 9. To relinguish or give up your position at a company.

_____ 10. Overuse of drugs or alcohol

_____ 11. Unwelcome sexual advances or remarks as well as inappropriate language or physical conduct

a. competent
b. conflict
c. customer satisfaction
d. discrimination
e. external customers
f. initiative
g. internal customers
h. learning
i. lifetime employment
j. mentor
k. organization
l. orientation
m. procrastination
n. resign
o. sexual harassment
p. substance abuse

REVIEW CONCEPTS

www.cengage.com/school/marketing/yourself

12. How can you prepare for your first day at a new job?

13. What are some reasons employees leave a position or a company?

14. Why should you be professional when resigning a position?

15. How should you view every task you're asked to complete?

16. Why is learning a continuous process?

17. How can you learn more about your new organization?

18. How can you manage your time more effectively?

19. What are some reasons people procrastinate?

20. What does it mean to be responsive to customers?

21. When is conflict negative?

APPLY WHAT YOU LEARNED

22. What does the term "discrimination" mean to you? What examples of discrimination in the workplace are you aware of?

23. Many employers are willing to spend money to help employees improve their general health. Why do you think this is so? Be specific about how a company might benefit.

24. Ken hated inventory time at Poe's Hardware. To complete an inventory, he had to count every nut and bolt in a bin and write down the quantity for each item. After he finished one bin, he had to go to the next bin and repeat the process, counting and sorting each size. He often lost count and had to start over—either because he was distracted by a customer or because Mr. Poe would interrupt him with something trivial, such as asking how he was doing. So Ken decided to show Mr. Poe that he didn't like to take inventory. He decided not to come to work during inventory week. And to avoid an argument, he decided not to tell Mr. Poe he wasn't coming in. What is the problem with Ken's action? How should Mr. Poe resolve the problem? How do you think a good employee would have acted?

25. Why would it be important for businesses to evaluate the quality of the customer service they provide?

MAKE ACADEMIC CONNECTIONS

26. **INTERVIEW** Interview a family member about his or her employer's expectations. What are the expectations in the areas below? Create a poster or PowerPoint presentation to report your findings.

   - Attendance
   - Punctuality
   - Completing assignments
   - Dependability
   - Teamwork
   - Follow through
   - Cooperation
   - Respect for authority

27. **CUSTOMER SERVICE** Many companies have a customer service area on their web site. Look at several companies' customer service areas and write a two-page paper describing how the companies serve their online customers and how they could improve service.

28. **SUCCESS SKILLS** Brainstorm a list of characteristics of a good student. Compare the qualities of a good student to the qualities of a good employee. Are they similar? Do school skills equal work skills? How? Be prepared to explain your answers to the class.

29. **RESEARCH AND APPLY** Think of a time you had a conflict with another person at work or school. Keeping that event in mind, visit **www.cengage.com/school/marketing/yourself** and follow the links to this activity. After accessing the recommended web site, click on "Interpersonal Skills." Read at least two articles, writing down the titles and authors. As you read the articles, take notes about any advice that you could have applied to your personal conflict situation. Answer the following questions based on your research: How could you have avoided the conflict? How could you have settled the conflict sooner or more smoothly?

Small Business Management Team Event

The Small Business Management Team Event requires teams of two to four members to provide advice to a start-up business.

Two stay-at-home parents want to start their own business, Gourmet Meals on Wheels, that will provide delicious wholesome dinners for busy families. Statistics indicate that working families spend a lot of money and time eating out at restaurants. The business will work directly with busy families to plan five healthy dinners for families during the week. The two entrepreneurs have set up an appointment to meet with the Small Business Forum to seek assistance and financing in opening this business operation. The two entrepreneurs have $10,000 each in savings that they plan to use for their start-up business.

Your team of two to four members will serve as consultants to the two entrepreneurs. You will provide them with information that they need for their presentation to the Small Business Forum. You must be aware of the location, competition, and the budget needed to successfully operate this business. You will help the entrepreneurs determine what makes their business unique and give them ideas to convince the Small Business Forum to provide financial assistance. You also must suggest ideas for growing the business. You have ten minutes for your presentation and an additional ten minutes to answer the judge's question

Dealing with Difficult People

You have probably heard the old adage, "You can please all of the people some of the time, and some of the people all of the time, but you can't please all of the people all of the time." Throughout your career, you are going to come across people that you find difficult. What makes someone "difficult"? Difficult people may be rude or discourteous, aggressive, angry, sarcastic, or maybe just nasty.

Incivility in the Workplace

Incivility refers to social behavior that lacks good manners, appropriate etiquette, or general courtesy. Incivility can be minor, such as failing to hold the elevator for a coworker or taking the last cup of coffee without making more. More significant examples include failing to give a phone message to a coworker, yelling at or taunting another employee, sabotaging an associate's project, spreading malicious information about a coworker, or numerous other examples of rudeness, verbal abuse, or harassment.

To address issues related to incivility, many organizations have formal and informal organizational policies, procedures, or rules for workplace norms. Codes of conduct or explicit policies formally outline expected behavior and may address organizational values and principles. These policies or codes commonly address issues such as discrimination or harassment, confidentiality, employee safety and health, use of illegal substances, or appropriate coworker interaction. Employees may be asked to read and sign an agreement to adhere to the code of conduct.

Informal workplace norms often are more subtle. While you can learn about formal workplace norms through reading the policies or codes, determining the informal norms can be more challenging. They often are based on organizational culture, and you might learn about these through observation or conversation with coworkers. For example, the organization may not have a formal policy regarding dating a coworker, but you might learn that it is frowned upon by the organization in conversation with a coworker over lunch.

Difficult behavior in the workplace often is marked by unwillingness to adhere to a code of conduct, or even total disregard for workplace norms, including argumentative, rude, or even threatening behavior in the workplace. This type of behavior can have serious consequences, as it can create a hostile working environment, damage relationships, or even lead to a loss of productivity on the job.

The common denominator is that difficult people often display a negative emotion or behavior. In fairness, keep in mind that what may appear difficult to you may not seem so difficult to another. It is valuable to consider the perspective of the so-called difficult person, as it may help you not only to better understand the behavior, but also to better address it. One effective strategy for dealing with difficult behavior is listening. Listen to the comments being made, ask questions to clarify the issue at hand, and then model a calm, appropriate tone and body language as you respond. It may be helpful to remember that you can't fully understand a person's motivation for the difficult behavior. Stress, fatigue, insecurity, and lack of information can contribute to difficult behavior. For example, a new mother whose baby was awake and crying for several hours during the previous night may be fatigued and stressed. She may have behaved differently had she obtained a good night's sleep.

Develop Your Skill

Consider several situations where you have encountered difficult people. Think about how you responded at the time. Prepare several options for a different response that could have been more effective. Work with another student to prepare several scenarios, and then role-play the situations for the class.

Chapter 12

The Entrepreneurial Spirit

12.1 Entrepreneurs In Our Economy

12.2 Starting a Small Business

12.3 Becoming an Entrepreneur

CAREERS IN MARKETING

Avon

A leading global beauty products company, Avon is the world's largest direct seller, with more than 5.5 million independent Avon Sales Representatives. Avon markets beauty supplies, fashion jewelry, and apparel to women in more than 100 countries. Avon began as the California Perfume Company in 1886, and its first sales representative, Mrs. P.F.E. Albee, pioneered the direct door-to-door selling method. The company now includes Avon Color, Anew, Skin-So-Soft, Avon Naturals, mark, and its flagship Avon brand.

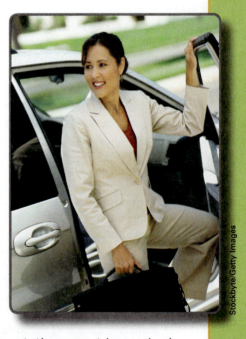

Stockbyte/Getty Images

Avon Sales Representatives operate as independent businesspeople, running the business according to the pace and schedule most convenient for them. They continue to sell Avon offerings by catalog directly to customers they recruit as well as through personalized web sites. Avon Sales Representatives must be goal-oriented leaders who are driven by success. They must provide proactive customer service, maintain a positive attitude, and deliver value with a personal touch.

Think *Critically*

1. Avon explains to sales representatives that they must be their own boss as their earnings potential depends on them and their ability. Why is it important for all entrepreneurs to set high standards for themselves?

2. Why is optimism such an important characteristic for entrepreneurs?

PORTFOLIO BUILDER PROJECT
Showing Your Portfolio

Project Objectives

You can use your career portfolio to provide evidence of your achievements, skills, and experience in a way that reflects the interests of your targeted employer. In this project, you will:

- Collect documentation of your achievements, skills, and experience.
- Select work samples related to employer interests and your career target.
- Practice presenting your portfolio to an employer.

Getting Started

Read the Project Process below. Look at the supporting material on the Portfolio Builder CD. Review the differences between specific workplace skills and SCANS competencies.

Project Process

Part 1   Lesson 12.1 Gather items that provide evidence of your workplace achievements. Locate all positive work evaluations and awards. Look for volunteer awards that show evidence of high work standards, commitment to helping others, and accomplishments.

If you have completed an internship or participated in job shadowing, include your own summary of the experience or a letter from the employer.

Part 2   Lesson 12.2 Gather samples of your work, such as graphic design pages, Power-Point slides, business letters, school newspaper clippings, or web pages. Try to include samples that showcase your ability to use advanced technology. Use the SCANS checklist to help you focus on samples that demonstrate general workplace skills, such as problem-solving, teamwork, and leadership skills. Use the workplace skills checklist to select items that document skills related to your career target.

Part 3   Lesson 12.3 Review your selections, and include only those items that will be meaningful to employers. Practice presenting your portfolio. Think of it as a flexible tool that can be adapted for different situations. You will not show every potential employer every item in your portfolio. Instead, you will use it to demonstrate specific aspects of your achievements, skills, and experience.

Project Wrap-Up

Some interviewers will not have the interest or patience to examine your entire portfolio. With a partner, role-play a tough interview situation in which you show only key portfolio items.

Photodisc/Getty Images

Entrepreneurs In Our Economy

Goals

- Explain how a free enterprise system encourages entrepreneurship
- Understand how entrepreneurship helps shape the current U.S. economy

Key Terms

- entrepreneur
- free enterprise system
- antitrust laws
- information economy
- knowledge economy

A Free Enterprise System

An **entrepreneur** is a person who starts his or her own business. Entrepreneurs whose small ventures become much larger companies are the ones we usually hear about in the news. Bill Gates started Microsoft, a computer software business, in his garage. Debbi Fields' Mrs. Fields cookie recipe is now patented and can be enjoyed by mall shoppers everywhere.

Your own family may be involved in an entrepreneurial venture. Perhaps your dad has the primary responsibility for a small business, such as a florist shop, a pet store, or a dry cleaners. If your mom is a doctor in private practice—she has an office, appointments, and patients separate from a hospital or clinic—she is an entrepreneur. Many entrepreneurs sell services, such as dog walking and grooming, executive search and placement, accounting and law, and computer consulting.

Entrepreneurs as a group have enormous influential power in political lobbying, purchasing, and shaping their communities. In the rest of this chapter, you'll learn about the privileges and responsibilities of entrepreneurship, as well as how you can start being an entrepreneur right now!

Entrepreneurs and Free Enterprise

Free enterprise system is another term for capitalism—a system in which most economic resources are privately owned and individuals are

marketing matters

Jacob has played in a youth football league for 10 years. Almost every year, he has grown and has needed to buy new equipment, even though his old equipment was in almost-new condition. He has read and heard that many kids don't play football because buying equipment can be very expensive. How might Jacob use his observations to start his own business? Who would be his suppliers? Who would be his customers?

©Zsolt Nyulaszi, 2009/Used under license from Shutterstock.com

free to decide what they will produce with the resources. A free enterprise system makes entrepreneurship possible by allowing business interactions to be governed by the laws of supply and demand and not restrained by government interference, regulation, or subsidy. This freedom gives business owners the opportunity to reap the full rewards—and risks—of the ventures they choose to operate, in the way they choose to operate them.

Governed by Laws of Supply and Demand While entrepreneurs can choose what businesses they want to start, the marketability of their products defines their success. A business cannot survive if there is not enough demand for its product.

Entrepreneurs can use knowledge of the laws of supply and demand to help them create successful businesses. For example, a service station that was the only one located near a busy highway exit (one supplier in a high-demand environment) would be more successful than a service station located at a small town intersection near three other service stations (four suppliers in a lesser demand environment). Just as marketers perform research to ensure their products will be bought, entrepreneurs must perform research to determine the skills and experience necessary for success. They also need to know when, where, and by whom their product is desired.

Not Restrained by Government Interference, Regulation, or Subsidy In a true free enterprise system, businesses are free to pursue opportunities, unrestrained by government interference, regulation, or subsidy. True free enterprise systems don't really exist, however. In the United States, some government interference and regulations have been implement-

ed to keep businesses from infringing upon the rights of others. One example of such government regulations is antitrust laws. **Antitrust laws** are designed to promote competition and fairness and to prevent monopolies and other

Digital Vision/Getty Images

unfair business practices, such as false advertising, deceptive pricing, and misleading labeling.

Did You Know?

A brand is more than just a logo. According to David Ogilvy, founder of the Ogilvy advertising agency, it's the way people perceive a business, including "its name, packaging, and price; its history; its reputation; and the way it's advertised."

Check Point

Give a specific example of how supply and demand can work to the benefit of a business.

America and Entrepreneurs

To people around the world, the words "freedom" and "America" are synonymous. Since the first settlers arrived, Americans of all backgrounds have been able to pursue the "American dream"—the freedom, equality, and opportunity available to all Americans. People who were penniless and in oppressive situations journeyed (and still journey) to America for a better life; others with wealth and status left the security of their homelands to pursue more limitless opportunities here.

Using the resources they brought to this country, as well as those they found here, immigrants carved out industries and businesses that created growth in their new communities. Although their industries may not be as strong as they once were and their resources may now be used for other purposes, many cities are still defined by the industries that created them. For example, Pittsburgh's football team is named the Steelers, after the steel industry that brought growth to the city.

Although people continue to rely on natural resources to define local businesses, technology-related changes have created a powerful new world of resources for people everywhere. Today's economy is transitioning from an **information economy**—one that is largely based on the trade of information and the management of the tools used to distribute that information—to a **knowledge economy**—one focused

marketing math connection

Managers like to compare the productivity of their department or company with the productivity of other departments or businesses. One way to do this is to find the cost of a single job (such as a letter or memo) or the cost for a single worker or workstation.

An order center has estimated the total cost of the workstations for 10 order clerks last year. Use the estimates to find the average cost of each workstation.

- Wages and benefits: $138,000
- Space: $8,590
- Utilities: $890
- Depreciation: $13,600
- Supplies, postage, and telephone: $17,098

SOLUTION

Total operating costs	= $138,000 + $8,590 + $890 + $13,600 + $17,098
	= $178,178
Average cost per workstation	= $178,178 \div 10$
	= $17,817.80

on knowledge-intensive activities. This is due to increased globalization and technological advances. Workforce competencies are evolving, as demand for skilled labor, not just in terms of advanced degrees, but also on the job training, is increasing. New communication and data technologies have enabled people to start businesses using resources that can be accessed and transferred independently of location, such as their own skills and knowledge and communication media (for example, telephone lines and satellites). According to Patrick Von Bargen, the executive director of the National Commission on Entrepreneurship, "Entrepreneurs are powering America's economic engine, and they do so in large part by going online."

Photodisc/Getty Images

American companies started by entrepreneurs have created the personal computer, biotechnology, and franchise restaurant chains; shattered AT&T's telecommunications monopoly; and designed innovative products with rippling benefits. Some of the large companies you may be familiar with today were started many years ago by entrepreneurs such as George Eastman (Kodak film), Henry Ford (Ford automobiles), and Henry John Heinz (Heinz ketchup).

Entrepreneurism affects businesses of all sizes and people everywhere. As technology provides increasing career, lifestyle, and location options and as large companies continue to change in size, direction, and ownership, the entrepreneurial spirit will be more important to our lives than ever.

Workshop

If you could start your own business, what would it be? Be creative. Make a list of the types of resources you would need to start the business. Is there any support available to help you obtain these resources?

Check > Point

What is an information economy based on?

careerbuilder®

Turn Your Hobby Into a Career in Five Steps

By Kate Lorenz, CareerBuilder.com
Copyright 2005 CareerBuilder, LLC.—Reprinted with permission.

Experts say that many of today's small businesses are a result of a person following their passion. So don't waste another day doing something you don't enjoy. Follow these five easy steps for turning your hobby into a career you love.

Step 1: Explore the possibilities.

Consider what types of moneymaking opportunities are available in your area of interest. Look online and check the Yellow Pages for business categories and listings of companies that do what you want to do. Visit your local library and seek out reference materials that relate to your hobby.

Let's say your hobby is dog training. Start your research by reading magazines, newspaper articles and books dedicated to dog obedience, pet ownership and animal behavior. In these materials, you are likely to find information that will help you think about what it takes to start a dog training business. Or, check out job search Web sites like CareerBuilder.com for possible openings in your field of interest by doing a keyword search. To perform a search, simply go to the "Quick Job Search" area and enter related key words or phrases such as "dog obedience" or "dog training." You may be surprised to find openings that are a close match to your skills right in your own backyard. If you don't find any, don't be discouraged. Check back often, you never know when a prospective employer will post your dream job.

Step 2: Get expert advice.

Visit your local office of the U.S. Small Business Administration. In addition to providing you with a wealth of information about starting and owning your own business, these offices usually hold conferences and have networking groups for new or prospective business owners. Be sure to ask about any government assistance programs for small business owners.

Experts also suggest that prospective small business owners take advantage of every opportunity to talk to local business owners within their communities by attending chamber of commerce meetings. Once you get to know some of the chamber members, ask them for startup advice or referrals to other sources of assistance. Take a class on starting your own business at your local college or university. You also should consider doing volunteer work or accepting a job in your area of interest. You'll gain firsthand experience and meet valuable contacts that you will need once you get your business up and running.

Step 3: Conduct simple market research.

Talk to people and businesses in your area and ask for feedback on your business idea. It would be very wise for a potential dog trainer to talk to local veterinarians, dog groomers and pet store owners/managers. These are the people

continued on page 321

who work with your potential clientele each and every day. Ask them for their opinions on your business idea and whether there is a market for your services.

Step 4: Draft a simple business plan.

There are scores of books that will walk you through the creation of a simple business plan step-by-step. The SBA can provide you with an easy-to-use format. Whatever you do, don't skip this step. You'll need to see in black and white the blueprint for your potential business.

Step 5: Just do it.

Once you've made the decision to turn your hobby into a job, go for it! That's exactly what one woman with a talent for floral design did. She had loads of floral design products lying around her home from years of making floral arrangements for friends and family members. One day she put all of those materials to work for her. She made up 10 floral arrangements, which she loaded into her van along with her young son and went from floral shop to floral shop selling her products. By the end of the afternoon, she had sold them all and gotten orders for more. Today, she regularly receives orders from area flower shops and has a successful small business all her own.

12.1 Assessment

THINK CRITICALLY

1. What are some recent examples of specific jobs or industries that were affected by supply and demand?

2. Why would an economy that supports entrepreneurship also support innovation?

3. Why is the United States not a true free enterprise system?

4. How has technological advancement encouraged entrepreneurism?

MAKE ACADEMIC CONNECTIONS

5. **ECONOMIC RESEARCH** Research the United States economy and the laws and regulations that prevent it from being a free enterprise system. What changes would need to be made to allow the economy to operate as a true free enterprise system? Present an oral report of your results to the class.

6. **COMPANY RESEARCH** Research a successful business that was started by an entrepreneur. Write a two-page report on the company's growth since operations began and on its contributions to its local economy.

Starting a Small Business

Goals

- Understand the risks and planning involved in starting a small business
- Describe the different types of businesses

Key Terms

- business plan
- franchise
- franchisee
- franchisor
- sole proprietorship
- unlimited liability
- partnership
- general partnership
- limited partnership
- corporation

Small Businesses

Entrepreneurial businesses usually start small. According to the Small Business Administration (SBA), small businesses are defined as businesses with fewer than 500 employees. The SBA's Office of Advocacy reports that small businesses:

- Represent more than 99% of all employers.
- Pay approximately 45% of the total U.S. private payroll.
- Generate 60–80% of new jobs.
- Are 52% home based and 2% franchises.

There were approximately 27.2 million private businesses in the United States in 2007. Of those, 17,000 employed more than 500 people. The rest were considered small businesses.

Taking Risks

Many risks are involved with starting a new business, but the biggest risks are losing money and compromising job security. Before you decide to start a small business, you should have a good understanding of the risks you will face. According to the SBA, two-thirds of new companies survive at least two years, nearly 50 percent are open at least four years, and almost 40 percent remain open after six years.

New businesses take a great investment of an entrepreneur's time and effort. Working long hours, investing personal savings, and borrowing money

marketing matters

DeShawn has always enjoyed landscaping. During warm weather months for the past few years, he has posted flyers and begun to build a business cutting grass and caring for flowers and shrubs. He has always worked alone, but, as his business continues to grow, he is thinking about hiring another person to work with him. Is DeShawn an entrepreneur? Why or why not?

Photodisc/Getty Images

Riser/Getty Images

Workshop

Have you ever mowed lawns, babysat, tutored, or worked in a similar manner? What were some of the rewards associated with working for yourself? What were some of the difficulties?

to cover costs are common. The investment of time and effort, along with the risks involved, can be stressful. But new businesses can also provide personal satisfaction and the opportunity for increased income.

Business Planning

New business ideas come from a variety of sources, including hobbies, interests, and market research. Once you have an idea for a business, the next step is to write a **business plan**. A business plan is a document that details the important characteristics of a business, including the type of business, its products, the industry, a marketing plan, the manner of operation, and financial information.

Your business plan can be viewed as your blueprint for success. Putting the plan together will force you to look seriously at all aspects of the business and how it is going to become successful. Small Business Development Centers, often located within universities, provide resources you can use as you create your business plan. You can also find many templates and sample plans on the Internet.

NETBookmark

Writing an effective business plan is the first step in creating a successful small business. Visit **www.cengage.com/school/marketing/yourself** and follow the links to this activity. After reviewing the information on the web site, write a summary business plan by answering questions 1 through 10 on the web site.

com·mu·ni·cate

Read a biography of a successful entrepreneur—such as Phil Knight, Liz Claiborne, or Sarah Breedlove Walker—and think about what characteristics contributed to that person's success. Write a two-page report explaining your findings.

Check Point

What is a business plan?

Developing a Business

In 2007, approximately 637,000 new businesses were started. If you became an entrepreneur, one of the decisions you will have to make is what sort of business you'd like to develop: a franchise or a new business.

Developing a Franchise

An entrepreneur can start a business by purchasing the rights to participate in an existing business as a franchise owner. A **franchise** is a written contract granting permission to sell someone else's product or service in a prescribed manner over a certain period of time and in a specified territory. Additionally, the word "franchise" is often used to refer to the product or service itself. A franchise involves a **franchisee**—the person or group who buys the franchise—and a **franchisor**—the company whose products the franchisor will sell. A franchisee operates under a franchisor's trade name, and usually with the franchisor's guidance, in exchange for a startup fee and a percentage of sales.

Subway restaurants, Play It Again Sports, and Hallmark stores are examples of franchises. Consultants who market Mary Kay cosmetics through personal selling are franchisees. Chances are you recognize these businesses and the products they sell. Franchisees pay to be associated with these high-recognition names.

Developing a New Business

Developing a new business means that you determine the concept for the business, select a location, and arrange operations. Unlike owning a franchise, owning a new business affords you a great deal of control. You will be responsible for every aspect of your business, including building a customer base, arranging for financing, and delivering your product or service.

You may be familiar with the following entrepreneurs who developed new businesses: Anita Roddick (The Body Shop), Michael Dell (Dell Computer), and Bill Gates (Microsoft). These entrepreneurs were able to turn their ideas into successful businesses, and they grew their small businesses into well-known organizations.

Legal Forms of Business Ownership

As a business owner, you can organize your business as a sole proprietorship, a partnership, or a corporation. The organization that you choose will depend on the type of business you start and your goals for that business.

Photodisc/Getty Images

Sole Proprietorship A business that is owned and operated by one person is known as a **sole proprietorship**. This type of business is both the oldest and the most common. It also tends to be the easiest and least expensive to start.

As the proprietor, you have the freedom to make your own business decisions. But, with this control comes **unlimited liability**—which means that you, as an individual, are responsible for business debts, and your personal property can be used as repayment. For example, if your business cannot afford to pay a supplier, *you* may have to pay the supplier from your personal assets.

Partnership A **partnership** involves two or more people who become responsible for the debts, obligations, and success of a business. In a **general partnership**, partners share equal responsibility for debts and all have unlimited liability. A **limited partnership** *limits* the liability of certain partners. These limited partners often are not involved with the management of the firm. However, at least one partner must have unlimited liability.

Corporation A **corporation** is a business owned by shareholders. It is a legal entity that operates separately from its owners. A corporation is a more complex form of business ownership than a proprietorship or a partnership. But, because a corporation is formed as a separate legal entity, shareholders, who are owners, have limited liability for business debts.

Check > Point

Do you think you would enjoy being an entrepreneur? Would you rather buy a franchise or start a business from scratch? Explain.

THINK CRITICALLY

1. Why do you think the federal government established the SBA?

2. Why is your career likely to begin in a small business?

3. A business plan can be described as a "game plan." What features of the plan justify that label?

4. Why is using a business organization such as a chamber of commerce a useful resource for a person who wants to start a business? What are some student organizations that develop entrepreneurial skills?

MAKE ACADEMIC CONNECTIONS

5. **TECHNOLOGY** What role does technology play in small business? Visit the SBA web site (**www.sba.gov**) and the U.S. Census Bureau web site (**www.census. gov**) to find information related to technology in small businesses. Create a PowerPoint presentation to report your findings.

6. **HISTORY** Research and write a two-page report about the history of corporations in the U.S. For example, what is an LLC? What is a subchapter S corporation?

7. **INTERVIEW** Contact the owner of a local franchise operation. Ask this entrepreneur what attracted him or her to the franchise. What benefits does business ownership bring to this person's life? What trade-offs has he or she had to make? Write a newspaper or magazine article to report what you learned from the interview.

Becoming an Entrepreneur

Goals
- Understand the qualities necessary to be an entrepreneur
- Learn how to become an entrepreneur while employed by someone else

Key Terms
- entrepreneurial personality
- self-starter

Could You Be an Entrepreneur?

Being your own boss is an exciting idea. And, given these three facts about entrepreneurs, it's no wonder that starting a business is a goal for many people.

- Entrepreneurs are the creators of wealth through innovation.

- Entrepreneurs are at the center of economic growth and are the primary job creators in the United States. (As you read earlier in this chapter, more than half of all new jobs are in small businesses.)

- Entrepreneurs provide a mechanism for distributing wealth that depends on innovation, hard work, and risk taking. Thus, entrepreneurs provide a "fair and equitable" method of wealth distribution.

It's also a lot of work—frequently more work than being an employee. As one business owner put it, "You go from having one boss to having many bosses—you report to every customer." Making sure the business has something to offer and keeping customers happy are the business owner's responsibilities. As an employee, you will continue to get a paycheck as long as you have a job, regardless of how well the business is doing. Business owners need to worry about paying for their resources, including employees, before they can earn a profit themselves. On the other hand, the long hours and sacrifices you experience as a business owner can give you personal and professional satisfaction you might not be able to find as an employee.

marketing matters

Larry Villella was only 11 years old when he got an idea that developed into a business. He did not like moving the lawn sprinkler when his chore was to water the lawn. So he went into the basement and cut a sprinkler into a c-shape that fit around trees and shrubs. Four years later, his company, Villella's ConServ Products, had sold about $70,000 worth of products. What personality traits did Larry exhibit when he pursued his idea? Do you have some of these traits?

©Maridav, 2009/used under license from Shutterstock.com

An Entrepreneurial Personality

Do you think you'd make a successful entrepreneur? The most important factor in a successful start-up company is not an incredible new idea or a bottomless bank account, but an **entrepreneurial personality**. While there is no one personality "type" that marks entrepreneurs, people who become successful entrepreneurs do tend to share certain characteristics. To be a successful entrepreneur, you should be a self-starter, an outgoing person, a lifelong learner, and an optimist.

Self-Starter
Do you know what you want and want it enough to get up every day and go after it? If so, you are a **self-starter**. Procrastinators are the opposite of self-starters. They don't allow enough time to complete tasks and end up feeling negative and guilty and avoiding future tasks.

Outgoing Person
Even though you'll be flying solo, you'll need to enjoy meeting people as an entrepreneur. You'll rely on more people than ever to help you accomplish your goals: Satisfied customers will generate good publicity for you, reliable suppliers will provide the resources you need on time, and experts will help you in areas such as accounting and legal matters.

Lifelong Learner
Marketers are always making sure their products are meeting—and anticipating—the needs of their customers. If you are the product, you'll need to reinvest your time, money, and training in your capital (your skills and knowledge) to be an attractive and competitive product.

Optimist
Your ideas and actions may not always take you where you expected, when you expected. Create your own self-fulfilling prophecy: If you believe that things will work out in the end, you'll steer yourself in that direction.

Photodisc/Getty Images

diversity in the workplace

Opportunities for all exist in small business ownership. According to the U.S. Small Business Administration (SBA), in 2002, minorities owned 18% of U.S. firms. Of that group, 6.6% were owned by Hispanic Americans, 5% by African Americans, and 4.6% by Asian Americans. The self-employment rate for women was 6.5%.

The Department of Labor's Office of Disability Employment Policy reports that people with disabilities are nearly twice as likely to be self-employed as non-disabled individuals. Nearly 15% of people with disabilities in the workforce are self employed, compared to 8% of those who are non-disabled.

Source: U.S. Small Business Association web site (www.sba.gov)

Other Common Characteristics   Other traits are also common among entrepreneurs.

- Creativity
- Willingness to accept responsibility
- Willingness to take risks
- An open mind
- A high energy level
- Strong desire for achievement
- A tolerance of uncertainty
- High standards, both personal and professional
- Flexibility
- Self-confidence
- Determination
- Persistence

Learn from the Experience of Others

You may have a talent or an idea you think would be a great new business prospect, but remember, you're new to being a business owner. Don't assume you can start a business without a little outside help. After all, "the wise man learns from his own mistakes—the wiser man learns from others' mistakes." Draw from the experience of seasoned business owners in your community through your local chamber of commerce, SCORE (the Service Corps of Retired Executives), or even your parents or other adults. You may even have friends who have started successful businesses. Most people you ask for advice will be flattered that you consider them experts. What's more, as you consult with the experts, you'll be developing a network of contacts and demonstrating that you have initiative.

Workshop

Do you have what it takes to be an entrepreneur? Visit **www.cengage.com/ school/marketing/ yourself**, follow the links to this activity, and take the entrepreneur personality test. What was your score? Do you believe you have the personal qualities it would take to start and run your own business? for the product?

What is one of the best ways to learn how to start a successful business? Become an employee. Even jobs that seem tedious or unglamorous can be excellent learning experiences, and they will be more bearable if you approach them that way. Additionally, every job is a resume entry and a potential source of a positive recommendation.

Check ▶ Point

If you are thinking about starting your own business, who could you go to for advice?

Entrepreneur or Employee?

Being self-employed or owning a business isn't for everybody: Some people are better suited as employees, which is absolutely fine because businesses need good employees. As an employee, you can enjoy a challenging, opportunity-rich career by using a few entrepreneurial skills in your employer's "marketplace."

You might wonder, "How can I be an entrepreneur if I'm working for someone else?" Workplaces, large and small, are ripe for entrepreneurial activities if you have an entrepreneurial personality. Larger companies know that providing opportunities to learn and grow through training, new experiences, and innovative career paths is one way to guarantee employee satisfaction. It's also good business: Employers reduce the cost of rehiring and retraining employees and are less likely to see their most important resources—knowledge and skills—walk out the door to their competitors.

Photodisc/Getty Images

Any manager who values employee development and coaching will support your entrepreneurial attitude, as long as you can keep up with your current responsibilities. The closer your manager's role is to owner or an executive decision-maker, the closer you'll be to learning how to run a business. This knowledge will make you more valuable in your current

Photodisc/Getty Images

position because you'll know the ins and outs of the organization. Also, it's something you'll take with you when you move on to your next job.

Whether you are looking to stay and make the most of your corporate path or are feeling out the possibilities elsewhere while you're still on solid ground, practicing entrepreneurship as an employee will give you the power to gain as much as you can from your in-house experience.

Develop Your Plan

Answer the following four questions as you develop a plan to become a successful entrepreneur while still being an effective employee: What do you want to accomplish? How can you meet your employer's needs? Whose support do you need? What is your plan?

What Do You Want to Accomplish? Is there a particular skill you want to learn, solution you want to create, or project you want to put in your experience portfolio that isn't one of your current job responsibilities? If it's directly linked to your current job or within the skills your company needs, finding a way to learn a new skill is quick work. Maybe you would like to teach swimming lessons in addition to being a lifeguard or take photographs in addition to writing for your yearbook.

If the skill you'd like to learn is not directly related to your current job, it's not impossible to find a way to create the experience you want, but you'll need to be creative. For example, if you are a sports-arena facilities worker but want more samples for your art and design portfolio, maybe you can talk the promotions or publicity manager into allowing you to design signs for the arena or work with the program publications team.

How Can You Meet Your Employer's Needs? An important part of your job is to make your manager look good. Your manager's job is to manage his or her resources well and to help the company be profitable. If you can adapt your ideas to support your manager, he or she will be more likely to promote them, and you, to higher management levels. Your manager might even help you obtain the resources you need to implement your ideas, including time to work on your project.

Whose Support Do You Need? The most important person on your support team is your manager. Before you begin stretching your entrepreneurial limbs, make sure your manager is receptive to your new direction, approves your ideas and actions, and is informed of your progress.

People who have the money and other resources to start their own independent businesses are in an excellent position as they take their first steps. People who are able to use *other* people's money to start a business venture are in an even better position. To be in this position, you must earn the confidence of those who will be funding your idea, be responsible with their investments, and deliver results.

What Is Your Plan? Once you have thought through the first three ideas, you can create a plan that explains how and why your idea will succeed. No one wants to be associated with failure, especially your manager-sponsor, so make sure that you plan your idea, ask your manager and others for feedback, and adjust your plan accordingly.

How do you know if a product you want to propose is desirable?

- Start your market research in the interview process. Ask the interviewer, your future manager, and future peers the following questions: Which of your products have been most successful? Why? What are some upcoming products? Have you hired people to work on new products, or are current employees working on them? Their answers to these questions will give you a sense of whether the company values the experience and knowledge of its employees who work on new ideas.

- Use your interdepartmental relationships to learn as much about the company as possible. Exercise a healthy curiosity about the rest of the company when performing your job responsibilities. For example, if you're a recruiting associate working with payroll to set up new employee accounts, make an extra effort to find out what your payroll contact does, whom he or she reports to, and how your departments interact.

Check Point

What four questions should you ask yourself before developing a plan to become an employee-entrepreneur?

THINK CRITICALLY

1. How do entrepreneurs affect wealth distribution?

2. What four qualities are critical in an entrepreneur?

3. Why do you think retired executives are willing to answer entrepreneurs' questions?

MAKE ACADEMIC CONNECTIONS

4. **WORKPLACE PRACTICE** One way to become an employee-entrepreneur is to apply a new skill, solution, or activity to your current job. Create an example venture in an existing job situation, and explain why this venture is applicable to the job.

5. **HISTORICAL FICTION** Read more about an entrepreneur from the last century. Write a short story with this entrepreneur as the main character. Map out the plot, setting, and supporting characters, including those who may have supported or influenced the entrepreneur, before you begin writing.

6. **INTERVIEW** Because small, start-up businesses are typically run in an informal manner, they may lack formal policies on many matters, such as sick days, dress codes, Internet usage, and working hours. Talk to owners or employees of three small businesses. What formal policies do these businesses have? What issues have they not addressed? Report your findings in a one-page paper.

VOCABULARY BUILDER

Choose the term that best fits the definition. Write the letter of the answer in the space provided. Some terms may not be used.

——— 1. A person who starts his or her own business

——— 2. A system in which most economic resources are privately owned and individuals are free to decide what they will produce with the resources

——— 3. Laws that are designed to promote competition and fairness and to prevent monopolies and other unfair business practices

——— 4. An economy that is largely based on the trade of information and the management of the tools used to distribute that information

——— 5. A document that describes the important characteristics of a business

——— 6. A written contract granting permission to sell someone else's product or service in a prescribed manner over a certain period of time and in a specified territory

——— 7. A business that is owned and operated by one person

——— 8. A business that involves two or more people who become responsible for its debts, obligations, and success

——— 9. A business owned by shareholders

a. antitrust laws

b. business plan

c. corporation

d. entrepreneur

e. franchise

f. franchisee

g. franchisor

h. free enterprise system

i. general partnership

j. information economy

k. limited partnership

l. partnership

m. sole proprietorship

n. unlimited liability

REVIEW CONCEPTS

www.cengage.com/school/marketing/yourself

10. Who owns and controls most of the economic resources in a free enterprise system?

11. How does a free enterprise system make entrepreneurship possible?

12. In a free enterprise economy, when does government get involved in exchange relationships?

13. What is the difference between an entrepreneur and a manager?

14. Why are small businesses an important part of the U.S. economy?

15. What types of small business owners are not necessarily entrepreneurs?

16. Why is it important to assess your interests, skills, and personality traits before deciding to become an entrepreneur?

17. What problems might result when an entrepreneur decides on a business idea based on skills, interests, and experience only?

18. What are the three forms of ownership to consider when starting a new business?

19. Why is it important to get assistance from a lawyer and others when starting a new business?

20. Why is it important for a new entrepreneur to have a written business plan?

APPLY WHAT YOU LEARNED

21. Why do you think some businesses started by entrepreneurs fail when they begin to grow?

22. Give an example of an entrepreneur using the laws of supply and demand to create a successful business.

23. Many employees face the problem of the "glass ceiling," an invisible or unspoken barrier that prevents them from advancing beyond a certain position. Women and members of racial and ethnic minority groups are most likely to bump into the glass ceiling in their careers. How do you think the glass ceiling has affected the growth in new business ownership by women and minorities?

24. Consider your skills and personality traits. Would you make a good entrepreneur, or are you more suited to be a manager or another worker within a business? Explain your answer.

25. Which personal characteristics do you think are similar and different between an inventor and an entrepreneur?

MAKE ACADEMIC CONNECTIONS

26. **LAWS** At the library, find newspaper or magazine articles about the federal government's accusation that Microsoft violated antitrust laws. Learn about the reasons for the accusation and the eventual outcome. Do you agree that Microsoft violated these laws? Do you think such laws are necessary for our economy to run smoothly? Why or why not? Report your findings in a two-page paper.

27. **INTERNET RESEARCH** Search the Internet using the words "American dream." What types of sites and information do you find? Find four web sites that mention the American dream, and describe them to the class. Which ones are dedicated strictly to business operations?

28. **COMPANY RESEARCH** Use telephone and Internet directories to identify specific businesses that provide the following services: finance, marketing, information management, and product/service management. Find out who founded these specific companies and how old they are. Are some of the companies franchises? Prepare a PowerPoint presentation of your findings.

29. **LEGAL RESEARCH** Identify legal problems that entrepreneurs might face when starting a new business. Identify at least four legal issues and suggest solutions. Try to find examples of legal issues in actual court cases to get ideas for the problem and solution activity. You might want to focus on a specific service or industry, such as the distribution of copyrighted music over the Internet. Present your findings to the class.

30. **COMPOSITION** Write a business plan for a specific business in which you think you would succeed, based on your own entrepreneurial characteristics. Choose the product or service that your business will offer.

Travel Tourism Marketing Management Team Decision Making

The airline industry has been struggling due to an uncertain economy, heightened security issues, and rising costs. Only one competing airline has shown a profit during the past year. One of the struggling airlines has asked you and a partner to develop survey questions to ask prospective airline customers. The answers to these questions will help the airlines develop marketing strategies for increased business.

You have also been hired to suggest promotional strategies to increase business activity for the airlines. You have 30 minutes to devise your survey questions and marketing plan for the airlines using a management decision-making strategy. Be sure to outline your strategy. You will be given 10 minutes to present your information, and the judges have five minutes to ask questions about your plan of action.

"I'm really excited that we joined the farm cooperative and are participating in community-supported agriculture this year. Because we purchased a share, every week we get a delivery of recently harvested vegetables and fruits. We'll get to try quite a variety, and I'm glad the co-op's web site has recipes for many of the foods. We're going to eat well all season!"

Have you ever thought about where your food comes from, and how it gets on the shelves of a grocery store or restaurant kitchen? Agricultural managers work with small and large farms, ranches, and greenhouses. They manage operations which include everything from land ownership or lease agreements and crop production methods to agricultural marketing and sales of farm output. They monitor weather conditions, farming technologies, regulations and legislation, market prices, and even farm workers.

Employment Outlook

The rate of employment is expected to remain steady.

Job Titles

- Farm Buyer
- Crop Production Manager
- Farm Manager
- Farm Supervisor

Needed Skills

- Managers do not necessarily perform farm labor. Instead, they hire and supervise production workers, establish farm output goals, plan marketing and sales initiatives, plan for transportation, and oversee maintenance.
- A bachelor's degree usually is required, and a graduate degree related to agricultural science often is recommended. Certification is available through professional organizations, and apprenticeships may be available.
- Managerial skills, including accounting or bookkeeping, knowledge of credit sources, and familiarity with safety regulations is essential.
- Skills in communication, personnel management, computers, and conflict resolution are important.

What's It Like to Work in Agricultural Management?

Mark is up before dawn. It's the middle of harvest, and he has a very busy day planned. He monitors crop production, and then plans for transportation to the distributor. The weather has not been cooperating, and he hopes to meet his projections. The farm needs additional laborers both during planting and harvesting, so he has scheduled interviews for the afternoon. He wants to hire several people who are willing to work long days doing physical labor throughout the season.

He has been interested in farming from an early age. He honed his interest helping his grandfather manage a large vegetable garden, and later majored in farm management in college. His knowledge of technology came in handy when he oversaw the adoption of farm management software to make it easier to track trends related to weather, irrigation, planting, and other related operational elements. The software also will make the budgeting process easier. Farming has many challenges, and Mark feels confident that, under his management, the farm will continue to be successful.

What About You?

What are some of the things you would like about working as a farm manager? What would you find challenging?

GLOSSARY

A

ABC goals goals that are actionable, bounded, and compelling

Accomplishment something that has been successfully completed; result of well-utilized skills

Actionable goals goals that can be acted upon and are behavior-related

Administrative management a management theory based on the work of Henri Fayol and Max Weber that focused on managing the whole organization for efficiency and effectiveness

Advertising a promotion activity that is characterized by communication with an audience through non-personal, paid media such as broadcast commercials and printed ads and flyers

Affirmative action programs that are put in place to encourage the hiring of diverse individuals and to discourage discrimination

Agrarian Society early society circa 7,000 B.C.; characterized by permanent settlements, agriculture on a large scale, work separate from family life, specialization of labor, and the use of plows and the wheel

Americans with Disabilities Act a law that requires employers to make reasonable accommodations for employees with special needs and discourages discrimination based on disability

Annual report a report that includes operational and financial information about an organization

Antitrust laws laws that are designed to promote competition and fairness and to prevent monopolies and other unfair business practices

Appearance one's visual impression

Arrogance the feeling that one is perfect or knows everything

Attachment an enclosure of another document related to a piece of correspondence

Attitude the way you think and feel about something; the most important factor in hiring entry-level employees

Audience the people who view, read, or listen to your material

B

Barter to exchange something of value (a non-monetary form of currency) for a good or a service

Basic skills skills that are important for life, not just work, such as reading, writing, speaking, basic math, and problem solving

Behavioral perspective a management perspective that emerged out of the Great Depression of the 1930s; it focused on the behaviors of individuals in the workplace and the ways managers could effectively motivate employees

Benefits the advantages a customer gets from buying a product; the advantages an employer gets from hiring a job candidate; financial, professional, or personal incentives offered as part of a position's compensation

Benefit selling the marketing practice of promoting products by considering the needs and wants of the customer

Benevolent-authoritative one of Likert's management styles that assumes managers hold the responsibility within the organization. Employees are motivated to work through rewards.

Body the main message or content of a letter or memo

Body art tattoos and body piercing

Bonus an addition to a base salary that consists of special earnings based upon performance

Bounded goals goals that are measurable and specific

Brand extensions offering many new varieties of a product to pique consumers' interests and satisfy changing tastes

Business an organization that uses labor, capital, land, and entrepreneurship to produce goods and services at a profit

Business casual a style of dress that is professional yet relaxed

Business correspondence letters, e-mail messages, phone conversations, and other forms of workplace communication

Business plan a document that describes the important characteristics of a business, including the type of business, its products, the industry, a marketing plan, the manner of operation, and the financial information

C

Capital an economic resource (factor of production); includes those items necessary to produce goods and services, such as buildings, machines, and tools

Capitalism economic system in which individuals are free to own property; individuals and companies are allowed to compete for their own economic gain; and free market forces determine the prices of goods and services

Career/placement centers offices in schools and colleges that offer career counseling, assessments, and job search and career advice

Chronological resume a type of resume that arranges work experience in reverse chronological order. It is used to show steady, relevant work experience or years of education related to a career.

Classical perspective management perspective that emerged out of the Industrial Revolution in the late 19th and early 20th centuries; includes scientific management and administrative management

Classified ads job listings published in a newspaper

Closed-ended questions questions that require only a "yes" or "no" answer

Code of conduct written set of ethical guidelines for an industry, profession, or company

Coercive power a leader has the ability to impose a penalty, such as firing an employee; this can be used unethically, and for leaders who abuse this type of power, it often results in low employee morale

Cold calls unannounced, in-person visits to potential employers

Cold cover letters letters used when your job-search network does not generate contacts in your preferred company; these letters

directly inquire about unadvertised employment opportunities

Command economy government provides answers to the three economic questions

Commission an addition to a base salary that consists of a percentage of sales

Commodity anything that holds exchange value

Common strengths abilities shared by most firms in a given industry

Communication process the basic process of sending and receiving a message

Communism economic system in which a centralized government owns all resources and determines what should be produced; also known as a "command economy," in which individuals do not directly benefit from their work

Compelling goals goals that are important to you and compel or force you to action

Compensation package total salary, benefits, and incentives offered as compensation

Competent properly or sufficiently qualified to do a job

Conflict a struggle or state of opposition that occurs when what one person wants is not compatible with what another person wants

Consultative one of Likert's management styles that assumes managers have some trust in the abilities of subordinates. Employees are motivated by rewards and are allowed some involvement in the organization.

Consumers people who choose to spend resources on goods and services intended for personal use and not for manufacture or resale

Contact information resume section that identifies your legal name, address, telephone number, and e-mail address

Contingency theory a contemporary management perspective that suggests that managers must respond to the environment, and that there is not one single correct way to manage an organization

Controlling function of management that involves monitoring a business to make sure its goals are met

Cooperate to work with others for mutual benefit

Corporation a business that is owned by shareholders and that operates separately from its owners

Cost of living the amount of money required to purchase the things you need to maintain your standard of living

Cover letter a business letter that introduces your resume and is used when submitting a formal application for a job opening

Customer satisfaction managing the perceptions that customers have of your company's performance in relation to their expectations

D

Decisional role a management role that involves making decisions, such as allocating resources and hiring employees

Demand how much of a product consumers are willing to purchase

Demographic information information about a customer that includes age, gender, and level of education

Differentiation a focus on uniqueness, or the differences between a product and its competitors

Direct mailing sending a marketing packet—a cover letter, a resume, work samples, and references—to potential employers

Discrimination inappropriate treatment of an individual based on a group or class that the individual belongs to

Displaced workers workers who are unemployed because of changing job conditions

Distinctive competencies the things companies or individuals do particularly well

Distribution one of the seven key marketing functions; the process of delivering products and services to customers in the best way possible

Diversity an employment trend characterized by the changing composition of the workforce to include people of different experiences, races, ages, and ethnicities

E

Early Modern Period economic era from the 1400s to the early 1700s; characterized by colonization, exploration by sea, and major inventions such as the telescope, printing press, and gunpowder

Early Trade Period economic era from 800 B.C. to 1400 A.D.; characterized by the development of early marketplaces, improved transportation and communication, bartering with items, and coined money

E-commerce the process of conducting business transactions over the Internet; an important employment trend that has changed the way consumers and businesses buy products and services

Economic conditions economic factors that influence consumer buying power and marketing strategies; factors include business cycles, inflation, resource availability, and income

Economic questions (1) What goods and services will be produced? (2) How will they be produced? (3) For whom will they be produced?

Economics the social science that deals with the production, distribution, and consumption of goods and services

Economic utility the amount of satisfaction a consumer gets from using a product or service

Education an employment trend characterized by the critical importance of lifelong learning and the ability to adapt to change in the workplace; a section of a resume that identifies the names of schools you've attended, degrees or certificates earned, relevant courses, graduation dates, and grades

Emotional motives reasons that relate to feelings

Employee assistance program (EAP) a program in an organization that provides a variety of counseling services and treatment options to employees

Employment agencies companies that are in the business of finding permanent or temporary assignments for job seekers

Entrepreneur one who organizes the start-up of a new venture and takes the risks necessary to start a business

Entrepreneurial personality a successful entrepreneur is a self-starter, outgoing, a lifelong learner, and an optimist

Entrepreneurship an economic resource (factor of production); includes the ability to envision new opportunities and undertake them

Environmental scanning identifying important trends in the marketplace

Equal Employment Opportunity Commission (EEOC) an office of the federal government that was created to deal with issues of discrimination

Equality a key American value; the belief that all people should have a right to succeed based on their efforts

Ethics a set of moral values that guides your behavior for many years

Etiquette rules of social behavior

Exchange a transaction in which two parties trade something of value for what the other has to offer. Two types of exchange are monetary transactions and barter transactions.

Expert power others believe the leader has expert knowledge or skills in a particular area (doctor, computer programmer, professor)

Exploitative-authoritative one of Likert's management styles that assumes top-level management has most of the responsibility. Employees are motivated to work by threats of job loss or pay cuts.

Export a good that is produced domestically and sold abroad

External communication correspondence from companies to clients and from companies to customers

External customers customers outside of the organization who purchase your products or services

External information information made available outside of an organization, as in directories, publications, and chambers of commerce

Extravert someone who enjoys being in large groups

Eye contact gazing directly at another person to show attention, sincerity, and confidence

F

Facial expressions the sometimes conscious and sometimes unconscious movements of facial muscles to communicate emotions or attitudes

Factors of production economic resources; labor, capital, land, and entrepreneurship

Family leave a certain length of time that employees may be absent to care for infants or sick or elderly relatives without jeopardizing their employment

Family Medical Leave Act a law that requires employers to allow eligible employees to take an unpaid leave of absence from their positions for up to 12 weeks per year to recover from an illness or to care for a child, spouse, or parent

Features factual characteristics of a product, such as its intended use; employees' skills

Feeling-thinking personality trait that shows how you make decisions

Filtering a barrier to communication; the process of shaping, shortening, or lengthening messages as they travel through the communication network

Financing one of the seven key marketing functions; the process of acquiring the financial resources needed to market a product or service. Financing also involves giving customers payment options.

First-line managers lower-level managers who manage the day-to-day operations of an organization, including employee supervision

Flexible work arrangements benefits usually offered to experienced employees who may have challenging schedules due to family obligations; includes flexible work hours, job sharing, and telecommuting

Follow-up interviews additional interviews for a candidate in whom an employer is very interested

Form utility the economic utility that exists when the actual form of the product attracts consumers

401(k) an employer-sponsored retirement plan in which an employee's contributions to stock or mutual funds are deducted directly from the employee's paycheck

403(b) an employer-sponsored retirement plan similar to a 401(k) plan, but available only to employees of government or nonprofit agencies

Franchise a written contract granting permission to sell someone else's product or service in a prescribed manner over a certain period of time and in a specified territory. Additionally, the word "franchise" is often used to refer to the product or service itself.

Franchisee the person or group who buys a franchise

Franchisor the company whose products the franchiser will sell

Free enterprise system a system in which most economic resources are privately owned and individuals are free to decide what they will produce with the resources

Freedom a key American value; liberties, as stated in the U.S. Constitution

Functional resume a type of resume that focuses on personal characteristics, skills, abilities, and work experience. It is used to highlight a job seeker's strengths.

G

General partnership a type of partnership in which partners share equal responsibility for debts, and all have unlimited liability

Geographic information information about customers that includes ZIP codes and addresses

Gestures hand movements

Globalization condition characterized by products, services, labor, technology, and capital moving easily between businesses and countries all over the world

Global village the phenomenon of drawing people and businesses together from across the planet

Goals things you want to accomplish

Good a physical product, such as a shoelace or refrigerator

Goodwill correspondence correspondence that expresses support, thanks, or care

Grooming clean, pleasant, and tasteful appearance

Gross Domestic Product (GDP) the total value of the goods and services produced in the United States

H

Horticultural Society early society circa 10,000 B.C.; characterized by cultivated plants and domesticated animals, bartering within tribal groups, a focus on strength and hard work, and the use of hand tools to grow food

Human capital individuals' knowledge and skills that are necessary to produce goods and services

Human relations a management movement that stresses the importance of relationships in organization

Human resources a management model that values the individual employee by focusing on how businesses can encourage communication and participation by workers

Human resources department a department in an organization that supports the hiring process by preparing job descriptions, screening applicants, scheduling interviews, and passing on qualified candidates to the hiring manager

Hunters and Gatherers early society prior to 10,000 B.C.; characterized by nomadic family groups following herds and vegetation and using primitive tools for finding food and survival

Hygiene cleanliness

I

Idea marketing the process of marketing an idea, social practice, or information, in which a need for the information is determined, a service is suggested, and a plan is put into place for promoting and distributing the idea

Import a good that is purchased in the United States but produced abroad

Inclusion involves respecting and valuing the uniqueness of others; rather than focusing on differences, unique qualities are acknowledged and appreciated; in the workplace, inclusion often is connected to diversity

Income the amount of money earned from labor or the sale of products and services

Individualism protecting your individual rights; the free association of unique individuals who cooperate as equals in order to maximize their freedom and satisfy their desires; an employment trend in which individuals take responsibility and are accountable for their personal efforts

Industrialization Era economic era from the 1700s to the 1950s; characterized by technological advances, mass production, and major inventions such as the steam engine, cotton gin, and electricity

Industry a specific employment field; a branch or segment of the economy, such as service, construction, management, or farming

Inflation economic condition characterized by a continued rise in the price of products

Information Age current economic era; characterized by a shift from the manufacturing sector of the economy to the service sector along with a focus on computers, the Internet, digital technology, and access to information

Informational interview an informal interview with a person who works in the occupation or for an organization you are targeting; an opportunity to learn more about an occupation or organization

Informational role a management role that involves gathering relevant information and making it available to employees

Information economy an economy that is largely based on the trade of information and the management of the tools used to distribute that information

Informative correspondence correspondence that describes or explains something

Initial interview a first interview, during which the interviewer assesses the overall impression the interviewee makes as well as his or her experience

Initiative the ability to take on work that needs to be done without specifically being asked

Inquiry letter a letter used to inquire about employment openings, career advice, job leads, or any other information related to a job search

Instrumental value a value that refers to behaviors such as honesty or perseverance. Instrumental values help you obtain your terminal values.

Internal communication correspondence between employees of the same company

Internal customers employees within your organization for whom you provide information, services, or work

Internal information information developed within an organization and made available through annual reports, company web sites, and informational interviews

Interpersonal role a management role that involves interacting with others, communicating with

employees, and coordinating with other departments in the organization

Introversion-extraversion personality trait that helps determine how you communicate with others and in what workplace environments you would be most successful

Introvert someone who generally likes to work alone

Intuition-sensing personality trait that explains how you learn and receive information

J

Job application a form provided by an employer that asks a job candidate to list qualifications, work history, and work-related personal information

Job banks web sites that offer databases of available positions that can be searched by job title, location, and keywords

Job objective a section of a resume that identifies the job you are applying for

Job-related skills skills that are specific to a position, occupation, or industry

K

Knowledge economy an economy that is focused on knowledge-intensive activities

L

Labor an economic resource (factor of production); includes human effort and work

Labor force all people who are working or looking for work

Law of demand an economic law that states that the amount of a product demanded relates inversely to price. Consumers tend to buy more of a product when it is sold at a lower price.

Law of supply an economic law that states that the amount of a product supplied is directly related to price. Businesses tend to produce more of products that they can sell at higher prices.

Leading function of management that involves getting people to work together to accomplish the shared objectives of a business

Learning the process of gaining knowledge or skills

Legitimate power others believe the leader has the right, or authority, to lead; this may be based on title (manager, president, owner)

Letterhead special stationery with the company's name, logo, and contact information

Lifetime employment staying employed with one company for the duration of a career

Limited partnership a type of partnership in which the liability and involvement of certain partners is limited

Low self-esteem personal insecurities that lead to uncertainty

M

Management using people, material resources, and technology to accomplish an organization's work

Management science a management model that uses mathematical models and computer simulations to represent systems or processes within organizations

Market any place where buyers and sellers conduct exchanges

Market economy the U.S. economic system in which market forces such as supply and demand move the economy with some government involvement. Individuals can own and profit from businesses and are free to choose their own purchases, schooling, and careers. The government owns some businesses and regulates certain industries but does not fully control economic forces.

Marketing the process of making one product more attractive than the other products a person may choose. Marketing also involves making that product satisfactory to both the consumer who buys it and the producer who makes it. Marketing is defined by the American Marketing Association as "the activity, set of institutions, and processes for creating, communicating, delivering, and exchanging offerings that have value for customers, clients, partners, and society at large."

Marketing action plan a list of planned marketing activities or tasks, including how activities should be completed and the dates by when they should be completed

Marketing Era era of the U.S. economy from the 1950s to the early 1990s; characterized by businesses producing items and services based on consumer demand. Products were increasingly visible in advertising campaigns during this era.

Marketing-information management one of the seven key marketing functions; the process of gathering and using information about customers to improve business decisions

Marketing plan a written plan that addresses a current situation, identifies marketing strategy goals, and outlines how to reach those goals

Marketing strategy the larger strategy that emerges from an organization's goals and mission statement and takes into account existing strengths, weaknesses, opportunities, and outside threats

Market opportunity awareness an awareness of circumstances or timing that allows action toward a goal

Market segments components of a market that are made up of consumers with one or more similar characteristics

Mass customization the process of providing products and services that more closely meet the needs and wants of individual customers

Mass mailing sending marketing packets with generic resumes and cover letters to organizations that may or may not have openings

Mediate to work as an objective outside party to help people resolve a conflict in a way that benefits them and the organization

Mentor an experienced employee who helps a new employee learn about the ways of the organization

Middle managers mid-level managers who implement the plans and decisions made by the top managers

Mirroring moving your body to mimic that of another person

Mission statement a statement of purpose that provides a view of what an organization is and what it wants to become

Mixed economies have elements of both command and market economies; most countries have mixed economies

Modified mass mailing sending marketing packets with customized resumes and cover letters to organizations that may or may not have openings

Mutual goals objectives shared by buyers and sellers

Myers-Briggs Type Indicator (MBTI®) an instrument used by career counselors and organizations to identify personality traits

N

Need something that is required to live

Network the people you know; your contacts and relationships

Networking actively making as many people as possible aware of your job search; reaching out to the people you know to ask for job leads, job referrals, and introductions to hiring managers

Networking letters letters written to the contacts you've generated from networking in order to request help with job contacts or career strategies

Niche sites web sites that specialize in listing jobs in particular industries or occupations

Nonverbal communication communication other than spoken language

North American Industrial Classification System (NAICS) a system for classifying industries in the United States, Mexico, and Canada

O

Occupational Outlook Handbook a government publication that provides detailed information on 11 major industry clusters and more than 250 occupations

Online resume an electronic resume document that is sent in an e-mail message or as an e-mail attachment

Open-ended questions questions that require a more detailed answer than "yes" or "no"

Operations management a form of management science that focuses on all aspects of production, such as managing inventory and planning shipping routes

Opportunities favorable circumstances or advantageous times that foster increased performance

Optimist one who feels confident and positive, believing that things will work out

Organization an orderly structure or system

Organizing a function of management that involves arranging work and grouping resources

Orientation an opportunity for new employees to learn about a company's policies, structure, culture, and expectations and to adjust to a new working environment

Overtime an addition to base salary that consists of dollars per hour for extra hours worked

P

Packaging includes attitude and appearance, and can provide a competitive advantage

Participative-group one of Likert's management styles that assumes that managers have confidence in subordinates. Employees help set organization goals, and communication and teamwork are highly valued.

Partnership a form of business ownership that involves two or more people who become responsible for the debts, obligations, and success of a business

Pension an accumulation of money that an employee can access upon retirement

Perceiving-judging personality trait that reveals your preference for flexibility or structure in your life

Perceptions mental pictures or images that come to mind when one thinks of a specific product

Personal inventory a personal document that lists the details of your education, experience, and other qualifications in order to identify your job-related skills

Personal mission statement individual statement of purpose that provides a view of a person's skills and accomplishments and what he or she wants to become

Personal selling a promotion activity that is characterized by direct contact and communication with an audience through paid sales personnel

Personal space the physical distance that feels comfortable for personal interactions, about two to four feet

Persuasive correspondence correspondence that attempts to convince the audience to believe or take action toward something

Pessimist one who tends to take a gloomy, negative view of situations

Place utility the economic utility that exists when products are available where consumers want them

Planning function of management that involves determining in advance what needs to be done to accomplish business goals

Portfolio a collection of work samples that represents one's abilities and accomplishments; used to demonstrate work readiness, to show eligibility for admission to colleges and organizations, and to showcase special talents

Positioning creating distance between products in the marketplace in the minds of consumers

Positive body language communicating a positive attitude through your posture, eye contact, nonverbal messages, and gestures

Positive communication relaying your message and image clearly with appropriate tone of voice, word choice, and respect

Positive self-esteem feeling good about yourself and projecting confidence in your abilities

Positive self-talk motivating and complimenting yourself; recognizing your own accomplishments and skills

Positive thinking visualizing your success and training your mind to respond optimistically to challenges

Positive work habits using positive behaviors on the job, such as courtesy, accepting blame, getting along with others, and volunteering for extra work

Possession utility the economic utility that exists when different ways are provided for a consumer to own or purchase a product

Precision targeting taking the needs and interests of different groups of consumers into account and targeting them

Pre-employment testing addresses issues such as aptitude, proficiency, personality, honesty, and drug use; tests may be done on-site before or after the interview, or you may be asked to complete the testing at another location

Price the amount of money that must be exchanged for a good or service

Pricing one of the seven key marketing functions; the process of deciding how much a product or service will cost the consumer. Price is the value placed on the product.

Primacy effect the notion that the initial impression one makes when meeting someone new has a greater impact than later impressions of that individual

Privately owned organizations organizations that do not offer shares of stock for public purchase

Procrastination deferring or delaying action; putting things off

Producers individuals or companies who create valued products and exchange those products with consumers for scarce resources

Production Era era of the U.S. economy prior to 1925; characterized by a focus on mass production, the affordability of products, and the belief that products would sell themselves

Product/service management one of the seven key marketing functions; the process of designing, creating, and improving products and services in order to satisfy customer needs

Profit maximization when businesses make the most money in sales of products with the lowest expenses possible

Profit sharing a share of the profits earned by the company

Promotion one of the seven key marketing functions; communications presented to consumers in order to inform, persuade, and remind them of a product's benefit, and encourage them to buy it

Prosperity business cycle characterized by higher incomes, increased production, and lower unemployment rates

Psychographic information information about a customer that includes attitudes, needs, and wants

Publicity a promotion activity that is characterized by communication through personal or non-personal media that is not explicitly paid for delivering the message, such as announcements, letters of recommendation, and newspaper articles

Publicly owned organizations organizations that make shares of stocks available for purchase on a stock exchange

Punctuality arriving at the scheduled time

Purpose your reason for communicating

Q

Quantitative perspective management perspective that emerged after World War II; it focused on techniques such as mathematical models for management

R

Rational motives conscious, logical reasons

Realistic requirements those requirements that you can attain (with some effort) in relation to employment

Recession business cycle characterized by increasing unemployment, decreased consumer spending, and fewer opportunities for businesses to sell their products

Recovery business cycle characterized by increasing employment and business opportunities and an increase in consumer spending

References people who will provide positive information about you to a potential employer

Referent power others identify with and want to be like the leader (athlete, celebrity, politician)

Related coursework section of a resume that is used to list relevant courses when the job seeker has little work experience or does not have a degree in the field of interest

Related experience resume section that is used to list relevant experience that is not part of a paid job, such as extracurricular activities, volunteer work, and unpaid apprenticeships and internships; also called activities

Relationship Marketing Era current era of the U.S. economy in which the focus is on building long-term relationships that benefit buyers and sellers and create satisfaction. The goal of relationship marketing is to attract new customers, keep current customers, and anticipate customers' needs.

Relationship selling a buyer-oriented sales philosophy, based on trust, needs satisfaction, and mutual goals

Request correspondence correspondence that makes a request or asks the audience to clarify something

Resign to relinquish or give up a position with an organization

Resume a brief summary of a job seeker's education, job history, and skills

Resume bank a site where job seekers can post their resumes to be viewed by recruiters and employers

Reverse chronological order listing information with the most current information first and the least current information last

Reward power a leader is able to offer rewards, such as raises, promotions, or other incentives (manager, owner, instructor)

Risk a possibility for loss

S

Salary compensation an employee receives for his or her services

Salary range identified minimum and maximum salaries

Sales Era era of the U.S. economy from 1925 to the early 1950s; characterized by an emphasis on using salespeople to convince customers to buy products

Sales promotions a promotion activity that is characterized by communication with an audience through a variety of non-personal, non-media vehicles, such as samples and coupons

Salutation a formal introductory greeting in a letter

Satisfaction the outcome of a successful exchange in which the performance of the product or service meets expectations

Scannable resume a printed and mailed resume that has been specially formatted so it can be scanned into a company's computer database

Scarcity the economic condition caused by unlimited needs and wants and limited resources to fill those needs and wants

Scientific management a management theory developed by Frederick Taylor that focused on management as a science centered on production and worker efficiency

Segmenting dividing markets into groups of consumers with common characteristics, such as needs and wants or previous purchase decisions

Self-awareness understanding the various factors that shape your personality and interests

Self-confidence knowing and understanding yourself and believing in your abilities

Self-esteem believing in yourself and having confidence in your abilities

Self starters people who know what they want and get up everyday and go after it

Selling one of the seven key marketing functions; direct contact with potential customers to determine their needs and satisfy those needs

Service a non-physical product; specific skills or knowledge

Service sector businesses that provide services (such as financial, child care, health and safety, or personal) rather than physical goods

Sexual harassment unwelcome sexual advances or remarks as well as inappropriate language or physical conduct

Sick leave an allotment of days for which an employee can be paid while being absent due to illness

Skill a proficiency of ability developed through training or experience

Small business a business with fewer than 500 employees

Socialism economic system in which the government owns most major enterprises and key industries such as health care and public utilities. Individuals can own less critical businesses. Socialism is also characterized by high taxes that are used to provide low-cost social services.

Social marketing marketing that encourages or discourages certain behaviors by attempting to influence attitudes that affect behavior; the marketing of ideas, particularly ideas that can benefit individuals, groups, or society

Soft skills workplace competencies that include teamwork, communication skills (oral, written, and electronic), time management, problem solving, ability to work as part of a team, attitude, adaptability, and the ability to work with diverse individuals

Sole proprietorship a business that is owned and operated by one person

Stock options an addition to base salary that consists of opportunities to invest in the company's stock at a lower price than the current price per share

Strengths skills and competencies

Structure organization and format

Subject line a brief section of an e-mail that alerts the reader to the topic of your message

Substance abuse an overuse of drugs or alcohol

Summary of qualifications resume section that lists special keywords related to specific jobs and skills that are used to search computer databases

Supply how much of a product is offered to the market

Sustainability meeting today's needs without compromising financial, human, or natural resources for tomorrow

SWOT analysis an analysis of an organization based on existing strengths, weaknesses, opportunities, and threats

Systems theory a contemporary management perspective that considers the organization as a system with four basic elements: inputs from the environment, transformation, outputs, and feedback about the process

T

Targeting seeking out those consumers who are most likely to buy a product

Target market a clearly identified portion of the market to which a company or job seeker wants to appeal

Technology the practical application of knowledge to accomplish a task

Terminal value a value that is an end in itself; it relates to a state of existence, such as a comfortable life

Theory X a management style theory that assumes that employees dislike work, need direction, and must be coerced or controlled into working

Theory Y a management style theory that assumes people do not inherently dislike work but view it as a part of life and can become committed to organizational objectives

Theory Z a management style theory that assumes people are committed to their jobs and can work together effectively. Managers with this style focus on the organization and long-term employment.

Threats factors in the marketing environment that might hamper performance

Time utility the economic utility that exists when a product is available at the time when consumers want it

Time wasters activities that limit productivity; may include interruptions, socializing, or even trips to the document shredder

Top managers upper-level managers who look at the "big picture" and plan the overall, long-term direction of an organization

Traditional economy answers the three economic questions according to custom or tradition

Traditional selling using memorized sales techniques to set appointments, overcome objections, and close sales

U

Unlimited liability personal responsibility for all business debts

V

Vacation days paid days off offered as an employee benefit

Values things that are most important to you that affect your choices and your behavior

Virtual office a nontraditional office in a home, hotel room, client office, or anywhere else a personal computer can be plugged in and connected to a traditional office network

W

Want an unfulfilled consumer desire

Weaknesses skills or competencies that may be lacking or do not support the mission

Work experience section of a resume that identifies the names and locations of previous employers, job titles, dates of employment, responsibilities, and accomplishments

Workplace competencies skills that effective workers possess and most employers desire; also known as *soft skills*

INDEX

Jordan, Michael, 57
Just-in-Time (JIT) inventory system, 22

K

Kerrigan, Nancy, 65
Keywords, job search, 168
Knight, Phil, 324
Knowledge economy, 318

L

Labor, 36
    force, 162
Land, 36
Leadership, 53
Leading, 48
Learning
    about your workplace, 290
    lifelong, 295
    from others' experience, 329–330
Legal forms of business ownership, 324–325
Letterhead, 237
Levitt, Julie Griffin, 136
Lifetime employment, 291
Limited partnership, 325
Listening, 276–277
    skill, 101
Liz Claiborne (company), 129

M

Mailing
    direct, 142
    mass, 142
    modified mass, 142
Management
    administrative, 50
    behavioral perspective and, 51
    classical perspective and, 50–51
    contemporary perspectives and, 52
    controlling and, 48
    defined, 47
    evolution, 50–52
    functions of, 47–49
    levels of, 49
    organizing and, 48
    planning and, 48
    purchasing power and, 34
    quantitative perspective and, 51–52
    roles of, 48
    styles, 52–53
Management science, 51
Market
    analysis of, 157–158
    consumers and, 35
    economic resources and, 36
    economics, defined, 34
    economic utility, 15
    needs and, 35

producers and, 35
scarcity and, 35
segments, 120
supply and demand, 36
target and, 120
wants and, 35
Marketing
    communication and, 18, 20–22
    consumer spending and, 34
    defined, 4
    features and benefits in, 77–78
    functions, 6–7
    goal of, 18
    ideas, 8
    individuals, 8–9
    information and, 20–22
    plan, 149
    social, 8, 91
    society and, 13
    successful, 9
    technology and, 17
Marketing action plan, 159
Marketing Era (1950s to early 1990s), 18
Marketing-information management, 7
Marketing Math Connection (feature)
    advertising rates, 234
    Americans with disabilities, 75
    average cost of workstation, 318
    career growth, 22
    comparision, 154
    employee theft, 111
    health insurance premium, 307
    interest rate, 42
    overtime pay, 264
    pricing merchandise, 219
    radio advertising costs, 188
    survey respondents, 141
Marketing plan
    creating own, 157
    market analysis and, 157–158
    marketing action plan and, 159
    marketing strategy and, 159
    strategic marketing and, 151
Marketing strategy
    goals and expected outcome and, 159
    positioning statement and, 159
    strategic marketing and, 151
    target market and, 159
Marketing trends
    innovative sampling and, 167
    precision targeting and, 167
    social media marketing and, 167
    sophisticated information gathering and, 166–167
    targeted information delivery and, 167
Market opportunity awareness, 162
Marketplace
    defined, 13
    exchange, 5
    history of, 14
    marketing functions, 6–7

marketing ideas, 8
marketing individuals, 8–9
marketing yourself in the workplace, 9
meaning of marketing, 4–5
planning, 6
satisfaction, 5
society and marketing, 8–9
Market segments, 120
Mary Kay cosmetics, 324
Mass
    customization, 22
    mailing, 142
    media, 177
    production, 16
Mathematical models, 51
MBTI. *See* Myers-Briggs Type Indicator (MBTI)
McCormack, Mark, 297
McGregor, Douglas, 52
Memos, 237–238
Mentor, 290
Microsoft, 316
Middle managers, 49
Mirroring, 279
Mission statement, 151
Mixed economy, 16
Modified mass mailing, 142
Monetary exchange, 5
Money
    coins, 207
    defined, 5
    paper, 207
    preferred commodity, 206
    price and, 208
Moody's Manuals, 131
Mother Teresa, 65
Mrs. Fields cookies, 316
Mutual goals, 263
Myers, Isabel Briggs, 64
Myers-Briggs Type Indicator (MBTI), 64–65

N

NACE. *See* National Association of Colleges and Employers (NACE)
NAICS. *See* North American Industrial Classification System (NAICS)
National Association of Colleges and Employers (NACE), 135
National Business Employment Weekly, 273
National Commission on Entrepreneurship, 319
National Compensation Survey, 215
National Education Association, 210
National Institute for Dispute Resolution, 278
Natural risks, 42
Needs
    in economics, 35
    satisfaction, 263